SCOTTISH HISTORY SOCIETY

FIFTH SERIES

VOLUME 9

The British Linen Company

A

ACKNOWLEDGEMENT

The Council of the Society is pleased to record that the publication of this volume has been assisted by generous sponsorship from The British Linen Bank and its parent, Bank of Scotland.

Founded by Royal Charter in 1746 as The British Linen Company, it gradually evolved into a financier of the linen trade, and in the late eighteenth century, into a fully-fledged bank.

Publication of this volume marks the 250th anniversary of the foundation of The British Linen Company.

British Linen Company one-guinea note, 1768.
Ebenezer Hill, the Company's teller, shortly after the issue of this note absconded with over £600 of the Company's money.

The British Linen Company 1745–1775

edited by
Alastair J. Durie

★

★

EDINBURGH

printed for the Scottish History Society *by*
PILLANS & WILSON LTD., EDINBURGH

1996

British Library Cataloguing-in-Publication Data:
A catalogue record for this book is available
from the British Library

ISBN 0-906245-18-4

Printed in Great Britain

CONTENTS

PREFACE

It is now more than twenty-five years since I was first allowed access, thanks to the kindness of the then Secretary to the British Linen Bank, Mr David Antonio, to the papers of the British Linen Company. Letter books, ledgers, day books, journals and miscellaneous papers were alike stacked in large and rather dirty piles in the vaults of the head office at St Andrew Square. It was a research student's dream to find such a remarkable hoard, amounting to the fullest set of business records for any manufacturing enterprise in eighteenth-century Scotland or indeed in Western Europe. Moreover it was a collection almost untouched, save for some examination of the early correspondence and the minute books of the Directors, which had been used by Dr C.A. Malcolm in his bicentenary history of the British Linen Bank published in 1950. But times have changed, and this collection is now carefully catalogued and cared for in the Archives Store of the Bank of Scotland at Sighthill, the Bank of Scotland having absorbed the British Linen Bank in 1971.

During the preparation of this volume, the present Archivist at the Bank of Scotland, Alan Cameron, and his staff have been of immense service in producing and copying documents, not to mention supplying much-needed cups of coffee. Their interest and knowledge has helped to sustain my enthusiasm for this project, first suggested to me by the late Professor Ian Cowan. And as a novice in the world of word-processing, I have drawn persistently on the expertise of the Manager of the Design and Implementation of Software in History (DISH) lab of the University of Glasgow, Mike Black, who himself undertook some transcription. Through the good offices of the Bank of Scotland, Sandra Morrison also provided a section, for which I am grateful.

The Pasold Research Fund was kind enough to provide some support towards the cost of travel, and the present British Linen Bank has made a very generous contribution towards the costs of publication. My wife Kate has done her best to heckle out the worst knots from my prose and the publication secretary for the Scottish History Society, Dr Julian Goodare, has scrutinised the text with an exactness and care much needed. It has been an immensely interesting project, and a delight to pursue.

A.J.D.

University of Glasgow
March 1995

ABBREVIATIONS

BLC	British Linen Company.
BOTL	Board of Trustees Letter Books.
BOTM	Board of Trustees Minute Books.
BSA	Bank of Scotland Archives, Sighthill, Edinburgh.
NLS	National Library of Scotland, Edinburgh.
SRO	Scottish Record Office, Edinburgh.

DALHOUSIE BLEACHFIELD,

Five miles ſouth from Edinburgh,

WILLIAM DOUGLAS bleaches at the following prices, viz. All plain Linen yard broad, or under, woven below 900 reed, not full white at 1½d. per yard, 900 white, 2d. 1000 2½d. 1100 3d. 1200 and 1300 3½d. 1400 and 1500 4d. 1600 and all above at 5d. Cambrics, Damaſks, and Tweels, 4d. Lawn, Cotton, and Diapers, at 3d. and all cloth above yard broad to pay in proportion.

Cloth taken in at Edinburgh, by Meſſ. Andrew Gilleſpie upholſterer, above the City guard; George Boyd cloth merchant, Lawn-market; Robert Smith merchant, oppoſite Fountain-well; William Bridges merchant, head of Canongate; Adam M'Leiſh merchant, foot of Niddry's-wynd; Alexander Thompſon merchant, foot of Old Fiſh-market; Peter Smith ſhoemaker, foot of Forreſter's-wynd; Alexander Roſs merchant, Graſs-market; Duncan Moir weaver, Siennes; Mrs. Anderſon, Chapel-ſtreet; William Haldane maſon, Nicholſon's-ſtreet; Miſs Straton milliner, foot of Tolbooth-wynd, Leith; Robert Maving ſtabler, St. Bernard's-ſtreet, ditto; Mrs. Cochran merchant, down the ſhore, ditto; James Baird ſhoemaker, Borrowſtownneſs; Baillie Johnſton merchant, Anſtruther; Convener Brown wright, Crail; John Cockburn merchant, Fiſherrow; Benjamin Simpſon merchant, Dalkeith; James Kinaird weaver, ditto; John Hunter weaver, Middleton; Baillie Hiſlop merchant, Peebles; Andrew Ballentine merchant, Weſt Linton; John Niven weaver, Pennycuick; John Kerr, taylor, Selkirk; Robert Mein merchant, New ſtead, near Melroſs; Miſs Nelly Chiſholm merchant, Jedburgh; Laurence Smith, Libertonkirk John Trotter merchant, Loanhead.

N. B. And at the Bleachfield, where there is fulneſs of pure water, and the cloth returned very ſoon.

A contemporary advertisement for a Scottish bleachfield, showing a bleacher scooping water over pegged-out cloth so as to wash out the bleaching solutions.

INTRODUCTION

The rise of the Scottish linen industry in the eighteenth century to become the leading manufacture of the country is a considerable success story, made all the more remarkable by the low level of proficiency from which the industry started, and the level of competition from the established industries of Ireland and Europe.[1] But grow the industry did in spectacular fashion, output doubling every twenty years or so between 1730 and the end of the century. And while there is debate over just how much of this linen was sold outside Scotland,[2] there is no doubt that appreciable quantities of coarse and medium quality linens found their way to markets in England or in North America. Success in external markets, rather than merely the domestic, showed just how far the Scottish industry had improved its products and competitiveness in a context of rising demand.

The linen industry had a long pedigree in Scotland, and had achieved a fairly substantial toehold in the English market by the later seventeenth century. Not surprisingly, therefore, linen along with black cattle featured prominently in the economic arguments of the pamphleteers in the debate over the question of Union with England. Unionists stressed the existing value of the English market and held out the prospect of much greater sales to the colonies in North America and the West Indies once these markets were laid open to the Scots. Quite how much weight their arguments carried is difficult to assess, but certainly some appear to have been influenced: the merchants of Edinburgh asserted in 1710 that 'it may well be remembered that the great inducement made use of to engage Scotland in this Union was the prospect of improving

1 A.J. Durie, *The Scottish Linen Industry in the Eighteenth Century* (Edinburgh, 1979). See also R.H. Campbell (ed.), *States of the Progress of Linen Manufacture in Scotland, 1727-1754* (Edinburgh, 1973).

2 Durie, *Linen Industry*, 147-55, argues the case for a very substantial export market by the 1770s, taking some 30 per cent of output; others, such as R.H. Campbell, *Scotland since 1707* (2nd edn., Edinburgh, 1985), 38, are more cautious.

and vending our linen in Manufactories by a direct exportation as well to the west of Germania as to the West Indies'.[1]

The reality, however, was that the Union offered no immediate transformation. Indeed, if anything, the evidence of the first twenty years after 1707 is one of difficulty for many manufacturers and depression in several areas, particularly in the finer and medium fabrics, with Dutch, German and French linen making substantial inroads. Only the east-coast coarse linens seem to have held their own and even they had their periods of difficulty: it was reported in November 1727 that Perth linen at London had seriously fallen in price as against three years previously, and that 'Dundee and Montrose linens go off very ill'.[2] Given this experience, the subsequent performance of the Scottish industry was all the more gratifying. Production grew slowly in the 1730s but began to accelerate in the following decades; the commercial output of linen doubled from an annual average of 3.5 million yards in 1728-32 to 7.8 million by 1748-52, and had reached 12.6 million by 1773-7. It was not uniformly uninterrupted expansion as there were periods of depression, as in the mid 1750s and the early 1770s, but it was overall an impressive progression which fully justified the hopes of the industry's supporters, such as Patrick Lindsay, whose pamphlet *The Interest of Scotland Considered* had argued firmly in 1733 that the Scottish linen trade would turn 'to a very great account'.[3]

In the development of this Scottish manufacture, three factors have been held to have been of major significance in improving the industry's structure and performance. The first was the work of the Board of Trustees for Fisheries and Manufactures, created in 1727, which devoted most of its time and limited resources to assisting the linen industry through regulation, instruction and promotion. Though some of its policies were of considerable value, others were much less so, such as the attempt to encourage the growth of more flax in Scotland so as to lessen dependence on imported supplies from Holland or the Baltic. While Scots farmers could and did grow good flax, it was not a popular crop, and the industry always remained highly dependent on imports from Holland or the Baltic. The Board was not always to blame for failure and waste; the Fund to encourage the manufacture of linen in the Highlands was given to it to administer in 1754, but the objectives were set by Parliament

1 *Records of the Royal Burgh of Edinburgh, 1701-1718*, ed. H. Armet (Edinburgh, 1967), 186. See also C.A. Whatley, 'The economic causes and consequences of the union of 1707: a survey', *Scottish Historical Review*, lxviii (1989), 150-81, especially 173-4.

2 NLS, Saltoun MSS, box 12: John Drummond to Lord Milton, 7 Nov. 1727.

3 P. Lindsay, *The Interest of Scotland Considered* (Edinburgh, 1733), 98. See also his later work, *The Linen Manufacture of Scotland* (Edinburgh, 1735).

without the Board being consulted, except in the most general way, as to what was practicable. The predictable outcome was an expensive scheme of little or no long-term value. One of the Managers of the British Linen Company, William Tod, was part of the initial team sent north in August 1754 by the Board of Trustees to survey appropriate sites for manufacturing stations in the Highland areas eligible for support. He and his colleagues submitted a detailed report as to how the development of manufacturing villages in the Highlands might civilise the inhabitants, and 'destroy by degrees the present dependence on their chiefs and make them loyal and useful subjects'. He was under no illusions as to the scale of the task, and made plain his reactions to what must have been his first visit north: 'The Highlanders live in so poor, so wretched and barbarous a manner that it would astonish mankind to be told such people inhabited Great Britain.'[1]

The Highland stations were, unfortunately, to prove both costly and ineffectual. By contrast, the Board's most effective instrument was relatively inexpensive: the network of stampmasters set up in 1727 in the main weaving districts.[2] The stampmaster's business was to inspect for a small fee every web of cloth offered for sale, to check that it was of consistent weave throughout, and to measure its length and breadth.[3] If satisfied, he then stamped it with his own personal seal, which bore his name and location, and the dimensions of the piece of cloth. Should a buyer find the cloth to be insufficient in any way, such as the inside of the roll being inferior to the outside fold, he had a right to sue the stampmaster. This system was both regulatory and educational; the stampmasters were selected from the ranks of practising weavers, and were in a position to help by pointing out how the weaver might improve his work. The system seems to have worked well and encouraged confidence in buyers. It was tightly policed by the Board of Trustees who took all complaints seriously, and did much to raise standards and ensure consistency in an industry with so many small producers. But for all the virtues of the stamping system, it did indicate the cloth concerned as having been of Scots manufacture, not always a marketing asset overseas, and there were times, as the British Linen Company's correspondence indicates, that it was politic to 'put the thistle out of sight as we have often done to oblige customers in England'.[4]

1 Letter and report from William Tod to David Flint, Secretary of the Board of Trusees, 28 Sept. 1754, printed in A.S. Cowper, *Linen in the Highlands* (Edinburgh, 1969), 33-41.

2 Durie, *Linen Industry*, 32-5, 67-9, 110-12.

3 See the Appendix, 'Note on the Manufacture of Linen' (pp. 225-6 below), for an explanation of the processes involved in linen manufacture. The Glossary (pp. 227-9) lists technical terms.

4 P. 90 below.

Another area into which the Board of Trustees put a good deal of effort and achieved some success was that of bleaching, a technique in which the Scots were lamentably deficient in the early eighteenth century. Cloth tended to be sent out of the country for finishing, either to England or Holland. The Board gave subsidies to help with the erection of large-scale commercial bleachfields in Scotland, though the sums involved seldom accounted for more than a fraction of the capital outlay incurred by the promoters. The field at Dunfermline, for example, received a grant of £200 from the Board of Trustees towards its construction in 1733, which represented only about one-quarter of the cost.[1] The Board also assisted with the training of Scottish master-bleachers to reduce dependence on imported Dutch or Irish bleachers. Grays' Green in Glasgow was used as the main training centre in the 1730s and 1740s but dissatisfaction with the Grays led to a switch in 1749 to the British Linen Company's new field at Salton where apprentices could be trained in both the Dutch and the Irish methods for bleaching fine and coarse cloth respectively. Men trained there did not hesitate to advertise the fact when they found employment elsewhere. An advertisment for Brechin Bleachfield carried by the *Edinburgh Evening Courant* in March 1756 made full play of the fact that its master-bleacher, Colin Smith, was 'late of Salton'. By the late eighteenth century, not only had the practice of sending Scots cloth for finishing outwith Scotland ceased, but Irish cloth in increasing quantity was starting to come to Scottish bleachfields, a clear indication of how radically things had turned round.

Government policy was also of great significance, particularly mercantilist legislation which intervened in the market to tip the scales in favour of British producers against their Continental competitors.[2] This took two main forms: putting up import duties on foreign linen brought into Britain for sale in the home market, and helping the position of British linens in the colonial markets by retaining rather than repaying (or 'drawing back') the import duties on foreign linen when it was re-exported to North America or the West Indies. The latter policy was politically sensitive as it would tend to raise the cost of living in the colonies. In 1742, therefore, a new approach was tried: the introduction of a subsidy for British linen exported. Financed in part out of higher duties imposed on imported cambric, a measure which pleased British fine linen manufacturers, the subsidy or 'Bounty' applied not to all types of

1 SRO, NG1/13/1, Records of the Board of Trustees, 'Bleaching Bonds'.
2 A.J. Durie, 'Market forces or government intervention: the case of the Scottish linen industry', *Scotia*, xv (1991), 1-12.

linen or in all markets but only to coarse and medium linens under 18d per yard in value exported to British colonies. The level of support was increased in 1745 by a second Bounty Act, and its assistance was seen by many contemporaries as essential in allowing home manufacturers to compete in the colonial markets. It was, however, resented by manufacturers of fine linen who argued that it gave the coarse sector an unfair advantage and pushed up the price of flax and of spinning alike to their disadvantage.

The bounty was temporarily withdrawn in the mid 1750s. The results, as we shall see, were catastrophic for the coarse and medium sectors of the industry. Output in Scotland fell sharply, exports were reduced by one-third, and many weavers, particularly in the export-orientated east of Scotland, were put out of work. Negotiations to restore it, in which William Tod of the British Linen Company played a leading part, were hampered by the intervention of Scottish fine linen manufacturers who pressed for its extension to all linens, something that was quite impossible. George Drummond, who was in London to lobby for the restoration of the bounty, despaired: 'William Tod last post has heard from William Murdoch [of Glasgow] that unless there is a bounty given on linen of 2/-, 2/6d, and linen above that, the manufacturers at Glasgow will vigorously oppose the bounty on the coarse linen as partial. We wish for that as sincerely as they do, but if it's impossible to obtain what they wish for, is it reasonable to refuse what we can get?'[1] The Edinburgh lobby, under the direction of Lord Milton, proved effective; the bounty on coarse linen exported was quickly restored, and thereafter retained until its final abolition in 1832. As exports rose, and 90 per cent of Scottish linen exported was eligible for bounty, the cost of this support rose substantially. The Board of Trustees consistently argued that the expenditure was justified:

> The whole expense of bounties on British linen exported has been more than repaid to the public by the addition to the Revenue of Excise and Customs from the importation of Rum and other commodities in return for home-made linens exported to America and also by the revenue arising on the consumption of persons employed in that manufacture and who on the failure thereof must turn a Burden on the Country till they can shift for themselves. The Manufacture is a Staple Influence and Connection in the support of many other branches of trade.[2]

This brings us to the third factor of significance: the work of the British Linen Company, which was brought into being by Royal Charter in 1746. At the peak of its operations in the 1750s, it was probably not just the largest single

1 NLS, Saltoun MSS, Box 186, Drummond to Milton, 29 Dec. 1755.
2 SRO, NG1/3/5: BOTL, Board to William Tod at London, 26 Mar. 1753.

firm in the Scottish linen industry but in the Scottish economy as a whole, handling as it did every stage of the manufacture of linen cloth from the importation of the flax to the bleaching of the woven cloth. It employed thousands of weavers and spinners in the east and north of Scotland, and marketed hundreds of thousands of yards of cloth annually. Its contribution to the Scottish linen industry included the introduction and promotion of some fabrics new to the industry, such as Osnaburg, which was to become a staple of east-coast manufacturing. Its bleachfield at Salton was a recognised training ground for a generation of Scots master-bleachers. Its financial support, of which more anon, underpinned the activities of many linen manufacturers. But its success was achieved with great difficulty, as the Managers' correspondence makes clear, and at considerable cost to itself. In the 1760s the Company began to make the transition from manufacturing to finance, and steadily reduced its commitment to the linen industry. But for twenty years or so, it was a major force within the industry, and in the development of what was becoming Scotland's premier industry.

It may be helpful to view the history of the Company over this period in four sections: formation and development between 1745 and 1753, a period in which the Company's manufacturing policies were worked up; crisis and recovery from 1753 to 1762 with the loss of the export subsidy, the consequent confusion and eventual recovery; delegation and debt in 1763-1764, with the short-lived experiment of devolving most of its linen operations to E. McCulloch & Co., and the discovery of the seriousness of its financial position; and finally the period of disengagement, between 1765 and 1775, when the Company gradually pared away its interests in linen in favour of banking.

1. Formation and development, 1745-1753.

The formation of the Company had its genesis in the early 1740s, when two young and enterprising Edinburgh linen manufacturers, Ebenezer McCulloch and William Tod, took over the Board of Trustees' expensive and unsuccessful colony of French fine linen weavers at Picardy Place in Edinburgh.[1] This brought them to the attention of the members of the Board of Trustees, who included amongst their number Andrew Fletcher, Lord Milton, a figure of great significance in Scottish politics.[2] While the third duke of Argyll

1 Durie, *Linen Industry*, 49.

2 J.S. Shaw, *The Management of Scottish Society, 1707-1764* (Edinburgh, 1983), ch. 7, provides a full analysis of Milton's career.

controlled from London the direction of government patronage in Scotland, Milton was his chosen and very able man of business on the spot. As a leading member of the Board of Trustees, Milton was conscious, as were McCulloch and Tod, that while the bounty seemed to offer an opportunity for the expansion of Scottish linen sales into more distant markets, what held the Scots back was a lack of finance. To be able to compete with foreign suppliers of linen required not just well-made linen but the ability to offer the standard period of credit required by wholesalers and exporters. And for this, much greater capital resources were required than were currently available.

Milton, who was to become Deputy Manager of the British Linen Company while Tod and McCulloch were its first Managers, drew up a scheme, with Argyll's support, for a company on a much bigger scale than hitherto seen in Scotland, to promote the expansion of Scottish linen production, a private enterprise to complement and carry through the publicly-funded work of the Board of Trustees. Declarations of support for this initiative came from the mercantile and monied classes of Lowland Scotland and related groups at London, and there was general enthusiasm for a 'grand manufactory' to supply not just the 'home market' with 'better linen and at lower prices than the foreign', but also 'the colonies and plantations in America'. A prospectus was drafted by Milton, and the Edinburgh Linen Copartnery, or 'The Company for Improving the Linen Manufactury in Scotland',[1] was accordingly launched in 1745. But, and this was a serious problem, it proved difficult to raise enough capital without a guarantee of limited liability for the shareholders, try as Milton might to find some acceptable legal formula, and so a Royal Charter was sought in the name of the British Linen Company. It was finally obtained on 5 July 1746. This cleared the way for the raising of substantial sums at both Edinburgh and London. The duke of Argyll, for instance, who became the first Governor, subscribed no less than £3,000.

By 1751, when the subscription books were finally closed, some £70,600 had been subscribed. Just under £50,000 had been called, and most of that had actually materialised. To the £46,000 of long-term working capital provided by the Proprietors, the Company was able to add to its resources by borrowing both in the short and medium term in and around Edinburgh. In 1755 it had borrowed no less than £55,000; amongst its lenders were a number of kirk

1 Royal Bank Archives, Edinburgh: The Cash Ledger of the Royal Bank for 1745-6 (No catalogue number) records the opening of an account for this enterprise on 28 Mar. 1745. Lord Milton, with Thomas Allan and Alexander Shairp, merchants in Edinburgh, were named as the 'present Overseers'.

sessions as well as monied individuals.[1] The Royal Bank made available cash credit support, and the cordiality of that relationship was doubtless not unconnected with the fact that several members belonged to both Courts of Directors. The issue of promissory notes which started in September 1747 was another mechanism for supplementing the Company's financial resources; it was asserted that by the early 1760s the Company had a circulation of no less than £96,000 of notes. In short, the British Linen Company was by contemporary standards a very substantial enterprise, rivalled in the manufacturing and trading sectors of the Scottish economy only by the largest of the tobacco partnerships and perhaps not even by them.

The Jacobite Rebellion delayed matters for some time, with the unfortunate McCulloch left on his own in occupied Edinburgh without funds.[2] His co-manager was in Germany on a undercover mission for the Board of Trustees to discover what he could of German techniques for making coarse linen, in particular the Osnaburg fabric so much in demand in colonial markets. Tod's trip appears to have been successful.[3] On his return, and under his personal supervision, a few hundred yards of Osnaburg were woven in one of the British Linen Company's weaving factories; armed with this experience, the Managers were able to place larger orders elsewhere. Within a short time the production of Osnaburg became an established staple in the east of Scotland, with over a million yards of this fabric being stamped in 1753.

The correspondence of the Managers in this early period of the Company's operations makes it quite clear what an uphill task it was to raise standards in the industry. There were problems at every stage of the manufacture, and improvement in one area tended only to expose deficiencies in another. As a result, the Company found itself drawn into involvement in every stage of the manufacture. Almost from the outset, it was decided to use imported flax rather than Scots grown, and every year ships were freighted out to the Baltic ports,

1 Durie, *Linen Industry*, 117-20.

2 John Campbell, *Leaves from the Diary of an Edinburgh Banker* (Edinburgh, 1881), 11, records that as cashier to the Royal Bank, he was approached on 4 Oct. 1745 during the Jacobite occupation of Edinburgh by Alexander Shairp with a letter from Ebenezer McCulloch to him as one of the Linen Manufactory's overseers, 'signifying the distress the work people were in for want of silver coin and desired I might assist him'. The original diary, which is held in the Royal Bank of Scotland Archives, records a further visit from McCulloch on 12 Oct.: 'Changed £15 notes to Mr McCulloch and gave him a bag of shillings of £10 and a bag of silver [?] of £5 for the same.'

3 The BOT Annual Report to the Crown, 25 Dec. 1746, included this reference to Tod's trip: 'The Trustees having last year sent a skilled manufacturer beyond sea to make what observations he was able on the different methods practised on the Continent in carrying on the linen manufacture, he this year returned and communicated what remarks he had made that might contribute to set forward the Linen Manufacture.' SRO, NG1/7/3.

some of which fell victim to storm or privateer, with consequent disruption to the Company's manufacturing operations. Finding a merchant house that could be consistently trusted to supply the right sorts and qualities of flax at a reasonable price was a perpetual problem, and the Company had its fair share of disappointment and losses.

The uneven quality of Scots yarn, and the tendency of prices to rise in the Lowlands as demand increased, led to an ambitious scheme to establish a number of spinning agencies in the North of Scotland. By 1749 contracts had been agreed with agents at Tain, Cromarty, Dingwall, Wick, Inverness and Kirkwall. Many of the workers there had to be trained from scratch, and while no firm figure exists as to how much employment was created in total, at least one of the master-spinners in the north claimed in August 1754 to have over 1,400 spinners under his control. The task of supervising the day-to-day business at Edinburgh, where the yarn was received, checked and sorted, proved increasingly demanding. In 1750, therefore, the Company devolved all its yarn operations to a subsidiary, the Edinburgh Yarn Staplery, under the management of David Doig, an arrangement that was wound up in acrimony a decade later.

If manufacturing was a prime concern, so also was marketing, and it will be seen just how hard the Company had to work to get any foothold in the key markets at London and Glasgow. Initially the Company's linens were consigned to a linen factor at London, John Goodchild, whose interest, it was hoped, would be strengthened by the fact that he had taken a shareholding of £700 in the Company's stock. But the results were not encouraging. It was accordingly decided in 1747 to open a warehouse there, and an experienced clerk, Nathaniel Child, was put in charge. Two years later a warehouse was established at Glasgow under the supervision of Robert Colquhoun. There were problems: demand from the export markets fluctuated according to the state of the colonial trades, and in bad years not only were sales depressed but payments delayed. And it proved difficult to anticipate the extent or nature of demand; one year the cry might be for better linens, the next for the cheapest. It was not easy to co-ordinate manufacturing and marketing for the export markets. Sales of linen did increase steadily from just under £23,000 in the year ending in May 1750 to nearly £35,000 three years later; London's share of sales in 1753 was about 35 per cent, Glasgow's 23 per cent and Edinburgh's 42 per cent.

2. Crisis and Recovery, 1753-1762.

The picture was to change dramatically, however, with the withdrawal in March 1754 of the bounty on coarse and medium linens exported to the

Colonies. Its loss had been anticipated and agonised over in the previous year, but there was no easy response for such an export-orientated company as the British Linen. Production had to be cut back sharply, and a determined drive was made to clear the Company's hands of all linens in the category which had been eligible for subsidy. Quite exceptional and sometimes commercially risky tactics were employed to shift the Company's linen on hand, and one way and another substantial sales were made, which was just as well because over the next eighteen months sales were at a very low ebb indeed, falling from £37,000 in 1754 to a mere £14,000 the next year and even less in the following. Moreover, some of the sales were to little or no profit. The much reduced demand for manufacturing meant that yarn from the North began to accumulate at Edinburgh, dead stock which did not improve with keeping. The Company's finances were not assisted either by the number of bad debts which the rush to make sales had almost inevitably generated. In partial compensation for the loss of the bounty, Parliament had set up a Highland Fund to establish the manufacture of linen in the Highlands, and the British Linen Company became heavily involved in its application, but that did little to offset the depression in the Company's affairs.

Negotiations at London, in which Tod played a prominent part, did eventually secure a return of the bounty in June 1756. The Company's prospects brightened, the more so as war promised to disrupt German competition. What also helped was that Tod took up permanent residence at London, and took charge of sales there, the warehouse keeper being dismissed. Sales began to revive, though it took several years before they regained their former levels. It proved no easy task to rebuild the manufacturing after the depression of the years without any export subsidy: in McCulloch's vivid image, 'the national manufactures were by discontinuing the bounty almost lost; by losing our hands we lost our trade; like a great ship run aground there is more labour and disagreeable trouble to refloat her than originally to launch her to sea.'[1]

The physical separation of the Managers, Tod at London and McCulloch at Edinburgh, also caused problems. Two central and related issues came to divide them. The first was how best the Company could manufacture its linens—whether by using its own factories or not. The other was the even more fundamental question as to whether the Company should produce linens on its own account, or be involved only in joint-ventures for the sale of linen with selected manufacturers. On the manufacturing front, the Company had

1 P. 85 below.

from the outset maintained some factories under its immediate control where standards of production were higher than in the country in general, and, as McCulloch argued, new fabrics or variant designs could be quickly and efficiently introduced. Linen was, however, also bought in from manufacturers and master-weavers at Dundee and elsewhere, and as the general standard of hand-loom weaving began to rise in Scotland during the later 1750s, some of the Directors began to suggest that it was time to phase out the Company's factories. William Tod was a vociferous proponent of this view, which led to an increasing tension between himself and McCulloch, which Milton tried without success to allay. Milton remained on good terms with both, but the Managers moved ever further apart. In a letter to Milton in May 1757, Tod argued that 'it is a truth that as soon as any fabric gets into the hands of the Common people, no man can carry it to a profit in a Factory. In infancy it must be nursed there, but the coarser a fabric, the sooner it leaves the factories.'[1] Tod, who was by this time wholly resident at London in order to handle the marketing of the Company's linens, had become very disillusioned with affairs, and in particular with McCulloch whom he accused of ignoring all criticism. 'Before I left Edinburgh', he complained,

> I did all in my power to impress the people concerned in the Company with a belief that their linens of all sorts wanted improvements and were inferior to others at this market. I found I could gain no credit; I found a self sufficiency and a presumption, added to [which] 'the vanity of managing for a great Company' had an influence which all the remonstrances I could use in prudence were not sufficient to remove. When I came here I found I had been too much in the right. I was daily told of goods sold cheaper than ours. I saw them and I found some of our oldest and best customers leave the warehouse. In these circumstances, My Lord, and considering the Company's affairs, I resolved to write plainly and freely to Mr McCulloch and Mr Doig in a private way. The consequences was that they were affronted but would not believe. I then wrote publicly; the event was that they bestirred themselves a little, but I was, and am kept ignorant of the Company's transactions below unless such as are ordered to be wrote me. When I complain of things, or desire such and such things to be enquired into they are shuffled off and my letters are either forgot and laid aside or it is not thought prudent to write me a public answer.[2]

Tod's arguments began to change the Company's strategy, and the numbers of factory weavers were reduced. The Company betook itself more and more to joint-ventures with selected manufacturers rather than manufacturing as much linen itself. The standard pattern was for the goods to be consigned to London for sale, and the net proceeds divided after the expenses of the

1 NLS, Saltoun MSS, Box 92, Tod to Lord Milton, 19 May 1759.
2 NLS, Saltoun MSS, Box 88, Tod to Lord Milton, 22 Dec. 1757.

purchase, transport and sale had been deducted, according to the share taken by each partner in the venture—usually half each, but sometimes a third or three-quarters. The Company's strategy was switching from the manufacture and marketing of its own linens to the financing and marketing of those manufactured by others, just as Tod had urged.

But the rift between the Managers was never healed, and Tod resigned in January 1759 in order to enter a partnership with a linen factor at London. To his house of Tod & Anderson was consigned the various joint British Linen Company ventures as well as those on the Company's sole account, and in 1762 his firm handled the sale of over 600,000 yards of linen on joint account, half of which came from Tod's relative, David Neilson at Dundee. Tod subsequently dissolved his partnership with Alexander Anderson to set up on his own, and continued to deal with the British Linen Company for many years, latterly more in bills and specie than in consignments of linen, the flow of which steadily diminished as the Company disengaged itself from the trade. In September 1776, for example, Tod was requested to purchase £1,500 or £2,000 of Navy or Victualling bonds.

With Tod's departure in 1759, McCulloch was left in sole charge, a situation that may not have been to the Company's best advantage, until George Goldie, a relation of his, was appointed as assistant manager in 1762. McCulloch had, or so it appears, a tendency to embark on great ventures for marketing linen, some of which came unstuck, such as the scheme with William Dalrymple to market linen at Cadiz, and there were other occasions on which his commercial judgement seems to have been less than sure. But that may be an unfair assessment; the business of marketing linen to more distant markets inevitably carried a degree of risk, and McCulloch did nothing of any significance without submitting it first to the scrutiny of the Court of Directors. If there were errors, the responsibility was a shared one.

3. Debt and devolution, 1763-1764.

The Company's recovery from the problems caused by the withdrawal of the bounty seemed complete enough by the early 1760s. But in 1762 a financial crisis hit Scotland, and one of the Company's more important manufacturer-clients, George Young of Coupar Angus, became bankrupt. Two of the Directors, George Drummond and Patrick Lindsay, were invited to make a full investigation of the Company's affairs, which they presented to the Court in July of that year. They commended McCulloch for his capability, zeal and 'indefatigable application' and in general endorsed the current structure of the Company's activities. But they were disturbed by a long list of bad and doubtful debts, some of many years' standing. They also pointed out that even in the early stages of operations, the proprietors had insisted on the payment of their dividends. The report deeply disturbed the Court, and led to serious divisions as to future strategy. Some Directors wanted the Company to withdraw entirely from manufacturing, and confine itself to lending on security and participating in joint-ventures when adjudged safe; others were totally opposed to this betrayal, as they saw it, of the Company's aims and objectives.

A few months later, on 5 March 1763, McCulloch handed in his resignation as Manager as from the end of the Company's financial year at 30 May. But with his letter he also handed in a proposal that he, in partnership with the prominent merchants William and Robert Alexander, take over all of the Company's production and marketing of linen in Scotland, including the northern spinning, the bleachfield at Salton, the weaving factories, and all the flax, yarn and linen on hand. His firm, E. McCulloch & Co., would handle all this business, insuring against bad debts, with the British Linen Company's involvement in the linen industry reduced to the provision of finance for their operations and the consignment on joint-account of linen to London. This scheme appealed strongly to a majority of the Directors and Proprietors, and a contract was signed on 30 May, with the agreement to run for nine years after a trial period of eighteen months at the end of which either party could terminate the arrangement.

In fact the arrangement lasted only for the minimum period. At the end of the first year of trading, the Directors of the British Linen Company, as was their right, called for an examination of McCulloch & Co.'s balance sheet for the year, but even before they had received it, intimated that the copartnery would be wound up at the end of the formal eighteen months. There was some word of a fresh arrangement but nothing came of it, much to the indignation of some Directors of the British Linen Company such as George Drummond, Provost of Edinburgh and a close political partner of Lord Milton. He thought that McCulloch and his partnership had been shabbily treated and wrote to the ailing Milton: 'Their sales this year will exceed £40,000 and might have been much more if we had not cramped them greatly. What reason can we offer to the general court for proposing to dissolve this copartnery when none of us can say that we have so much as once looked into the books to see whether it has been advantageous to the company or not?'[1]

The real reason for the dissolution of the contract appears not to have been the trading performance of E. McCulloch & Co., which was in fact quite reasonable, but the progressive uncovering by McCulloch's successor as

1 NLS, Saltoun MSS, Box 62, George Drummond to Lord Milton, 16 May 1764.

Manager, George Goldie, of the Company's true financial position. The level of known debt had already forced a suspension of the dividend in 1762; Goldie found that the situation was much worse than initially acknowledged. A daunting list of bad and doubtful debts had been presented to the Court in May 1763, amounting to £8,609. Further enquiry revised this upwards to no less than £22,809, of which only a fraction appeared recoverable. The *Scots Magazine*, in December 1763, carried a bitter attack on the British Linen Company and its policies, alleging that their sole aim had been to use their stock and credit to monopolise the linen trade of Scotland; this called forth only the lukewarm defence that if this great house had in fact failed in its original design, 'they have hurt themselves more than the misapplication of so great a stock could hurt the country'.[1] Indeed so serious was the Company's financial predicament that some of the Directors felt that it could not continue: George Drummond informed Lord Milton in his letter of 16 May 1764 that Mr Young, a friend and fellow director, had thrown out to him on several occasions that he was afraid 'that the best and justest thing we could do was to wind up our bottoms, and honestly divide what was left of the Company's capital amongst the proprietors'.[2]

The decision, therefore, to dissolve the partnership with E. McCulloch & Co. was forced by the need of the parent British Linen Company to realise whatever assets it could as quickly as possible, even if it meant forcing the sale of the partnership's assets at less than might have been achieved with a little more patience. All the pressure the Company could bring to bear was exerted, but even in May 1766, over £11,000 was still owing by E. McCulloch & Co. to the British Linen Company, a marked improvement on the previous balance when just under £31,000 was outstanding. Many of the Directors felt that McCulloch was to blame for all their troubles, and were therefore inclined to give him and his firm no leeway. A long dispute ensued in which the Directors lodged a claim—*inter alia*—for damages of £10,000 from McCulloch. They argued that he had induced them to make dividends when there were no funds for doing so, in order to increase his own premiums. He had failed, in their view, to pay due attention to the persons to whom he had made sales, or to make sufficient effort to make the Company's debts 'effectual', and so on. McCulloch, for his part, denied these allegations, which he said were made 'only with a view to bully', and suggested that the whole of their conduct 'was levelled at one general object vizt. to give up the trade for good, to betake

1 'On the present state of our linen manufacture', *Scots Magazine*, xxv (Dec. 1763), 649-56.

2 NLS, Saltoun MSS, Box 62, Drummond to Milton, 16 May 1764.

themselves to their banking system, and to possess themselves of the Company's whole capital by purchase from ignorant and frighted proprietors at a very low rate'.[1]

The litigation was inconclusive, but the failure of McCulloch's firm in 1769 was not. Deeply financially embarrassed by this misfortune and by his subsequent invòlvement with the Ayr Bank (Douglas, Heron & Co.) which became insolvent in 1773, his stock in the British Linen Company was sold by roup in April 1775 for the benefit of his creditors. His latter years until his death in 1788 were spent in the service of the Board of Trustees, as a general riding inspector of the linen manufactures on a modest annual salary of £60. By contrast, his former joint-manager William Tod flourished in business at London, and retained his links with the British Linen Company, becoming Deputy-Governor in 1795, a connection severed only by death in 1799. His widow and children inherited his very substantial shareholding in the British Linen Company, some £23,000 or nearly one-quarter of the paid-up capital.

4. Disengagement, 1765-1775.

An immediate consequence of the dissolution in November 1764 of the copartnery with E. McCulloch & Co. was that the Company inherited back its northern spinning, and, after a year's delay, the bleachfield at Salton, which in the interim had continued to be run by McCulloch. The directors had long since decided that their primary business for the future was to lie in the provision of banking services to the linen industry, by discounting bills, circulating notes, and advancing money on reasonable security to linen manufacturers and others. Linen manufacturing was no longer a core activity. The northern spinning was gradually wound down and the last connection with the spinning agents finally severed in 1770, much to the Company's relief. Periodic attempts were made to sell off the bleachfield at Salton while it was still a going concern, but without success; eventually it was sold in 1772 to Lord Milton's son for conversion to a pleasure ground. By then the British Linen Company's interest in the linen industry was purely nominal. Cash credits, for example, had been granted with an increasing widening of focus; the first, arranged in April 1765, was for a linen firm in Kirkcaldy, John Fergus & Son, but after that they were granted to a wide range of undertakings with no connection to any aspect of the linen industry—general merchants,

1 BSA, 'Report by Archibald Trotter on the dispute between the British Linen Company and Mr Ebenezer McCulloch, May 1772'.

coalmasters, brewers, farmers, the town of Montrose, even to a Invernesshire cattle drover.[1]

The transition from linen to banking was complete by the mid 1770s; the Company's correspondence reflects this, with its preoccupation with rates of exchange, the circulation of its notes and the security of its advances.[2] Agencies were set up, such as that at Montrose. There were problems aplenty: the embezzlement of over £680 by the Company's Cashier in 1768, and the forgery of some £1 notes in 1773. There were challenges from other banks, the Aberdeen Banking Company (opened in 1767) proving particularly troublesome. The Aberdeen Bank's declared intention was to arrest the 'circulation of variety of banknotes from distant and remore parts of the Kingdom issued and signed by people for the most part unknown in this part of the Country',[3] and it tried to put pressure on the Edinburgh banks. A significant step forward for the British Linen Company as a bank was its acceptance in May 1771 into the weekly exchange of banknotes by the Bank of Scotland and the Royal Bank.

This phase of the Company's life was one of retrenchment, with all profits on their business ploughed back into the capital. It was not until 1774 that a dividend could again be paid—not on the share capital which had actually been paid in, but on the Company's current valuation of its stock, which was much less than half of the subscribed figure. Not until 1789 was the stock back to par, and for those proprietors who needed to sell, or their heirs, these were hard times. In 1774, for example, £500 of stock changed hands for a mere £245.[4] The state of the stock, slowly written up as it was over time, was used by Adam Smith in the *Wealth of Nations* as a prime example of the incompetence of joint-stock companies in trade.[5]

The financial difficulties in the 1760s must partly reflect lax accounting practices in previous years, but it would require an accounting historian to assess whether the management of the Company's affairs was worse than par. Annual accounts were certainly prepared and submitted for scrutiny, but long-overdue debts were carried on the books at face value for years without

1 BSA, BLC Register of Cash Credits, 1765-85.

2 S.G. Checkland, *Scottish Banking: a History, 1695-1973* (Glasgow, 1975), ch. 5, gives an authoritative account of the banking and financial issues of this period.

3 J. Douglas, *Scottish Banknotes* (London, 1975), 15.

4 BSA, BLC Court of Proprietors, 5 Sept. 1774. The stock was bought from John Forrest, merchant in Edinburgh, by George Goldie, the Manager, on 'behoof of this Company'; he held it until a purchaser could be found.

5 Adam Smith, *An Inquiry into the Nature and Causes of the Wealth of Nations*, ed. R.H. Campbell & A.S. Skinner, 2 vols. (Oxford, 1976), ii, 758.

any attempt to write them down. Unsold linens or those damaged at the bleachfield and ill-made northern yarn alike were valued at cost price year after year, though they lay unwanted and rotting in the Company's warehouses. Little allowance was made for depreciation in stock or equipment, whether in the factories or at the bleachfield. Things were to change after McCulloch's departure, and it is not surprising to find the Company's accountant looking in August 1772 for a substantial increase in his salary, given the additional work required of him.

But even if the Company had had a much tighter financial regime, losses would still have been inevitable. It took time to establish the Company's products in the market, and the loss of the bounty was a crushing blow just as some success was being achieved. The Company found itself faced with an impossible dilemma: either to let its bounty linens lie on hand unsold, and without any prospect of sale, and incur sure loss that way, or to offer more credit and take more risks, knowing that this would produce some sales and also some losses. The markets in which the British Linen Company was operating were highly competitive, with Continental and Irish linen keeping margins of profit down. At no market was this more true than at London, and whereas over the period 1748-62 sales at Edinburgh realised a profit level of 18.9 per cent, those at London barely broke even and Glasgow's were not much better. It was a hard proving ground for the Company. The linen trade, Tod wryly observed, was not 'like merchandise which sometimes has great gains to recompense great losses'.[1] The British Linen Company did indeed make a major contribution to the surge forward in the Scottish linen industry during the late 1740s and 1750s, but it was fortunate nonetheless that it had sufficient flexibility in the terms of its Charter to allow it to develop a supplementary and ultimately alternative role as a banking society. That was what was to ensure its long-term survival.

Editorial Method.

What follows is a selection from the Company's records. The task of selection is made all the more demanding because they have survived in such remarkable profusion. There are not just the Managers' outgoing letter books and the Minute Books of the Court of Directors and those for the Proprietors; there are also ledgers, day books, waste books and even a scrap book or two. Some of the records of two of the Company's subsidiaries, the Edinburgh Yarn

1 NLS, Saltoun MSS, Box 88, Tod to Milton, 4 Oct. 1757.

Staplery and Salton bleachfield, have also survived, along with the letter books of E. McCulloch & Co., the partnership to which the British Linen Company hived off its linen manufacturing interests in 1763. The challenge, therefore, has been to select a representative range of material so as to open a window on the Company's day-to-day business and concerns, its longer-term plans and policies, the debates and dealings. What has been selected is only the tip of the iceberg, perhaps less than five per cent of the whole, but is, I hope, sufficent to give an insight into the operations of this Company and its management.

The main source on which I have drawn is the Company's outgoing correspondence. All the letters cited, unless otherwise indicated, are from the joint Managers at Edinburgh, prior to Tod's resignation in 1759: where it is known and of particular significance as to which Manager was writing, that is made clear. McCulloch as sole Manager is the principal correspondent thereafter, until 1763 when he was succeeded by George Goldie. Most of the letters have been topped and tailed in order to focus on the meat of the correspondence. In similar fashion, selected extracts only have been taken from the Directors' Minute Books and the Meetings of Proprietors. A necessarily very limited use has been made of the Company's business journals, particularly those relating to Salton bleachfield, as indicative of what is to be found in them.

Much of the handwriting is very clear, but occasionally words are indecipherable, or a tired or bored copy clerk has lost a word, in which case either an omission has been noted by three dots ... or a guess word supplied in square brackets. Punctuation and spelling could be very erratic and in places I have had to intervene in order to bring coherence. Some familiar abbreviations have been left unaltered, while others have been expanded either silently or in square brackets.

British Linen Company Records.

The surviving records of the British Linen Company (later the British Linen Bank) are located in the Bank of Scotland Archives at Sighthill, Edinburgh. Application to view any part of this archive should be made to the Archivist of the Bank of Scotland, Head Office, The Mound, Edinburgh. For the purposes of this volume, selections from the following series have been used:

The Edinburgh Linen Copartnery, Letter Book, 1 Apr. 1745 to 26 Jan. 1749 (BSA 3/2/1).
Minutes of Meetings of Proprietors, 17 Sept. 1746 to 5 Sept. 1803 (BSA 6/5/1).
Minutes of Meetings of Directors, 2 Aug. 1746 to 9 June 1778 (BSA 6/6/1-3).
Report by Archibald Trotter on the Dispute Between the British Linen Company and Ebenezer McCulloch, 11 May 1772 (BSA 6/15/1).
British Linen Company Letter Books (main series), 27 Apr. 1748 to 19 Apr. 1776 (BSA 6/19/1-29).

British Linen Company Scotch Letter Books, 24 Aug. 1749 to 14 May 1761 (BSA 6/23/1-8).
British Linen Company English and Foreign Letter Books, 30 April 1748-2 June 1763 (BSA 6/24/1-7).
British Linen Company Letters to William Tod and Messrs Tod & Anderson, London, 14 Feb. 1758 to 2 July 1763 (BSA 6/26/1-3).
Salton Bleachfield Journal, 20 Feb. 1768 to 1 May 1773 (BSA 5/1/2).
British Linen Company Stock Ledgers, 29 Nov. 1746 to 25 Dec. 1798 (BSA 6/32/1).
E. McCulloch & Co., Letter Books (BSA 20/1-3).

There is in addition (of which no direct use has been made in this volume) other archival material for this period, including:

Cash Books, 24 Sept. 1746 to 30 May 1774 (BSA 6/49/1-25).
Journals of the Daily Transactions, 23 Dec. 1746 to 9 Oct. 1769 (BSA 6/47/1-24).
Ledgers of Accounts Current, 1748-1781 (BSA 6/39/1-14).
Ledgers of the Daily Transactions, 31 May 1750 to 30 May 1776 (BSA 6/37/1-27).
Register of Cash Credits, 24 Apr. 1765 to 19 Apr. 1797 (BSA 6/53/1).
Waste Book, 25 Jan. 1751 to 18 Apr. 1752 (BSA 6/56/1).

Chapter One
FORMATION AND DEVELOPMENT, 1745-1753

To John Goodchild, London

6 April 1745

This day tonight we sent for you 100 pieces Brown Cambric each 19 yards in length in three small bales. And so soon as we shall receive the London waggoner's receipt at Newcastle then it shall be forwarded to you by post.

The Success of our Linen Bill[1] in Parliament gives great joy to everybody, and the more so as it was unexpected from its former ill success and the many petitions put in against it. We refer you to Lord Justice Clerk[2] for full information either as to the forms or clauses of the Company's contract to be signed at London, or as to the plans laid down for employing the Company's cash.

To John Goodchild, London

9 April 1745

We hope by this time my Lord Justice Clerk will have removed all objections as to the difficulties raised anent the 13th article of the contract. But if the opinion of the ablest judges and lawyers of this country that that clause will save every particular person from being affected with the Copartnery's debts to a greater extent than his share or shares paid in should not prove altogether satisfying to answer these doubts stirred up pray would not a Royal Charter effectually do it? This we beg leave to hint to you and at the same time desire you would see to get every thing relating to the contract settled and signed while my Lord Justice-Clerk is in town, so that we may be able to get on with

1 18 Geo. II, 'An Act for allowing certain additional duties on the exportation of British and Irish Linens', which increased the level of export subsidy on coarse and medium quality linen exported to the American and West Indian colonies, and also those to Spain and Africa.

2 Andrew Fletcher, Lord Milton, who had been appointed Lord Justice Clerk in 1734.

the affairs of the Copartnery which this delay in signing, and our London partners not paying up their quota, has in a manner entirely put a stop to.

Enclosed is also the Carrier's receipt for for the three bales of Cambrick, which we hope you'll find turn out pretty nigh the Valienciennes Fabric. And we flatter ourselves that our Holland this year will give entire satisfaction. But of that you'll please write us afterwards. But in the meantime we beg the favour you'll let us know what is meant by the prohibition of Cambrics as by all the accounts we can learn of it here it seems contradictory of the design of giving us a Bounty on Coarse British linen.

To Mr Adie, Dunfermline

16 May 1745

I have examined your piece of cloth and cannot help observing the sundry faults of it to you although the stampmaster has passed it as sufficient. If ever our country is to have any considerable business or trade in this manufacture, the linen must be made so as to give content to the wearer. The piece you have sent here has been very ill-sorted and the yarn before sorting not half-boiled, if at all, and the woof as slightly put on as if the goods had been designed for buckram. But I am of the opinion that this last general evil will not be remedied till our country weavers can be persuaded to turn their treddles and to use better, that is firmer made looms with heavier lays than at present they use. At the same time the weaver ought to beetle his woof yarn before he winds it on his quils. That you may see what sort of cloths we want made and what sort of goods are brought to market from Germany, I have sent you a sample enclosed to what if this nation does not come up, we can never expect either business, character or credit. I have likewise sent you a table of directions which has been approved of by the Board of Trustees how to sort and make these coarse cloths.

William Tod to Messrs Sandeman, Perth

12 July 1745

Our Copartnery having some thoughts of buying a quantity of brown Perth linen if altered only a little in the breadth which we imagine will easily be got done, and thinking likewise to contract for some coarse brown Hollands of 12, 13 and 14 hundreds such as I saw in your factory, we should be glad if you could conveniently come this length that we may have a conversation concerning these things sometime next week which we hope will turn out to your advantage and that of our Company.

To John Goodchild, London

18 July 1745

We being very much straitened for cash just now have adventured to draw on you for £200 at 30 days in favour of Jas. Manfield in part of the balance due us on last year's account. What remains after this draft is honored, Mr Tod will settle with you at London someday soon, he intending to set out for Hamburg by way of London on Saturday first. But this is desired by the Board of Trustees to be kept secret lest our good friends the Hamburg merchants should take care to prevent his having any instruction or benefit of the journey. The General Meeting of our Copartnery have agreed to advance 10 per cent more on their subscriptions till such time as a Charter is procurred from the Crown, which is now paying in to the Royal Bank of Edinburgh.

To Mr Watson, Ceres

2 August 1745

We have received your cloths by your man and observe that Number 2, 4 and 10 are generally thin with sundry holes in each piece, some in the selvedges and one of these pieces has very ill sorted yarn for waft to it. The rest are all tolerably good only we would have you for the future to make out your invoices in sterling money, not in the old Scotch calculation and likewise we find your pieces do exceed the rate of a penny sterling for the hundred after the rates we apprehend Mr Tod bargained with you to furnish the Copartnery at. There is one rule which you must observe, never to exceed in your drawing for money on us that sum for which you have found security to the Copartnery, four drafts on us dated at Perth June 11th having lain unpaid till this date for that very reason.

To Mr Walter Nicoll, Aberdeen

14 October 1745

Yours of the 9th we have received and provided you can send the yarn with absolute safety to the other side of the Forth, we desire you may send it to the care of Provost Whyte of Kirkcaldy and write him to whom it belongs and desire him to keep it till he advise us of its being come to hand. But if you shall apprehend that there is any risk in sending the goods you may defer it till the Country is more at quiet.[1]

1 The Jacobite Army had seized the city of Edinburgh on 17 Sept., although the Castle, where the Company's specie was lodged, remained in Crown hands throughout the six weeks' occupation until the Highland Army left early in Nov. to march south.

To John Goodchild, London

22 October 1745

Yours of the 16th ult should have been answered before this, had not the disturbances of the Country, nay of this city, prevented me of doing any manner of business. As to our lawns being charged much higher than those you have had from Mr Dassaville[1] and I make no doubt of it. But then you'll please to know that all sorts of yarn and flax have been much scarcer these two years bygone than formerly, besides if you'll compare any sett of ours with one of the same from Dassaville you'll find that is as fine as any of his that is made in a reed one or two setts finer, that is to say a fifteen hundred of ours is as fine yarn as what they formerly made at Piccardy into a 16 or 17oo, and likewise you'll find ours to be considerably broader than what you had from this Country. When that manufacture was put into Mr Tod's hands and mine, the great objection was that our Scotch Lawns were made much narrower than the French and made much too thick; so that they would not answer the uses of Cambric, both of which evils I flatter myself are remedied by our present Scale of Weaving.

To John Goodchild, London

16 January 1746

By next week I shall forward you by land 5 bales of fine linen, Lawn and Cambric Holland, and shall send you the invoices. Mr Tod would tell you that thr' the trouble this Rebellion has occasioned the Country, we have been obliged to dismiss about 100 looms in this town only of the Fine Manufacture and since the 1st of September we have not had any correspondence with the people the other side of the Forth, where all our coarse manufacture is made from a 7oo to a 12oo. Amity and friendship.

To Alex[ander] Christie, Perth

6 February 1746

We have received two pieces of our ⅞ linens from Ba[illie] Mansfield that were sent you last season to be whitened and have no complaints with the colour but must observe that you have acted contrary to our agreement with

1 Nicholas Dassauville of St Quentin was the chief figure in the colony of French fine linen weavers established in 1729 by the Board of Trustees at Picardy Place in Edinburgh: SRO, NG1/3/1, BOTL, 22 Oct. 1728.

you in putting the linens through a callender. And packing and folding them before we have them examined in the waterfold and before they are stamped which by the late act of Parliament you'd see obliges us to have them stamped here when we have an opportunity of giving our oath upon the goods being the manufacture of this country conform to the Law for Drawing the Bounty upon Exportation. Therefore the dressing and finishing them in any way before they are stamped and oath made as above is quite an unnecessary charge and trouble of which we informed you when last here.

We would have wrote you long before now of this but by no means thought it prudent for us to mention the least thing of any effects being in your custody when lying at the mercy of a parcel of lawless, robing Highlanders.

To Mr Hugh McVeagh, Huntly

5 March 1746

As I am hopefull by this time the communication with your country is open and safe I would be glad to know the lowest price of best yarns with you from 8 to 16 hanks per lb, and if you could furnish me a parcel soon and at what price. I would propose paying you ⅔rds in cash at 30 days after shipping and the remainder in flax to be delivered you at Leith of which I dare say great quantities are sold with you; the kind is of the best Russia 12 head plescow which can be afforded you at 42/- per 112 lb and will with ease spin to three or four hanks per lb of which sorts of yarn you sell great quantities to London and Manchester.

The great stop to trade and circulation of cash that this civil war has occasioned, makes that I cannot deal with you in the same way as formerly. But this method I presume will be no inconvenience to you who can retail the above goods to advantage through the country. Below is a note of the last prices of yarn from Aberdeen. But I doubt not of their being considerably cheaper from the want of demand.

To Alex[ander] Christie, Perth

7 April 1746

When you wrote us the 4th ult that you had shipped 77 pieces of our linen on board the William & Mary of Perth, Graham master, for Leith, we daily expected the arrival of the vessel but as yet can learn nothing of her which is a very great loss to us as this is the season for disposing of low priced linens for exportation. We must therefore desire of you to inform us what is become of her.

We have just now 55 pieces of about 21 yards each which we shall send by any carrier from your place bringing a line from you fixing the price we ought to pay for carriage which we doubt not you'll make as cheap as possible. But upon this condition likeways that you agree to send us the goods by land when whitened by reason that we lose more by this tedious method of sending by sea in not getting our sales made in time than if we gave somewhat more for whitening here.

To Mr David Knox, Errol

17 April 1746

Your first letter desired us to remit you £20 or £25 which is not in the Copartnery's power at present or will not be this month or two occasioned by the delays we have met with in procuring our Charter which this plaguey rebellion has stopped us from ever since the month of September last, tho' now we expect everything will be put to rights in the above mentioned time.

To William Tod, London

27 May 1746

Pray write me the numbers of those pieces that turned out very ill of last year's parcel. I wrote you that there was some few bad pieces taken in while the rebels were masters of this City and want now to be satisfied whether it's owing to bad flax or bad workmanship that this has happened.

To John Goodchild, London

2 August 1746

'His Majesty having been most graciously pleased at the desire of sundry of the Nobility, Gentry and Merchants of Great Britain to grant them his Royal Charter incorporating them into a Body Politic for the more effectually promoting the linen manufactures of the Kingdom by the name and style of the British Linen Company and having appointed for their first and immediate Governors and Directors—His Grace Archibald Duke of Argyll Governor, the Right Honorable Andrew Fletcher Esq, Lord Justice Clerk Deputy Governor, Patrick Crawfoord & Wm Beckford Esqs, Messrs John Coutts, Thos Allan & Alexr Shairp Merchants in Edinburgh Directors.

'They therefore in consequence of the powers vested in them by the said charter give notice that a general meeting of all those who have agreed to become proprietors will be held at the house of Ebenezer McCulloch merchant in Edinburgh upon Wednesday the 17th Day of September next at 3 o'clock afternoon.'

By order of the Court of Directors of the Linen Company I sent you the above advertisement which you will be pleased to have inserted in the first London Gazette after this shall come to hand conform to the will of our charter which obliges us to give such notice 30 days at least before any general meeting can be held.

Court of Directors

2 August 1746

The Court having under their consideration what may be the most proper and necessary steps for commencing the operations of this Company have resolved and agree that a cash account or credit for Three Thousand pounds shall be applied for and taken out with the Royal Bank of Scotland and that the Managers shall have liberty of drawing on the said bank from time to time as the affairs of this Company may require and it's ordered that the Managers shall pay in all money they shall receive on the Company's account into the Bank within at least three days after such money shall be passed to them excepting that the affairs of the Company shall require their instantly paying away the sum or sums so received or that the sum or sums paid them does not exceed £50 stg.

The Court have likewise resolved that the Company shall purchase from the Proprietors of the Edinburgh Linen Society or Copartnery all their effects upon hand.

The Managers have represented that as there is a great probability from the experiments already made by the above named copartnery of making considerable progress in manufacturing and improving that species of linen called Osnaburg or Sprigg linen so much wanted for exportation it would be absolutely necessary to import a large quantity of Russian flax, which is the best for that manufacture, and that by their latest account from thence flax was fallen to so a price as fifteen and sixteen roubles per birquit for the kind called twelve head plescow and so in conformity for nine head ditto. The Court therefore ordain the Managers to write Mr Thomas Allan merchant in St Petersburg that he would buy up and contract for Two Hundred tons of twelve and nine head flax for account of this Company provided that these kinds does not exceed the above mentioned price, and in case flax should exceed sixteen roubles that he should not buy more than one hundred tons and that they give Mr Allan a credit for drawing on George Clifford and Sons at Amsterdam for three Thousand pounds in case he shall require it. And that Mr Claude Johnston be wrote to honour Mr Clifford and Sons their bills on him and son and advise the Company so they may put Mr Johnston & Son in cash for paying said drafts. And the Court does further allow the Managers to make purchases of flax from time to time till the above shall come to hand so that this useful branch of manufacture may be increasing as quick as may be.

The Managers having represented to the Court that in the present method or way they have been in use to provide themselves with warp yarns for the fine linen, they have experienced it to be of great loss to the manufacture, which is by purchasing the different sorts they may want from the dealers in yarn in this place who supply themselves with flax from the Dutch factors at six months' credit from the time of shipping by which means they buy in their goods at an advance of ten or twelve per cent above its real worth which obliges them to beat and heckle up their flax to a fineness much beyond its natural strength or quality and this occasions the cloth when whitened to have a bare thin hungry look, the threads of such overspun flax not being able to stand the severe operations it must go through in the bleaching: to remedy which it is ordered that the Managers shall immediately write to Mr James Craufurd at Rotterdam to buy up for the Company a quantity of flax for the above purpose not exceeding ten tons or thereby and that Mr Craufurd have liberty to draw on London upon his buying the above or any part of that quantity or that the Managers shall remit him the value as shall be most for the Company's interest. And it is ordered that the Managers shall cause the same to be heckled in such a proper way as not to exceed the natural strength or quality of the flax which flax when so dressed shall be given out to different persons in the country about to get the same spun into yarn of such a fineness as they shall be directed and that they the Managers may be at liberty to allow these agents for spinning a premium of two pence per spindle, they being always answerable to make good any losses of flax and that they shall defray all charges of carriage out and home.

To Andrew Ross, Depute Steward of Orkney

11 August 1746

In consequence of what Mr Farquharson would write you anent my Lord Morton's resolutions about employing the poor in Orkney in useful branches of manufactures and agreeable thereto that the Directors of the Linen Company had resolved to risk a large parcel of dressed flax and tow to be spun into yarn with you, conform to the directions of a spinning mistress to be provided by the Company at the Earl's charge, I have shipped this day 3679 lbs dressed flax and 1137 lbs tow to be spun for our account, on board the Isobel of North Leith Richard Alison master, to be delivered at Kirkwall to your order and likewise have sent on board the same vessel 42 wheels and 6 check reels which are the property of my Lord Morton. The spinning mistress, whose name is Christian Harrison, will present you this; I have engaged her a year from July last at the rate of six guineas per annum certain and two more provided she gives content to you by application to her business in instructing the people you will present to her for that end. But in case there shall be such a number instructed by next March or April as will be sufficient to spread the art of spinning yarns fit for the Osnaburg linen for which this is designed then she may have liberty to return home if she wishes.

I doubt not Mr Farquarson would write you that the fixing of the prices for spinning at Orkney is left entirely to you after comparing the prices we pay for spinning such yarns here and at Orkney which am apt to think are fully one half cheaper with you. You will be pleased to intrust this flax with some one person or other of credit, who is to keep of what he receives and to charge us again with what yarn he shall ship for the Company and his bill or draft on the Company at sight for the charges of freight and spinning shall be duly honoured and we shall leave it to you to fix a proper salary or premium to be paid him for his trouble which if this trial succeed may be very considerable. I have no further to add but I look upon the succeeding of this project to be for the interest of the Earl, the people employed, the Company and of the Kingdom in general.

To Henry Gilles, Brechin

25 August 1746

The great objection we have always had to your yarn is that its being spun beyond what the strength of the flax will admit of which is the occasion of yarns wasting much in strength and and substance when boiled and much more so when it goes throughout the several trials in bleaching. We therefore would desire you to make trial of spinning six pounds of flax of a superior quality to what you have been in use to spin. We would have it understood that the flax when rough or undressed is not to be beat into a finer quality than it naturally ought or to be exceptionally cut down through finer heckles than it should. This would have another effect, provided you was at pains to choose right flax and not over heckle it, in preventing the vast numbers of thumb knots we are plagued with in your yarn.

To Mr Cunningham, [Falkirk?]

29 August 1746

We received yours and have given each of the men you sent yarn for a piece of cloth and if we had more of that kind would have given it them but our method with coarse linen is to show them the fabrics of cloths we want and to pay them so much per yard agreeable to the hundreds and kinds of linen we have occasion for. What we understand from the people sent is that they have not money to buy yarn but if they had they are willing and could furnish us the linens at our prices and as it is impossible for us to trust so many different hands we would propose for the good of the country that any man who has money in your town should buy and give out yarn to these poor people to be wrought and we could give him ready money for the cloth or if there is none such with you we shall on your security lend any one of them you think proper £30 or £40 which person might lend in small sums or buy yarn and trust it to these people till their webs should be wrought and upon return of their webs for which they should be paid ready money they should have credit for as much more yarn or money to buy it. If when you come next here you'll bring one of your most knowing weavers with you and to him would point such a way as we doubt not would answer all your inclinations and ours in this affair.

To Mr John Goodchild, London

20 September 1746

We in course expected a invoice of the copartnery's goods on hand that as we wrote you we might know how to set them to the Company which in some respects is only a continuation of the copartnery, yet there are some who fearing that there may be loss to the copartnery by the troublesome times, incline rather to buy the goods at a certain price than on a venture at what they cost, and on the other hand some members of the Copartnery expect profit and say as the new members of the Company would not have borne the loss last year if there had been any, therefore they ought not to have the profit upon the whole. There must be an inventory of all goods on hand made and those sold to the Company as two neutral men shall judge.

To Mr George Chalmers, Dunfermline

10 October 1746

After inspecting the 10oo cloth you left here, we find the yarn pretty well boiled but so unevenly sorted and wrought that we cannot put it to your account till we have the pleasure of seeing you here. We doubt not such pieces you make for the future will be free from such faults and that you endeavour to introduce in the country such a creeks [sic] of linen as may be saleable and lasting. Pray cannot you introduce the Osnaburgs with you? If you have spinners we will send you a woman for ten days to teach your spinners and will pay you for these goods all your charges in manufacturing and 5 per cent more for your trouble, or if you think sending a woman here would do better, she will be taught in eight days and may teach these with you when she returns and a weaver, if sent here, might be taught the working in two days as there is no difficulty in it.

To Mr Henry Kennan of Carolina, at London

8 February 1747

We can just now supply you with a large assortment of linens of the same fabric you saw at Mrs Young's from 2/5 to 4/- a yard and by next summer will be able to deliver quantities of white linen ⅞ and yard wide from 9d to 18d per yd of as good a fabric in either the the Irish or foreign linens and likewise in 2 or 3 months be able to bring a pretty large assortment of Osnaburg linen to market which we flatter ourselves will be nothing inferior if not better than the foreign linens of that name upon both which last mentioned there is a bounty of 1½d upon exportation.

The Company will do everything in their power to cultivate and establish a correspondence with gentlemen in the American trade. And you may depend on having what goods you are pleased to order from them charged at as low & reasonable a rate as possible. There's a convoy to sail with the trade to London about the middle of this month so that your orders in course of post will hit that opportunity.

To Thomas Shairp of Houston, Esquire, one of the Proprietors

25 April 1747

The British Linen Company being informed that the town and barony of Leadhills belonging to the Right Honorable the Earl of Hopeton contains about 400 families where the women are quite idle and depend solely upon the labour of the men for their subsistence.

The Company therefore in order to promote industry and extend the linen manufacture thro' the Kingdom propose to send there a person skilled in the heckling of flax who will give out dressed lint to those women to be spun into yarn for the Osnaburg manufacture and pay them weekly for what yarn they shall return at the rates usually paid in other places for spinning. Provided my Lord Hopeton will countenance to the undertaking and particularly that he would cause a woman to be sent from Leadhills to be instructed at Edinburgh in the method of spinning this kind of yarn which will cost no more than her maintenance for two or three weeks at most as in that time any experienced woman will learn it and be capable to instruct her neighbours at home. And further that My Lord would allow his factor to lay out the money for the wheels which will cost about 4/6 per piece and distribute them amongst the miners who should be obliged to take a wheel for every woman, (or if that shall be thought too much) for every two women in his family betwixt the age of 10 and sixty years and this advance can easily be replaced to his Lordship by ordering the factor to deduct the value of the wheels out of the first payment that shall be made to the workmen.

We judge it will be quite proper at first to get my Lord to interest himself in this affair as above. But are of opinion that in a few months practice the people will need no authority to be interposed or any other spur to industry than the benefits accruing from their labour as they will be able (in conformity to their industry and application) to earn from 16d to 2/4 per week. So that if the town have 400 families and each to produce only one spinner who we shall suppose makes at a medium 20d per week or £4 6/8 per annum, the returns in general for spinning to Leadhills will be £1733 6/8.

From the experiments made by the Company in the Osnaburg manufactures, we have the pleasure to acquaint you that they have not only given satisfaction to our own West India merchants in Scotland but what is much more material to both the West India merchants and linen drapers at London. Now the Company is resolved to push that branch of the linen as far as it's possible. And for that end the Court of Directors have ordered us to ask your assistance in procuring an answer to the enclosed proposal from my Lord Hopeton who you see (if we are rightly informed) will have it in his power at a very small expence to make all of his people at Leadhills very useful to themselves, the Company and their country.

Court of Directors

12 July 1747

The Managers this day reported that agreable to their desire Mr Hume had drawn up a memorial which had been presented to the Convention of Royal Burghs met on Tuesday the seventh current which was approven by them, with orders to the clerks to transmit a copy of the said proposal to the Magistrates and Council of each burgh in Scotland.[1]

Which being read it was ordered the thanks of this Court should be returned to Mr Hume, for the service he has done this Company, and the trouble he had taken upon himself without fee or reward.

The Proposals to the Royal Burghs are as follows Vizt.

As this Company is composed of Gentlemen who in laying out their money upon the manufacturing of linen cloth have in view the service of their country, the Company has had nothing more at heart from the beginning than to encourage private manufacturers by the assistance of ready money to extend their business as much as possible. This measure has already had a good effect. Many private manufacturers have credit for considerable sums in the books of the company. They draw out their money as they have occasion for it, and pay it back in linen cloth. This is so great a conveniency that the manufacturers who thus deal with the Company have, for the most part, put more cloth

1 *Extracts from the Records of the Convention of the Royal Burghs of Scotland, 1738-1759*, ed. J.D. Marwick (Edinburgh, 1915), 240-1, states that the proposal was received at the Annual Convention on 7 July 1747; copies made at the Company's expense were transmitted to the burghs for their consideration with a letter desiring them to report their opinion to the next convention. The matter then appears to have lapsed.

through their hands in six months than they were formerly in use to do in thrice that time.

The prospect of promoting the linen manufacture by this scheme is so fair that the Company have an inclination to make it universal. To this end they submit the following proposals to the Convention of Royal Burghs, to be promoted by them with such alterations and improvements as they shall please to suggest.

The Company proposes to set aside £5000 sterling of their capital stock for advancing the linen manufactures within the Royal Burghs of Scotland, and to enter in to contracts with the Magistrates of every Royal Burgh upon the same plan that has hitherto been carried on with private dealers. Every burgh which chooses to accept of the proposal shall have credit in the Company's books for the sum agreed on, upon condition of employing what they draw out in manufacturing of coarse linens and offering the same to the Company at an equal price.

In order to lay out to the best advantage the sums to be contracted for, 'tis proposed that the indigent children of both sexes, with which most of the burghs of Scotland but too much abound, shall be taken up, and taught to spin and weave, for doing which the magistrates of Royal Burghs have sufficient authority by repeated Acts of Parliament; that others should be received who offer themselves; and that a proper person be chosen in every burgh skilled in the manufacture to have the charge of educating the girls to spinning and the boys to weaving to whom the Managers of the Linen Company will be assisting, by giving directions about the manufacturing the different kinds of coarse cloths.

Such contracts with the Company will be still more advantageous to Royal Burghs than private dealers. Royal Burghs will find the sweets of such a commerce in several particulars. In the first place, a boy of any capacity may be brought in the course of three months to weave from five to six yards of Osnaburg in a day. The boy's labour, even in that coarse cloth, will be worth to the employer a penny a yard, and proportionately more when he is carried on to finer sorts. A girl in less than that time, may be brought to earn by spinning from fourteen to twenty pence a week. This will afford a considerable profit to the undertakers, as will be evident from the scheme annexed, which has been put in practice several years by a gentleman in the neighbourhood of Edinburgh, who maintains his boys at 14½d a week; and at a distance from the capital this expence will be proportionately less; at the same time the charge of erecting a loom and providing utensils for these boys will not exceed twenty eight shillings. And if profit can be made of the work of such young creatures, almost from the beginning, how great must be the profit of their work on the whole when the town that has set them to work is entitled by the law to the benefit of their labour until they are thirty years complete.

In the second place, the Royal Burghs instead of being oppressed by the poor, and being considerably out of pocket by their maintenance, will not only be relieved in a great measure of the burden but turn their poor to great account.

In the third place, a stock of working poor will be raised in every town, who will be attached to the town by getting their education there, and who may be made a happy beginning of promoting not only the linen manufactures to the greatest degrees of fineness, but also other branches of trade. And lastly every artificer and workman within the town must find his account in this scheme by the additional demand for all necessaries of life occasioned by so many people employed in this linen manufacture.

The Company will oblige themselves to purchase all the goods made as above proposed at the same price they pay to private manufacturers; and to that end will enter into bargains for three, five or seven years. And to put the matter on as fair a footing as possible, they are satisfied in the case of any difference about the price, that the same be fixed by indifferent persons, mutually or separately chosen. It does not readily occur that there can be a doubt of the benefit that must redound to the burghs by following out such a scheme.

Court of Directors

7 March 1747

The Managers having represented that Thomas Boswell, dyer, and Patrick Anderson weaver in Musselburgh, proposed to borrow ten pounds stg on their joint bill, to enable the said Anderson to increase the number of looms he has going in the Company's service, the Managers were to write Baillie Lindsay of that place theranent and to act agreeable to his answer.

The Court being likewise informed that Mr Thomas Allan, the Company's correspondent at Peterburg, desired that twenty pieces fine linen might be sent him upon twelve months credit and that if the Company would agree to go one half concerned in the adventure to send him fifty pieces, the first the Court agreed to, but deferred going into the last proposal till they could be in some sort ascertained to what advantage they could carry on such a trade to Petersburg, it being probable that the Dutch could not only afford them cheaper goods at that market, but that they likewise saved a good deal on their insurance that we are now liable to in time of war.

The Court being informed that from some conversations the Managers had had with several Highland gentlemen they had reason to believe that the Company might make advantagious contracts with the more considerable persons in the Highlands, for a term of years certain, for the delivery of large quantities of coarse linen yarn, they ordered the Managers to proceed in their correspondence with persons proper to bring about such contracts.

To Mr David Stiven, weaver, Dunfermline

22 April 1747

You have but small reason to complain of our returning you the linens you call Huggabags, as they were not only ill manufactured but made of the worst tow yarn we ever saw and no sort of care had been taken to boil the yarn with ashes before they were wove. We desired you to make some Huggabag of either 3/4, 6 quarter or 2 yards broad of good sufficient yarn, and we should be determined by the price at which you could afford the samples if or not we might give you an order to go on and enlarge your trade in that way. But surely you cannot say we desired you to rake together all the trash of ill made linen of that sort in your town?

The great fault of all your town made diapers is that the figures are by no means square, being much longer waft ways than they are by the warp. Pray mend that on your next pieces you send us which will encourage a future correspondence.

Court of Directors

8 February 1748

The Managers acquainted the Court that as the season for bleaching both fine and coarse linens draws near, they had wrote to Mr William Gray at Glasgow and Mr William Colvin at Denovan in order to know at what rates they would bleach the Company's linens, but as yet had received no return. The Court approved of the same, and directed the Managers further to write Mr Andrew Wight at Ormiston, Mr Andrew Dickson at Haddington and Mr William Neilson at Roslin to the same effect and communicate their returns to the Court.

The Managers informed the Court that through the increase of the Company's affairs it would be absolutely necessary to hire a much larger warehouse than that which the Company presently had, and one better situate so as both to give access for carriages and if possible to have it disjoined from any neighbouring houses, that thereby the Company's effects might be in less hazard from fire. And as the Earl of Murray's house in the Canongate seemed in every way well adapted for a warehouse for the Company where at the same time there would be as much spare room as would lodge the Managers, and perhaps more of the Company's servants under the same roof with their effects, they had wrote a letter to Mr John McKenzie of Delvin, agent for the Earl, offering him a rent of £50 stg yearly for the use of his house and gardens, upon his lordship's agreeing to enter in to tack for some few years.

To Nathaniel Child, the Company's warehouse keeper at London

12 May 1748

We will carefully note your observations on the various kinds of linen mentioned in yours dated 5th May current. All we can just now say is that we are conscious that there is nothing wanting on our part to bring these fabrics to what you would wish them, but the difficulty in accomplishing this in a country where the manufactures are yet in their infancy is greater than any can imagine who has not been here to observe it. The Osnaburgs are not what we wish or expect them but would gladly hope many of those you reckon the second sort is more owing to the colour than fabric, if so we shall be less hurt abroad, tho' we may suffer a little in the sale at home.

We are sensible such a quantity of fine Hollands as are with you will be a drug and many of them hardly saleable in London, and therefore wish you would by first opportunity ship 25 or 30 pieces more for Jamaica.

To Alexander McKenzie, Dingwall

19 May 1748

Mr John Dingwall, writer in this place, having proposed to the Court of Directors that you should be constituted and appointed the Company's agent or factor for carrying on the spinning of Osnaburg yarn at Dingwall on the same footing with Mr John Reid at Tain, please know that the Court have agreed to the same upon Mr Dingwall's joining with you in a bond of security to the Company for a faithful account and reckoning being made of all goods and cash that shall be entrusted to your management. And for which purpose have extended a bond for your and Mr Dingwall's signing which he will transmit you.

The conditions of employing Mr Reid are; the Company keeps him supplied for flax fit for that manufacture, the sea hazard, freight, charges of unloading, heckling and spinning together with the charges of reshipping the yarn when made and all the other risks and expences of bringing the yarn to Leith being entirely on the Company's account. And further the Company allows him to draw on us for what cash is necessary to carry on the spinning. The premium allowed him in full for his trouble is at the rate of one penny stg for each spindle of yarn he shall so spin.

The Company has allowed Mr Reid to lay out some of the Company's cash on spinning wheels in order to enlarge the spinning more expeditiously. But then this money is to be recovered from spinners how soon they are capable from their work to repay the same. It will certainly be necessary for you to go to Tain for some days to observe their method of carrying on the spinning which will be of much more service than any instructions that can be communicate to you in a letter, and therefore have enclosed you a letter to Mr Reid which you see will procure you a spinning mistress, or the opportunity of teaching one there, as you shall like best. And at the same time by looking through their affairs and Mr Reid's advice will be able to judge what flax & utensils will be necessary for you to begin with.

To William Gellatny, Arbroath

24 May 1748

We have this day again looked through your country linens which are much worse when open than on the outside. In short they are so extremely thin and raw that we are sorry to tell you they will answer at no price. This we can assure you Sir, gives us uneasiness as you are a young manufacturer, but you had better make few goods and well than many and bad made linens. We are determined to be very careful to take nothing but very well made linens, and give a price accordingly.

To John Wemyss, weaver in Dundee

26 May 1748

We have yours of the 25th current and are much at a loss to understand what you mean by an agreement or bargain made with this Company for Osnaburgs at 6½d. And that it is by a letter wrote you on the first of January last. We see no such letter in our books nor do we remember any such agreement. It's true we wrote you the 1st of December last that we would give you 6½d for the goods then sent, from which we took no discount, but at the same time told you they were not worth that money. We will not continue to purchase bad goods visibly to our own loss as well as that of the manufacture. The custom in many places as well as of your town is to make a few yards of the piece better than the rest, and folding that good piece on the outside makes it absolutely necessary for us to see the whole piece from end to end which makes the lapping with you needless.

The difference in measure which you mention, we imagine, has been owing to your measuring these goods when first out of the loom, by a yard which running along the selvage (which is looser commonly than the middle of the piece) always measures more than by a machine with which all linen goods ought to be measured and in case any of the stampmasters measure in any other way for the future, it's the resolution of the Board of Trustees to deprive them of their office. The prices affixed to your linens were truly more than we thought them worth when taken together, but if you think otherwise we shall be extremely well pleased to return them and we desire your answer concerning them in course of post. We have as little doubt of your coming soon into the right fabric of such goods, as of most people of your country and for our parts will be willing to give you as much as any other manufacturer in Scotland for such goods.

To Walter Orrock, Methil

27 May 1748

If we remember our conversation with you today about the freight of your ship, it was this. That you was willing to charter her with this Company from St Petersburg to the Firth of Forth. That she was to be at St Petersburg some time in July next, there to take in her loading of seventy-five tons hemp and flax, or five tons more or less, each ton weighing 2000 lb weight at the King's Beam here. That she was to lie thirty work weather days at Petersburg in order to take in her loading there, and twenty such days at Leith for unloading her cargo. The first to be accomplished from the middle of July or from her arrival at Petersburg, if that be after the middle of the month, and the last from her arrival in the harbour of Leith. That the iron for kiltage or ballast to the ship should be at your own account. And lastly, that the freight should be at the rate of three pounds eight shillings per ton, deducting therefrom whatever you may save from the difference of insurance on your ship from what you paid last year, and may this voyage. And if any greater allowance than the difference of assurance as is given at London on account of the present cessation of arms, you are willing to make an allowance proportionally.

If these, Sir, are the terms, we are willing to enter into charter party with you accordingly and desire the favour you'll write us your answer within a few days that we regulate ourselves in conformity. If in anything we are mistaken, please advise & oblige.

To Messrs Allan & Shairp, St Petersburg

28 June 1748

We are exceedingly glad to find you have succeeded in your application for appointing a braak[1] in your port on the same footing as at Riga, and can assure you that if that had not been timeously remedied, the trade of your port would have been greatly sunk; at least we judge from comparing the goods we had

1 The brack was an official scheme for the inspection and grading of all goods from the interior—such as timber, linen, ashes and flax—prior to shipment. See J.R. McCulloch, *A Dictionary of Commerce* (London, 1859), 986.

last season from Riga and Petersburg together, the preference being greatly in favour of the former.

We have now principally to confirm to you what we wrote you on the twentieth instant per the ship the Helen of Methil. That we have again freighted the said ship, George Lumsden master, which now being enlarged is estimated to contain about 75 tons flax and hemp, and desire you may give him complete loading of flax after allowing Messrs David Deas and Company to ship forty tons flax or hemp on board the Helen on their account and five tons on the shipmaster's account if he shall desire it.

We have agreed for thirty work weather lie days at your port to be computed from the 20th July or from the day of arrival if after that time. And with regard to the kiltage, we have agreed with Mr Walter Orrock the proprietor of the ship that he shall load the same on his own account so that we have no instructions to give you concerning the iron for kiltage as Mr Orrock will give the necessary orders concerning it himself. And further we have agreed to advance the shipmaster Forty pounds stg on his receipt at Petersburg in part of freight with all of which we crave your compliance.

We have the rather chosen to freight this ship as the master last year suffered considerably thro' his own inadvertancy and ignorance of the customs at Russia, as he is in hopes by a proper representation and the aid of the British Ambassador to procur a redress for which cause we have got My Lord Justice-Clerk, our Deputy-Governor to transmit his case to My Lord Hyndford[1] begging him to use his interest and intercede for the poor man. We would therefore beg you would give Captain Lumsden all the favour and assistance in your power either with My Lord Hyndford, the British Consul or with whom else it may be necessary to make interest.

We have sent you by Captain Lumsden a box containing 17 clubs and 6 dozen golf balls which were bespoke by your Mr W. Shairp when here value in all £2 9s 4d stg which have paid and placed to your account.

14 play clubs @ 14d	£0 16/4
3 iron clubs @ 2/6	7/6
6 dozen balls at 4/-	£1 4
A box	1/6
	£2 9/4

1 The diplomat John Carmichael, Lord Hyndford (1701-1767), later ambassador to Vienna, had been sent on a special mission to Russia in 1744 from which he was to return in Oct. 1749.

To Mr Richard Oswald, London

12 July 1748

The other day we had an order from Messrs Dennistoune Herries and Company for three pieces of our first 2nd 3rd kinds of Edinburgs[1] as samples. These are sent, and if they please these gentlemen write us they are to take 2000 yards for a trial and will do all in their power to introduce them in America.

This trial we understand is owing to your recommendation but as it is only one instance amongst many your friendship has given us we will trouble you with no other return than assuring you we are sensible of your concern and gainers by your friendship.

You know I never concealed from you any difficulties I foresaw in undertaking this new manufacture and one of them I told you was that Mr Child was not a judge of the Osnaburg linen and I am very sure if I had not been at the opening of the warehouse last year, the fear he had from his ignorance of these goods would have prevented the sale of them altogether, for having no judgement of his own to depend on, he was always of the same opinion with the last man who looked on these linens and elated or dejected as he met with judges and honest men, or ignorant and designing people. While I did all in my power to impress him with a good opinion of these goods and I hoped that the success I had in the sales would have confirmed it, I now find it otherwise for tho' the fabric is much better, his complaints are louder, and tho' each cargo is better than the former still his fears and cries increase.

If I can judge the man's temper, I take this is owing to the deadness of trade and little export at this season of the year, and as he is unacquainted with the exporters of these goods, he is much afraid the quantities we are sending will be greater then he can sell and therefore would gladly have us stop sending any more goods for sometime. This you know would be attended with many difficulties for was we to stop purchasing the country would be so discouraged as to throw up that new manufacture altogether, and if we shall reduce the price of such linens as are now made the effect would be the same for I know the manufacturers from the price they paid for flax cannot afford it. It is true our flax will now be cheaper, and sometime hence we can lessen the price but if from Mr Child's fear and ignorance or otherwise any damp come on our sales at London, the market will not easily be regained, and the consequence

1 The Board of Trustees had just launched a campaign to give the various fabrics of linen Scottish or patriotic names. Thus Clear Lawns were termed Carolines, striped muslims Glasgows, and Osnaburgs were dubbed Edinburgs: SRO, NG1/1/9, BOTM 4 Aug. 1748.

very hard on this Company and country. As this is our situation I beg the favour you'll go and look on these goods, particularly the last sent by Pollock and converse Mr Child in such a manner as your prudence shall direct without letting him know that you have heard from me.

If he shows these goods in the low warehouse they will appear to great disadvantage for I am sure it is much too dark and a bad light to show such linens in. We have written him of this, but I wish you would notice it and advise him either to show these goods above stairs at a stronger light or get the under warehouse better lighted.

In short, Mr Oswald, you'll either be so good as to continue your care of this new manufacture, and by your conversation get it into repute in London otherwise all we can do here may be frustrated above. These linens I'm sure are extremely good and sufficient, and the same from end to end with the outfold; it is true they may be a little more cottony than the foreign or there may be a stripe in a piece blacker than the rest of the web but can this be a reason for such a reduction in price as discourage the manufacturer or will they be of less service to the wearer. Please deliver the enclosed after reading to Mr Turner. I much wish his friendship, and am persuaded that if half a dozen friends such as you and he were to join in recommending these Edinburgs it will be in your power to introduce them against all the private interest, malice and ignorance that may appear against them.

To Mr Galfridus Mann, London

8 September 1748

You have herewith a draft on Nathaniel Child for £16 14 5d payable at sight to your order being a dividend of 5 per cent on the stock paid in by you to the Society for Promoting the Linen Manufacture in Scotland and established at Edinburgh prior to receiving his Majesty's Charter for erecting the B.L.Co on receiving of which charter the said Linen Copartnery was dissolved and the goods sold in such course and the nature of the thing and the distraction of the times during the late rebellion would admit of. The gentlemen who became proprietors of the B.L.Co not choosing to have the effects of the copartnery rolled over on them alleging that during a rebellion and the infancy of a manufacture there behoved to be a considerable loss. However we have now the pleasure to acquaint you that that after paying the capital stock paid in together with the debts of that copartnery there are now funds in our hands for paying a 5 per cent dividend and if no loss happens on some debts still outstanding we hope to be able to make another dividend of 1 per cent more.

Court of Directors

10 February 1749

Sundry of the manufacturers here having represented that by the present high price of yarn they were unable to furnish their shirting linen at the prices formerly contracted for with the Company which the Managers being fully sensible of, had agreed to pay them an additional price of 3 per cent on the value of the shirting linens they shall deliver in from the eighth day of February current to the fifteenth day of May next. Which the Court acquiesced in seeing that without such additional price the manufacture behoved to stop but recommended to the Managers to think of some method for preventing the weavers being subjected to such sudden rises in the price of yarn which in the present case was no ways owing to the rise of flax.

Sundry of the Company's friends at Glasgow having proposed sending quantities of their goods to be sold there and Mr James Johnson having accepted of that trouble till such time as the Company should determine the opening of a warehouse at Glasgow, the Managers had accordingly sent him sundry bales of Edinburgs which he had received and now writes that in order to establish the trade, it would be in the Company's interest to allow him to sell the best made Edinburgs at seven pence one farthing per yard and so in proportion for the inferior kinds. Which the Court agreed to.

Court of Directors

16 March 1749

Mr Tod, one of the Managers now at London,[1] having proposed by his letter dated the ninth current, that the Company should make contracts with some of the considerable drapers at London for the Edinburg linens as that would in a great measure enlarge and ascertain the sale of that species of linens, and as the value of them was to be payable at three or four seasons in the year, the Company by such frequent returns would be enabled to sell at very low profit, and these drapers put in a capacity of serving the export merchants with advantage to themselves. Of which proposal the Court approved and ordered that he should be wrote to make trial to bring about such contracts.

Sir Alexander Mackenzie of Coull by his letter of the eighth current having proposed to carry on the spinning of Edinburg linen yarn on his own estate

1 While at London, Tod was also active on behalf of the Board of Trustees in lobbying for a continuance of the bounty, something which was strongly urged: 'You will be able to show that the Bounty on low-priced linen has of late years improven and set forward this manufacture in surprising manner'. SRO, NG1/3/3, BOTL 18 Mar. 1749. The Trustees rewarded him for his success with a vote of £100 towards his expenses: SRO, NG1/1/10, BOTM 9 June 1749.

by way of agent for the Company, being on the same plan as was first made use of for introducing the spinning in the North, the Court ordered that he should be furnished with what flax he wanted on the same footing as is now done with Tayne and Cromarty, and the yarn to be taken off his hands on the same conditions, and he be wrote accordingly.

The Managers represented to the Court that for some months bygone the manufacturers had brought into the warehouse their Edinburgh linens of a much inferior quality than what was formerly delivered in both colour and substance. In order to check which practices the Managers had been in use to take them off their hands at certain discounts conform to their quality but that still they found this had not the desired effect of improving that manufacture or even keeping it up to its former goodness of fabric. It was now proposed that the Court should give orders for the receiving in two pieces only of an inferior make along with twenty pieces of the best kind which it's thought will prevent their continuing to manufacture goods of an inferior quality. And that the manufacturers may suffer nothing by this stoppage in their sales, they might be indulged till Whitsunday next with an advance of three-quarters of the value of what goods they may deliver in, and that one-fourth only shall be applied for extinguishing their bills to the Company, the present practice being to apply one-half for payment of their bills, and the other to the credit of their current account to be drawn out by them as they had occasion. The Court considering of how great consequence it is to establish and maintain a right fabric of goods, on which the well-being of the country depends, orders the Managers for the future to receive in only two pieces of an inferior make along with twenty pieces of a good quality.

Court of Directors

2 June 1749

The Managers represented to the Court that in order to be thoroughly informed of the proper methods of fabricating any linens conform to the foreign patterns that are from time to time sent from London and required to be made by the Company, and likewise for ascertaining the precise cost of all the different kinds or species of linens in conformity with the rise and fall of the prices of yarn and flax aggreeable to which the Company's bargains or contracts with the manufacturers must vary, it would be for the interest of the Company to have a few looms of their own constantly employed in making such experiments. Of which proposal the Court approved, and ordered that a house proper for holding six or eight looms should be provided at the Company's charge to be employed as above proposed.

Court of Directors

29 March 1750

The Court taking into consideration the reference from the General Court of the 5th current as to affixing the forms of, and ascertaining the amount of the sum for which promissory notes should be issued by the Company for payment of goods purchased. A question arose whether such notes, when sealed and issued would not be constructed to be included in the clause in His Majesty's charter allowing 'The taking upon money by bonds, bills, or obligations at such rate of interest as they shall see fit, so as the principal do not exceed at any time the sum of £100,000 pounds'. Or that the affixing of the Company's seal to such notes would only be comprehended under that privilege in the Charter of having 'A common seal for the business and affairs of the Company' whereby every public deed or writing of the Company, was directed to be ascertained as such by the seal.

The Court was of the opinion the issuing of promissory notes for goods purchased was in no ways comprehended in the allowance in the Charter for borrowing under the seal at a certain rate of interest since the proposed notes were to be issued for goods bought only and the same to be expressed in the body of these notes. But on the whole deferred proceeding any further until such time as the advice and opinion of Mr Henry Hume and Mr James Ferguson Advocates was had on this affair. And the Managers were directed to lay this case before these gentlemen and to report their opinion to the next Court.

The Managers represented that for some time past, there had been a vacancy in the office of porter to the Company, William Sim the last in that office having been turned out on suspicion of fraudulent practices; the Court appointed Colin Cromby to succeed the said Sim in the office of porter with a salary as formerly of twelve pounds stg per annum.

To David Flint, Secretary to The Board of Trustees

21 April 1750

Mr Andrew Ross and Thomas Lindsay in Orkney who have been employed for some years bypast in introducing the spinning of linen yarns in that country, have represented to the British Linen Company, that in two or three years there would be no less than than two thousand spinners raised in Orkney, provided each spinner had a wheel and reel given them, that those already taught have been induced thereto, solely by the few wheels first given by my Lord Morton, then by the Company, and lastly by some few distributed by themselves, & unless the public take in hand to enlarge that article, private adventurers must leave it off.

Sir Alexander McKenzie of Coull Bart, writes the Company that a small experiment he had made in his country last year with between two and three tons flax was now completed, he having got all that quantity made into yarn. That he is so sensible of the benefit of industries being brought into the country that he would engage to spin up twenty tons of flax this year provided the Company will allow him the same price as was given before the reduction was made by the Board of Trustees, and without that or some such indemnification, it will be not possible for him to effectuate it. The Company has already lost very considerably by introducing spinning at Orkney, Tain, Cromarty and Inverness, not only in the value of utensils given away and in the value of their flax in teaching the people of the country to heckle, and in salaries to master hecklers and agents for spinning, but in taking back bad for good all the ill-spun yarn that must necessarily be made for the first 12 or 18 months, the last of which tho' not valued or brought to immediate account of immediate loss in their books, is by much a more considerable loss than the first, as it is thereby reduced the value of goods when made into cloth. The Company had sundry instances of persons whom they have taught to carry on the heckling and spinning in the North, their taking advantage of a rising market to sell their yarns for even a triffle more than was proposed by the Company to be paid on contract.

The Company cannot therefore continue to launch out their stock in teaching the Kingdom the different branches of the linen manufacture, seeing the benefits of the instruction being reaped equally by others who contribute nothing to the expence. Wherefore this memorial is humbly presented to your Board, desiring their assistance & advice how this spirit for promoting industry in the Highlands and Northern parts may be best preserved without hurting the particular adventurers.

To Gilbert Barclay, Cromarty

1 November 1750

When you was here, we signified the misfortune of the George and Jane, Captain Cuff, her having been put ashore on a desert island in the Baltic, and that she could not be put off again, or could such part of the cargo as was saved be transported this season to Cromarty, concerning the delivery of which cargo we had sent you instructions. We have now now other method left for supplying the undertakers for spinning with you, than by ordering the cargo of the ship the Blagedon, Captain Timothy Whinny, which will be about 70 lasts,[1] different kinds of flax from Riga to be wholely unloaded at your port. We had directed this ship to call at Cromarty to put out about 20 lasts in order to give the undertakers a proper assortment, along with the flax from Petersburg by Captain Cuff but now notwithstanding the unsuitableness of the Riga packages for your country, we are obliged to order the whole of the cargo to be unloaded at Cromarty. We have therefore sent you a bill of loading for the cargo on board the Blagedon, on the back of which you'll find a specification of the goods, and an indorsation to you for receipt of the cargo, which we desire you may unload as well hemp as flax at Cromarty, and pay the necessary fees, duties and charges of unloading. As also we desire you may pay the freight of the cargo to Captain Whinny, being fourty shillings stg per ton with two-thirds of his bill of port-charges. And for the amount of freight & charges you may take your reimbursement by bills on us at what date shall best suit your conveniency.

With respect to the iron on board, we can give you no sort of instructions, the same not being for our own account; but we presume Messrs Cornwall Greathed & Co of Riga will write you by the ship concerning it. In the charter party with the shipmaster, there is an agreement that he shall have fourty shillings a ton for freight in case we oblige him to unload at two different ports. You'll therefore take care that the instructions given by Messrs Cornwall Greathed & Co be not to our own prejudice; for we are now to pay no more than fourty shillings as all our goods are to be unloaded at one port.

As to unloading and delivering of the cargo of the Blagedon to the sundry undertakers, we desire the same rules may be observed as were signified to you by our letter of the 27th ult for delivering the cargo per Captain Cuff, and have only to add thereto that to the 100 tons there mentioned to have been bespoke by the sundry undertakers you would now add thereto twenty tons for your own account, and in proportion to the 129 bespoke, you would now deliver of this cargo of the Blagedon, and it shall be our special care to have your remaining qualities completed in the spring or early in the summer.

Court of Directors

8 November 1750

The Managers gave it as their opinion in Court that in consideration of the increase of spinning in the North, and the demands otherwise made on the Company for flax, it would be their interest to secure three hundred tons at least upon contract during the winter season in the different ports in the Baltic.

1 A last of flax was 1700 lb in weight.

The Court taking the same into consideration ordered that the Managers write their correspondents at St Peterburg to contract there for one hundred and fifty tons of flax, and their factor at Riga for one hundred and fifty tons more, if it can be execute at these ports with safe men and upon advantagious terms.

Court of Directors

15 November 1750

The Managers having proposed to pay the the undertakers for spinning in the North by the Company's notes, not only to prolong the circulation of them, but likewise to prevent their drawing on the Company for cash to carry on their spinning, the Court the better to accommodate the undertakers ordered remittances to be made them partly in bank notes and partly in the Company's. It being represented to the Court that the Company's notes were printed on such thick paper that most of them were already wore out in the circulation wherefore it was necessary to have new notes cast off in their place and a form appointed for cancelling the the Company's old notes.

The Court ordered that four thousand twenty shilling notes, and four thousand ten shilling notes be immediately printed and bound up in books as formerly, and remitted it to Messrs Whitefoord & Shairp to make out the form for cancelling the Company's old notes.

Court of Directors

20 December 1750

It being represented in Court that Samuel Hart of Edinburgh proposed to serve the Company as clerk and cashier at their bleachyard at Salton for the term of three years and will engage during that time to instruct the Trustees' apprentices[1] in keeping proper journals and accounts necessary at a bleachfield, provided the Company get him presented as one of the Trustees' apprentices to be instructed in the art of bleaching that thereby he may be entitled to the Trustees' premium of Fifty pound stg on laying out a bleachfield himself, or on being appointed first manager to any new field that may be erected and that the Company appoint him on such salary for these three years as they shall

1 The Board of Trustees had become concerned about the cost of bleaching in Scotland, which they considered to be much higher than elsewhere in Europe. To increase the supply of master-bleachers, they launched a scheme to train apprentices at Salton, a bleachfield which practised both the Irish method for lower-priced linens, and the Dutch for finer. Hart and two other apprentices were presented in 1751 for three seasons' training: SRO, NG1/1/11, BOTM 21 Nov. 1750.

think reasonable which he expects will be not less than thirty-five pounds stg with lodging, coal and candle free.

The Court, taking the proposals above mentioned into consideration agreed to the same and appointed Samuel Hart the Company's cashier and accountant at Salton Bleachfield upon the terms proposed.

To Nathaniel Child, London

8 January 1751

We wrote you last post to know how some of the ¾ wide linens and some sheeting shipped from Dundee had turned out. But are sorry to find by yours of the 3rd, enclosing an account of sales from the 1st of October to the 31st ult that these goods have been sold upon credit for less money than they cost the Company, although bought with ready cash; as this is the case it will be needless for us to employ more either of our time or of the Company's money in improving or extending that branch of the linen manufactures.

The Fifeshire linens too, we find, have turned out very poorly, having only sold upon an average at about 5 per cent profit though bought with cash and sold upon credit. And yet we took as much care in the buying in of those, as we did of the Angus linen of which we see you have sold a part (bale N10) to better advantage. It is not a little discouraging to see that your sales have only amounted to £1125 13/- for the space of two months and the profits upon the sales not at all tempting, so as to enlarge our consignments to London, or to launch out the Company's stock in the manufacture here. We are sensible that you will have difficulties in the sales, having so many rivals in the linen trade to compete with. And we are not without our difficulties here, having the bad conduct and mismanagement of young manufacturers and the prejudices of the old to struggle with in our attempts to introduce or improve any branch of the linen.

It must therefore be our joint study how to increase and keep on our hands, the Company's manufacturers and customers. We apprehend it would be of great consequence to the increase of the sales, if you would take the trouble of going frequently to the drapers and merchants' houses; and though you should now and then be at some little expence in going with them to the tavern, we are persuaded it might give the Company a large share of their orders, which other people prevent us of, by taking those methods of being intimate and familiar with them.

To Nathaniel Child, London

12 February 1752

On the other side you have invoice and enclosed the bills of loading for 21 bales on board the Isobel & Mary, John Haxton master, and for 5 bales and 3 chests on board the Jno and Margaret, George Wilson master, the value amounting in all to £532 11/-. Enclosed likewise we send you the original invoice of one bale brown linen shipped by Mr David Sandieman of Perth value £43 3/8 on board the Friendship, Mungo Oliphant master, D.S.no 1 to be sold by you for the joint account of this Co & David Sandieman.[1]

The agreement entered into by the Company with Mr Sandieman is this; Mr Sandieman is to buy up such goods as are wanted without charging any commission and the Company are to make sale thereof without charging commission on the sales, the purchase money being advanced jointly and the risk of sales with profit or loss being equally on the Company's and Mr Sandieman's joint account. This is our first trial in this new method and we hope will turn out to our mutual advantage as thereby the Company shall save 2½% of commission (or being ½ or 2 more that is not publicly acknowledged).

To Baron Wolf, Resident for His Britannic Majesty at St Petersburg

11 April 1752

We had the honour to receive your much esteemed favours of the 18th Feb in reply to ours of 14th January and are much obliged to you for the kind declarations therein and of the regard for the success of our linen manufactures which you are pleased to make. We shall be expecting to hear from you from time to time as purchases of flax shall be made and your directions when to forward a ship for bringing home the cargo.

The chief intent hereof is to notice to you that in bleaching our linens in the country we labour under some disadvantages (that may possibly be in your power to remedy) by being obliged to purchase our ashes called Russia Markoff and Russia Blanc from the Dutch who by engrossing the whole of these commodities subject us not only to the duties paid in Holland on import and export and the additional freight and insurance that necessarily must be paid from thence to Britain, but to whatever exorbitant profits they are pleased to demand and this Company will reckon themselves under particular obligations to you for supplying them with what ashes may be wanted upon equal terms with the Dutch, our correspondent in Holland having directed us to you as the only proper person in Russia for supplying us therewith. The Company would want annually from 150 to 200 casks of these ashes, reckoning each cask at from 8 to 10 cwt averdupois but least it should prove any inconvenience to you at the first to supply us with the whole that may be

1 It was standard practice to mark the bales of linen consigned for sale with the consignor's initials.

wanted and least any mistake should happen by our commissioning these goods from Russia by the designation they go under in Holland where possibly they may be known by another name we shall trouble you with half the quantity only. We therefore desire you may purchase for this Company 60 casks of Markoff and 40 casks Blanc Muscovia ashes and for your reimbursment of the value draw as usual on Mr Ja[me]s Craufurd of Rotterdam payable in Amsterdam who in a post or when we have occasion to write him shall have orders to confirm the same to you. You will be pleased to reply to this how soon you possibly can because if you can favour us with the above desired purchase we shall make use of the less quantity of iron for trimming our ships and make use of these ashes for that purpose. We intend by the ships that go from hence to Petersburg to send you a specimen of each of these kinds of ashes; at present we can only say that what's called markoff is of a darkish blue colour, the other of a white colour somewhat ressembling powdered sugar.

To Nathaniel Child, London

28 April 1752

We are glad to see the dealers in linen have resolved to petition the parliament for a repeal of the Cambric Act,[1] if they'll agree to a reasonable duty's being laid on, and seal affixed upon importation, we will most cheerfully join them in the petition and endeavour to persuade all friends of this Company that are in parliament of the benefits that would arise from such an act.

We are extremely sensible of what you write concerning the yarn. It has been our close application since the erection of this Company to promote and enlarge the spinning of all sorts of yarn from our own flax, and at present have got a good deal done, and in a year or two hence hope to have most if not all of our goods made from yarns of our own spinning and suitably proportioned to the quality and fineness of the cloth. In the Highlands and Islands we have at present about 2500 spinners at work and daily increasing, and as these people were totally ignorant of the business, you will easily judge the attempt has cost a great deal of expence and trouble, and will yet take time to finish it. The Company had pushed the spinning in the low countries, considering their demands for yarn would have heightened the price beyond what the London

1 By an act (18 Geo. II c. 36), as of 24 June 1748 the importation (except for re-export), wearing and selling of cambric had been prohibited. This measure was circumvented either by smuggling or by entering the linen to the Customs as a fabric of lower quality. The Managers consistently argued that it was more beneficial to the Scottish industry to have a modest duty imposed on imported cambric and other fine linen fabrics, which would actually be collected, rather than a prohibition that was simply evaded.

and Manchester people give at present, and therefore in order to preserve ourselves are obliged to go on cautiously. We think your proposal of laying a duty on yarn exported to Ireland in proportion to what they charge upon yarn exported from thence to Britain is very reasonable, and we hope something that way may be attempted next session.

To Mr William Tod, London

24 February 1753

Mr Doig is to keep all his good yarn from 4 hanks per lb downwards upon hand until you give further directions or are satisfied that the bounty is to be continued.[1] We do not well know what to make of the undertakers for spinning in the North. Mr Forsyth says that the spinning is decreasing. Mr McKay of Tordarroch says that he loses £10 stg on every ton manufactured. Both of which accounts seem to me void of truth; because in every other part of Scotland from the high price that provisions are giving a good deal of spinning is carrying on now and it would not seem probable that anyone but a downright fool (of which I will not accuse Mr McKay) would carry on our trade at such disadvantage as £40 per cent loss.

There is great demand at Glasgow for Edinburgs of which article we are like to be run out altogether for want of yarns, and yet from the former accounts from the North do not well know what quantity to order from the Baltic for next year and now is the right time. The flax on hand here and at Dundee may in all probability be disposed of before the next comes home, but you know we have 80 tons locked up at St Petersburg. Mr Doig and I have been talking of this matter and we think that at present 150 tons may be commissioned from Riga to be bought at such price as the market will admit of vizt 50 tons Cutt Marienburg, 70 tons Lithuania and 30 tons Drujaner flax; but it is my opinion that even that quantity might be doubled if the last year's crop be good and the price under 18 Rix Dollars per shippound for Lithuania and so in proportion for others. You will therefore take the affair under consideration and write Mr Mudie according to what you think best and let us have a copy of the letter you write in order to be registrated in our letter book. Below is a note of the sales, Glasgow and London included. Amount of Sales tot. 23rd February, 1753 £32,409 9/6.

1 The question of whether the bounty would be renewed was becoming of pressing concern. Tod reported in Mar. that there were 'many unforeseen difficulties ... [and] that the last resolution of the Ministry seemed to be that the Bounty on Irish linen [exported] should be discontinued and the Bounty on British reduced to 1d per yard and that no other fund could be given for the whole British than the Scots window tax': SRO, NG1/1/12, BOTM 26 Mar. 1753.

To William Tod, London

13 March 1753

There was lately a trial made from hence by Mr James Grant of sending some of our Hollands and Table linen to Bristol which answered very well. This with the great demand that is made for linens at their fairs of Bristol every half year; together with the quantities of Scotch linen that are carried there from Glasgow annually, not to mention the great resort of Scots and English pedlars to these fairs, make me hope that something considerable might be done by our Company for the consumpt of our linens; either by erecting a warehouse there on the footing of London, or as at Glasgow or by sending one we could trust to attend with a cargo at these fairs which happen annually at Xmas and midsummer or in July. You know we have a large stock of goods upon hand and until such time as we are better known in trade, I am afraid we must carry the goods to the market instead of the markets coming to the goods.

I desire you may have your thoughts on this subject and write me your thoughts thereof before I mention anything of it to the Directors. As you desired me I have shown all civilities in my power to Mr David Campbell at Dunoon, and have recomended him to Mr John Mudie at Riga, because Mr Mudie now knows the kind of flax that will best answer our manufacture, and will still better be able to serve his employers, as the clerk he has hired from this place knows what flax will stand the heckle and what will give the best colours in bleaching which was a principal cause for his hiring Mr Weir.

To William Tod, London

24 April 1753

I wrote you in my last that I was to be with my Lord Milton on Saturday bypast, but it happened that on the Thursday he was seized with a smart fit of the gravel at Salton which has reduced him very low. I saw him on Sunday when he was eased of pain, but so weak as not to be able to walk thro' his room. In this condition you know it was by no means proper to talk to him of any business. He of himself mentioned to me his disatisfaction with the late resolutions of Parliament about the linen manufacture, and said that unless the drawback on foreign linens was taken off, he foresaw this country would be in a worse situation than before the granting of the bounty. That therefore he wished you to make up to and be well with both the English and Irish that usually interest themselves in the manufactures so as against another session our forces might be united in parliament for obtaining a reduction in the drawback on foreign linens, and of this you are desired write him.

In order to form some plan to his Lordship what might be proper for the Company now to follow out in the North and what kind of effect the granting bounty or premium on the importation of flax and spinning of yarn in the Highlands in proportion to the 3000£ allowed[1] would have on the manufacture of coarse linens for export, I drew up the enclosed memorandum, of which you will write me your opinion.

Hollands in this place have been a very dead article, greater quantities than usual having been made this last year, and all last winter there sales by auction of these goods for the creditors of Scot & Stewart and the Messrs Jackson of Dalkeith etc which has prevented the sale in the usual manner. In a few days I am to sell two or three hundred pds value of them. The sales now amount to £35,000 and by the time of balancing will be much what they were the foregoing year. But how the profits for last year's trade may prove, I cannot give you the most distant guess. The Directors have fixed the time of balancing to the 30th prox.

1 By way of partial compensation for the loss of the bounty, and in response to the Scottish arguments that its end would discourage the coarse linen manufacture in the North of Scotland with the risk that idleness would breed disaffection, an act was passed allocating £3,000 per annum for nine years to the Board of Trustees 'for encouraging and improving the Manufactury of linen in the Highlands of Scotland'. It was to be used only in those parts where the manufacture had either not been introduced or had not arrived 'at any stage of perfection': 26 Geo. II, c. 318. See also Durie, *Linen Industry*, 89-91.

Chapter Two
CRISIS AND RECOVERY, 1753-1762

To Sir Alexander McKenzie of Coull, Dingwall

7 June 1753

We entirely agree with you that the withdrawing of the bounty will greatly affect the manufacture of coarse linens in all the branches of spinning & weaving etc, and must still affect in a greater degree the Highlands where industry has but very lately been introduced, and where the distance of places and the difficulty of access for carriages must render it both expensive and hazardous. The only comfort is that the Parliament have put the small funds they have thought proper to bestow into the hands of the Board of Trustees, a set of Gentlemen who both know the true interest of their country and who will be at all pains to distribute the £3000 per annum given them to the best purposes for promoting and continuing industry in Highlands.

As yet no plan has been settled for that purpose or indeed can there well be any till about Christmas next, against which time the Board will have fully informed themselves what are the best methods for promoting industry in the Highlands. But as a stop from this Company in employing the poor in these places where it has already been begun might prove of very bad consequence, we are resolved to continue the spinning with all of our undertakers in the North on the same conditions as last year for this ensuing year with this difference only; that we must have our yarns to be mostly from 16 to 24 cutts per lb; and very little if any to be of a grist less than 12 cutts per lb: by reason that these grists of yarn can be turned into some cloths fit for home consumpt. But we are afraid that can never be made a general trade of for export, unless either the bounty is renewed or the drawback on foreign linens when exported is taken off, and our own manufactures put on an equal footing with the foreign of which we are told there is some reason to expect that in a session or two hence it may be got effected. We can assure you that no pains was spared to have the bounty continued; but ineffectual! excepting as to the £3000 per annum for 9 years for promoting the industry of the Highlands and Islands.

William Tod to David Campbell, Esquire, Dunoon

28 August 1753

I am entirely of your opinion with regard to the linen manufacture of Scotland. If a proper and vigorous application was now made this ensuing session I flatter myself that something may be obtained. But if it is neglected, I do think with you that the manufacture and industry of this country will receive a blow which cannot be recovered in our age. Everybody seems sensible of this but no spirit appears to preserve the manufacture; I have long thought that the merchants in Glasgow ought to espouse a matter of such consequence in trade. In this part of the country we have little trade and few merchants; and to be plain tho' I wish well to my country I am truly weary of public applications, and my private affairs cannot afford the time these things require nor am I alone able for them. It is the manufacturer and all the poor people under him who must suffer most and in their ruin the country will be hurt. The merchant will not give out £100 but in such a manner that he can sell with gain and if one article will not afford that he will turn away.

I wish you would write your mind to Provost Cochrane[1] on this affair and I truly think you should represent to the Duke of Argyle the dismal effects the withdrawing the bounty must have even in the Highlands as well as in the low country. Lord Milton is just now with his Grace and I am sure will greatly approve of your talking to the Duke on that matter. I shall be ready to do you all the service in your undertaking in the Highlands that is in my power. I think you deserve of your country all the emcouragement the Trustees can give you and I wish I may have an opportunity of convincing you how much.

To Alexander Speirs, merchant in Glasgow

15 November 1753

We are favoured with yours of the 14th signifying your intention to purchase two bales Osnabriggs from our warehouse at Glasgow provided we will take our payment for the value from a debenture for about £80 lodged with Mr Colquhoun in June last; as also advising us you shall want a quantity next month, provided we shall take debentures registrated in June last to the amount of about £511 stg. In answer to which you'll please know that our instructions

1 Andrew Cochrane of Brighouse (1693-1777), Lord Provost of Glasgow. Cochrane was jointly appointed with William Tod in Nov. 1754 to represent the convention of royal burghs at London in the negotiations to secure a restoration of the bounty. They were charged 'to take every lawful measure that shall appear to them most proper for obtaining such parliamentary aid and encouragement to the linen manufactures of this part of the United Kingdom as can can be obtained from the legislator'. *Extracts from the Minutes of the Convention of Royal Burghs, 1738-1759*, ed. J.D. Marwick (Edinburgh, 1915), 466.

from the Company are to take the debentures for our own goods and discount the value from the purchaser's invoice, but without any allowance or discount as formerly on the debenture. And as for debentures for other goods than those of our own, we are to accept of them only in payment for and on the delivery of goods above the value of 18d per yard which are not entitled to any bounty on exportation.

These instructions to us are in consequence of the dilatory payments of linen debentures at the Board of Customs here, which are never paid sooner than 18 or 20 months after presentation, and it is more than probable those presented since the additional demand made for the whale bounty, and payable out of the same fund must be an act postponed 18 months longer; and we persuade ourselves you will be of opinion the Company cannot do more, every circumstance considered for the support of the export trade. If those debentures you mention are registrate here before the late inundation of Greenland debentures,[1] we shall deliver you goods to the value, one-half thereof in goods entitled to the bounty and the other in goods above the price of 18d per yard. The Company knows that there are a great many Scots made linens above 18d yd exported to America. And as they are persuaded no person can furnish better goods or upon better terms than they can, for this reason they are willing to have their manufacture known and introduced abroad, though even upon such disadvantageous terms in the beginning.

With regard to the complaint you mention of Scots Osnabriggs from your Virginia factors, we are sorry to hear it, but flatter ourselves such complaints cannot apply to those goods that are the manufacture of, and have the seal of this Company affixed, as it is hardly possible to take greater care of the quality of all linens received in from the weaver than we do.

Court of Directors

29 November 1753

George Young at Coupar Angus who for many years past has dealt considerably in the linen manufactures of that country, and who says that the demands for their linen are now greatly at a stand, owing to the late bankruptcy of some

1 As this letter makes clear, the bounties due to the exporters of linen were usually paid a long time after the presentation for payment of the vouchers or 'debentures' to the Board of Customs. The situtation had been made worse in 1749: in a bid to stimulate the British whale fishery, the subsidy paid to returned whalers was doubled to 40 shillings per ton of measured capacity. This measure stimulated much more activity and therefore demand on the government subsidy, which was also paid through the Board of Customs. As in the case of linen, whaling debentures were the subject of bitter complaint as to tardiness of payment. See G. Jackson, 'Government bounties and the establishment of the Scottish whaling trade', in J. Butt & J.T. Ward (eds.), *Scottish Themes* (Edinburgh, 1976), esp. 49-51.

of their most considerable factors at London. And therefore in order to support the trade in that country, he proposes that the Company and he should enter into an agreement for purchasing linen cloth to such extent from time to time as shall be thought proper; and to be afterwards to be shipped and sold at the Company's warehouse at London. And he proposes that the same should be bought up by him without any commission for his trouble, and thereafter sold at London without any commission to the Company for their trouble in selling the goods. But he would have the Company run the hazard of all debts, and for that hazard is willing to allow them a consideration of one and a half percent, to be deducted from the account of sales made on their joint behoof. And for what of his own proper money is not advanced for the purchase of goods at Coupar is satisfied to allow the Company to charge him with 5 per cent interest during the currency of such advance to be made by them on his account. The court in so far approved of the proposal that they ordered the Managers to advance three hundred pounds stg to be laid out by Mr Young in the plan above proposed, and ordered the Managers to write to London to know what is the usual premium paid to any person who sells goods for account of another, for running the hazard of what debts might prove bad; as also to know what allowance ought to be made in consideration of the extraordinary charges of warehouse rent, taxes etc at London.

To David Flint, Secretary of the Board of Trustees

7 December 1753

Some weeks ago there was laid into this Company's warehouse a parcel of linens belonging to Mr Sam Garbet which had been bleached at Salton with an acid of vitriol instead of sour milk. As also there was lodged here 6 half pieces of linen, one half of which it is said was done with vitriol, and the other with sour milk, in order to have as full an experiment as could be made of the different effects of these two kinds of sours upon the cloth either as to its colour or quality. Mr Christy at Kinchey, I am told, was the person who bleached these six half pieces and will produce the journal when desired of his process in bleaching them. Mr Hart at Salton did the others and will when called upon lay before you his process in bleaching with the vitriol.[1] Mr Garbet by his letter

1 These experiments at Salton concluded that the use of oil of vitriol or sulphuric acid did greatly accelerate the bleaching process, but that 'the principal objection that lies against the use of vitriol is that the executive part of bleaching being committed to ignorant people they might be apt to err greatly in the conduct of it, which would prove of fatal consequence': NLS, Saltoun MSS, Box 329, 'Reply from Salton Bleachfield in answer to Mr Garbet's enquiry to be informed how far Vitriol might be a saving in Bleaching', 27 Sept. 1753. In practice, oil of vitriol came to be quite widely used as a bleaching acid.

directed to Mr Tod and me of date the 10th November desires us to lay these linens before the Honorable Board which shall be done how soon you think it proper to have them sent up to the Office; and he in that letter has some remarks on the nature and use of vitriol. I take the liberty to enclose it herewith for the perusal of the Honorable Board of Trustees.

To John Watson, writer, Edinburgh

17 December 1753

The Company is charged by the officers of window lights with no less than 94 windows for the Earl of Moray's lodging and David Doig with 20 for the part occupied by him, making in all 114 windows. We are persuaded there is a great overcharge made on the Company by these officers of the window lights, as we apprehend no warehouses, counting houses, or other offices for public business are chargeable by law with this tax. We must beg of you to apply to the proper judge for a redress in this particular and to desire that a new survey may be made whereby it will appear that no part is liable but the East wing of the lodging presently possessed by the managers as a dwelling house, to which there is a private entry, and in every respect distinct from the Company's warehouses and offices. We beg this application may be made as soon as possible as the advertisement in the newspapers intimates this money must be paid betwixt and the 20th.

Court of Directors

20 December 1753

The Managers having laid what follows before the Court for their consideration viz

'That the bounty on all home made linen will determine with this session of parliament, and it is now said, this session will certainly rise the 1st of March next; that this Company will in all probability have at that period from £5000 to £6000 value of linens upon hand at their warehouse in Edinburgh over & above what can be expected to be sold there, or demanded for sale at either the Glasgow or London warehouses. Of which goods, there may be from 3 to £4000 value in Osnaburgs, one half of which from the bright colour are only fit for the demand of the Sugar Islands, the other half being purposefully made of a buff or brownish colour, are entirely adapted for the demands of the North American colonies. The remainder of the linens entitled to bounty are white linens of of various breadths and kinds from 8d to 18d per yard. That the sale of exportation goods does not come on till the month of March in any great degree, and continues usually for what is called the spring trade from March to the middle of May thereafter; that as it seems probable the bounty will determine before the ordinary demand comes on, the Company by having such goods on hand may lose from £1000 to £1200 stg; that considering the present scarcity of cash and the general dullness of trade in Scotland, it does not seem probable that any persons will undertake such a risk as that of exporting 5 or £6000 value of linen goods only on their own account and on the other hand it would appear that any risk attending the exportation or chance of the sale of such goods in North America, even in a dumping or wholesale way to merchants there, cannot be equal to the certain loss this Company would sustain by their not sending these goods abroad in due time, seeing that on the determination of the bounty, and whether the discontinuance of the drawback on foreign linens shall take place, yea or not, foreign linens of the same quality will rise in price all over America; That upon the whole therefore, it would seem advisable for the Company to be the exporters themselves for what of the goods cannot be sold before the expiration of the bounty; That it is against the rules of the Company to be exporters of goods themselves, to grant credit to persons residing out of Britain, or in any shape to interfere with the interest of the foreign merchant, yet in this case of necessity it certainly would be very allowable for the Company to take care of their own interest, even tho' that could only be attained in a way so different from the ordinary rule and practice.'

The Court ordered the same to be laid before Messrs Richard & Alexander Oswald at Glasgow for their advice, and to propose to them the shipping of what goods could not be sold before the expiration of the bounty for America by way of Madeira & the Sugar Islands and to endeavour the sale of them in a wholesale way for bills of Britain, and at last to land at Philadelphia with what of the goods could not be sold at these other places during the voyage; and to desire their opinion as to such a scheme, or in what other way they would advise the Company to dispose of their bounty goods as could not be sold in time.

To the Dundee manufacturers[1]

17 January 1754

As the bounty on the exportation of coarse linen will in all probability cease about the first of March next, and as we are resolved to take in no more linens called Edinburgs from any manufacturer after the 20th of February next. We therefore give this timeous notice so as you may send here what webs are now amongst your hands on or before that time and we hereby hold ourselves

1 A standard letter to all those listed at the end.

noways obliged to take any of the Edinburg linens from you after that period till further orders.

James Duncan James Farquharson
Robert Smith Wm Walker
Wm Lamb & Co. Robert Leighton
Robt Guthrie Jnr & James Guthrie, Craigie
David Walker at Rathillet
David Walker at Dundee
Thos Barclay James Wighton
David Simpson David Bowman
William Smith Thomas Mudie
James Young

To Robert Colquhoun, Glasgow

31 January 1754

The Directors have this day had under their consideration the proposal of allowing 5 per cent discount to such persons as shalll take to the amount of £500 value of bounty goods or upwards; & 7½% discount to such as shall purchase to the extent of £1000, & they are satisfied you make such abatements to the Company's customers for all linen goods that shall be bought from the Company and shipped before the 20th March next; and you are hereby empowered to take back all such goods as shall be refused to be admitted to bounty, if bought and entered for exportation betwixt and the said 20th of March. As also you may accept of linen debentures (other than for our own linens exported) in exchange for bounty goods when any purchase is made to the extent of £500 or upwards, but to allow no discount from such purchase, seeing it must be from 24 to 27 months before one can get payment of such debentures, whereas the utmost length of credit for goods upon personal security is from 12 to 14 months.

To David Campbell, Dunfermline

2 February 1754

This serves to convey to you a paragraph we have received from London concerning the diapers sent there. 'The 7 qrs diapers received by said ships are refused by the buyers on account of their being so very narrow, many pieces being scarcely more than 6 qrs wise and the widest not above 1⅝th yds whereas all diaper tabling should be kept up to their full breadths because the foreign generally are so and these are mostly sold as foreign to the consumers; some of these cloths are longer than needful and if the same quantity of yarn had been put into the breadth it would have made them just as they ought to have been, which must be observed against next year'. We hope you'll advert to the above directions.

To Robert Whyte, Kirkcaldy

19 March 1754

The repeated complaints against our Scots checks and other coloured linen goods for their mean colour both as to blue and white and complaints being sometimes made that even what colour they have does not stand the washing, occasions our giving you the trouble to enquire what has become of the project for erecting a dyehouse and a proper bleachfield for the yarn of which these goods are made. It appears to us that without something of this kind be speedily done, our check trade will greatly fall off and centre entirely in the hands of the Manchester dealers. Be so good as to give us your sentiments on the matter and to let us know if the Company can be any way useful to you either by taking a share with you in the undertaking or by aiding you in such other way as you shall require. If you had occasion to be this side of the water, a conversation about this matter would be of more use than a literary correspondence.

To William Tod, London

2 April 1754

As you desired, there is herewith sent an invoice of the 120 pieces hollands in two cases, marked A.B. per Captain Main value at the selling prices, and consigned to Mr Archibald McLane, amounting now to £777 10/2, but we still keep the the former valuation of £678 7/4 at his debit in our books, as it really appears to me a very wrong method of charging goods when consigned at the highest prices one can expect to bring for them, seeing by that method, one buoys themselves up with high fictitious profits before they are ever made good, or the charges deducted for selling them.

Mr Doig and I, after considering your letter from Ireland with the prices of yarns, and after comparing them with what are the present prices of sale yarns at Falkirk and Linlithgow do not believe it would answer the end to import any yarns from Ireland. The prices at Dundee are presently higher in proportion, but that will no doubt be regulated by the other markets. I have bought from Mr Shairp about £50 value of Jamaica cotton, the price of which I have agreed shall be fixed at what the same should give at London; the bargain was made last week, so you will have to enquire and write me. Our Osnabrigg warehouse now being empty, I have brought in the cotton spinning mistress and her scholars into it and am setting them to work with the cotton bought from Mr Shairp.

I am sorry Captain Main's ship is not arrived as yet on account of the bounty goods she had on board. All I can say is that everything was done that could be got done to dispatch them for London. And you may be assured that had there been any more at the time of her sailing to have sent you up to London, these should likewise have been sent. What were consigned to Mr Miller of Virginia were such as came in from the looms thereafter, and what Mr Shairp was obliged to give us back on account of the Customshouse people's assuring us no bounty would be paid, but on such linens as were exported before the rising of parliament, or at least that the ship was cleared out and ready to sail; neither of which could be done as to his ship for Jamaica. The value sent in Osnabriggs and Sheeting to Virginia amounts after deducting the bounty to £1203 and which Mr Miller may take upon his own account at 6 per cent more and paying for them by bills of exchange in 3, 6 & 9 months after arrival. If that is not aggreable, may sell them @ 50% advance of currency, but not for less until further orders.

To William Tod, London

11 April 1754

In answer to yours of the 6th, the flax wrote for was chiefly intended for Richard Neilson for the Manufactury at Cranston; and for which purpose he tells me it will be necessary that we have at least three tons to keep his people employed till the middle of June next, when it's to be hoped Captain Pillans, this day sailed for Riga, may be returned with a cargo of flax. Mr Neilson would have nothing coarser sent him than Lithuanian Rakitz and which would require to be of a bright colour and equally so throughout the package. Upon enquiry of Nicholas, the Sacking weaver, we find that a loom employed in that manufacture will consume at least five tons of hemp in a year. And we find it will be impossible to carry on the Sailduck manufacture to profit unless the first three numbers are made of hemp as it is considerably cheaper than flax. And therefore it will be necessary to commission from 50 to 70 tons of hemp of different sorts this season for these two purposes. James Mudie by his letter of the 6th ult says the price of flax and hemp are as under. Pray enquire what of these kinds of hemp are used in those branches of Sailcloth and Sacking; because if the hemp from Riga will do on equal terms with the Petersburg, we should prefer the first. I am to write from hence on Saturday for Riga and shall enclose the letter open for you to peruse, and add what may be necessary after making the enquiry above desired. I heartily wish you may succeed in your application for the payment of debentures. We have here about £4000 value and no appearance of funds for payment.

To George Young, Coupar Angus

11 June 1754

We have yours of the 8th current and from what you write are well satisfied the goods you have bought are good of their kinds, and very cheap when compared with the purchases of former years. It is very certain that linens are falling daily at the London market, in so much that hardly any judgement can be made in purchasing, and as we have hitherto always lost by the goods bought at your market, we are determined to make no purchases at this time. If there is any better prospect of good markets some time hence, we may then buy and will advise you.

Court of Directors

20 February 1755

The Managers informed the Court that there would be from 180 to 200 tons of finest Riga flax called Drujaner and Lithuania wanted for carrying on the Company's spinning in the North and supplying the manufacturers there. As also there might be wanted about 300 matts of one hundred pounds each of Dutch flax for supplying the manufacture of linens from about 20d to 2/3d value.

The Court ordered that Mr John Mudie at Riga and Mr James Craufurd at Rotterdam should be wrote to provide the above respective quantities of flax at such times as they judged the best for the Company's interest both as to quality and price.

Mr Robert Baillie, merchant in Edinburgh who is still considerably indebted to the Company and who tho' often pressed for payment could not yet make any and therefore had offered over and above the security the Company had of his brother Mr George Baillie of Haddington to grant them a right to his share being one-half of his ship the Planter, Robert Wilkie master, now abroad in Spain, and of which share the Company might dispose of at their pleasure. The Court ordered the same to be accepted of and to stay the use of any personal diligence against him till further orders.

The Court taking into consideration the state of the sales of goods at their Glasgow warehouse for some time past, and of the payment of debts due there, and finding that the sales were chiefly such goods as were entitled to bounty on exportation and that the payments for most of the sales had been postponed by the purchasers for sundry months after the time agreed for payment and that ever since the discontinuance of the bounty on goods exported at the rising of last session of parliament, the sales made from thence were not able to defray the charges of the establishment and that the applications made to this parliament for putting the home manufacture on an equal footing with the foreign linens as to export was delayed until next session. The Court of Directors therefore resolved to give up their warehouse at Glasgow.

To John Magill and Robert Whyte, Kirkcaldy

1 March 1755

Mr David Doig who I find has been over at your place acquaints me of his having made a conditional purchase from you of what checks you have on hand just now which he says may be about thirty or thirty-four thousand yards at the rate of 6⅙ per yard for the ¾ wide, and rising one penny per yd more for the ⅞ and yard wide in proportion; provided this Company will advance one third part of the purchase in cash, and deliver Riga flax for the other third at the usual prices, or reduce it to the ready money prices by discounting 2½ per cent. And for the other third value of the purchase he is to deliver yarns himself at certain prices agreed upon.

I own I think his appetite for trade is stronger than what the present stagnation of commerce would encourage, from any prospect at present of much profit attending full commutation. But I think it will serve the purpose of lessening the burden to any one particular, and it will surely serve the purpose of David's selling his yarn of which I think he begins to grow sick. However seeing he has gone such lengths, and that you are satisfied so to do; I agree on part of this Company to the conditional purchase he has made. And for that end have sent over James Drummond to make choice of the checks, and to see them put up in bales for shipping. And I desire the favour you'll cause them all to be shipped by first vessel for London, for here at present I cannot sell one yard, and what they may do at London I cannot yet tell; for everything there seems almost as dead as here. As to the time of paying the money, I suppose it is the usual time of six weeks from the delivery, but I would rather pay it twice; that is, one half of the sum in a month and the other in two months from the delivery. There is hereto subjoined a state of the prices of our Riga flax at 6 months' credit, and from which I am to ship thirty five tons for Cromarty in about ten days hence. If you please, you may chose your parcel before that time.

Meeting of the Court of the Proprietors

3 March 1755

Present the Honorable Andrew Fletcher Esq, Lord Milton, Deputy Governor and sundry others of the proprietors.

The Deputy-Governor having acquainted the Court with the present state of the Company's affairs in trade; and his own and the Directors' opinion thereupon having been reduced into writing, the same is by order of the Court inserted as part of their minutes and is as follows.

The discontinuing of the bounty on home made linens has not only put an end to the demand for these goods to America, but likewise to the demands for finer kinds, usually bought for assorting their cargoes outwards. The more than ordinary great importation of Germany linens into England for these twelve months past (owing as it is said to the stop of their sales to Spain) has lessened the demand for our home made linens thro' England, in so far that few or no sales could be made but at a loss. For these reasons a great part of the Company's stock of linens are still on hand, it being thought more eligible to keep the goods till the glut of the market is over than to sell at a considerable discount. Trade seems now to be somewhat on the reviving hands, more demands having been of late made than for a considerable time bypast; there are however some particular branches of our linen manufacture that labour under other and very great difficulties and until remedied cannot be carried on to advantage vizt Clear Lawns, Carolines and fine Shirting Linen or Hollands above 3/4 or 3/6d per yard owing to the fraudulent entry at the Customhouse of foreign goods of the same kind and for the same use as these; for instance they have fallen on a practice of late of entering French Lawns and Cambrics (tho' prohibited) in the package and form of German Lawns and Linens, and paying duty accordingly of 3d $\frac{1}{4}$ and 1d $\frac{3}{8}$ instead of 15d and 7d $\frac{1}{2}$ per yard, being the duty appropriated to such goods when enterable and of entering likewise Dutch Hollands, chargeable with a duty of 10d $\frac{18}{20}$ for broad Germany Linens, which pay a duty of only about 4d $\frac{1}{4}$ per ell.

To the first mentioned of these fraudulent practices, it is owing that the late flourishing manufacture of Clear Lawns and Carolines in this place is now almost totally ruined; and this Company are still possessed of a large parcel of these kinds of goods which cannot be sold but with difficulty and no profit. And to the second mentioned instance it is owing that we have but little demand at any time for fine linen above 3/6d per yard, the duties accepted at the customhouse bearing no proportion to the value of the finer kinds, or to the duties appointed by law. Things being thus situated, few or no goods were made last year, but such only as were necessary for an assortment, or such as were in constant demand. The Company has not been singular in these misfortunes; the country in general has suffered, and it's believed there are not now in many places of Scotland perhaps above one-third of the looms employed that there was about twelve or eighteen months ago. And we are told, and have good reason to believe that things are no better in Ireland. How soon it was known that Parliament had delayed till next session, the putting of our home manufactures on an equal footing with the foreign when exported, or of remedying the above mentioned practices at importation, the Directors resolved to lessen the expence of the establishment in so far as regards our export trade; for that end they have discharged the officers, and given up the warehouse at Glasgow, and proportionately reduced their establishment here. The Court likewise resolved to collect and have given orders to call in all sums outstanding and due the Company, and with their conveniency to pay off debts due by the Company. But it must be observed that this measure of lessening the sum employed cannot take place immediately on account of the stock of goods remaining unsold, the difficulty of recovering payment of debts in Scotland, and that likewise a great part of the bounty goods sold off last year were given at a more than ordinary long credit of two years.

As to what may be a rule of acting for this ensuing year, taking every circumstance into consideration, it would appear proper for the Directors to continue the plan of collecting in the Company's debts, and launching out only into such branches of the manufacture as can be done with safety, and to endeavour as much as possible the sale of stock on hand.

The Company having some years ago introduced the heckling and spinning of flax into the counties of Inverness, Cromarty, Ross, Sutherland, Caithness and Orkney to the great benefit of the poor of those countries; it is with pleasure that it can now be said that the spinning in those places is brought to a very great perfection, much more than could have been expected in the time, and is now become of considerable profit to the Company, not only as it affords them cheaper and better yarns than can be commonly be had at the Southern markets, but prevents their raising these markets by the Company interfering with others in the purchase. And notwithstanding of the great decrease of the linen manufactures and a general stop in trade, it is a particular satisfaction to say that this branch of the Company's trade, which has cost so much care and expence in the rearing, can still be supported with profit as well as reputation to the Company (but indeed it cannot be any further extended as things are at present). The people there have been for some time past, and can still be maintained in the spinning of flax into yarns fit for Diapers, Dowlas and fine Edinburgs, and the refuse of it into such stuff as is fit for the dyed kind of Edinburgs, none of which goods are dependent on any bounty or encouragement for export, being chiefly in demand for home consumpt, and for which the Company have a ready enough sale. The Directors have therefore resolved to continue and support that branch of trade as to the spinning in the North and manufacturing it therafter in this place and the neighbourhood into Diapers, Dowlas and Edinburgs. And for what further kinds may be wanted, such as low-priced Hollands, Sheetings and Linens from 12d to 2/- in the Irish fabric, they have given orders only for such to be made as will serve for an assortment to the stock on hand.

The Court of Directors are apprehensive it may be necessary to continue Mr Tod at London for some time further, in order to facilitate the Company's sales there, but that expence will only be incurred in the event of the Directors being satisfied that his stay there can be of use, or until the greatest part of the goods on hand can be sold off.

On account of the sundry disadvantages the linen manufacture is subjected to at present, the Directors, as has already been observed, have it chiefly in view to collect in the Company's funds, to lessen expence in proportion to the present state of trade and to sell off the present stock of goods on hand; so as that they may be enabled to embrace the earliest opportunity of the parliament's establishing the home manufactures upon an equal footing with the foreign, which it's believed will be done this ensuing session. Yet by these general maxims, the Directors do not mean to tie up their hands from making use of the Company's stock or credit to its advantage when any evident or even promising prospect of profit in trade shall occur. In the present uncertain situation, either as to what extent, or in what manner the Parliament may think proper to grant an encouragement to home manufactures in general, the Directors are of opinion some attempts and experiments should be made in the manufacture of such goods as [have] not hitherto been made in this part of the Kingdom, and that are either still entitled to a bounty on export, or are in demand for home consumpt, so that whatever turn our application to Parliament may take, they may be in some sort ready to employ the Company's stock to the best advantage in their power. For that end they have caused make some hundred pieces of a species of linen called sailcloth No 9 & 10, on the exportation of which the Law allows a bounty of 2d per ell; these goods are nearly of the same quality and use to which our strongest and best Edinburgs were applied; part of these have been exported to America, and part have been sent to London for samples, and from the esteem our Edinburgs have gained abroad, it may be hoped that this manufacture, so similar in quality and use, will come in time to be likewise in demand.

The Directors have likewise had a trial made of introducing the manufacture of hempen sacking cloth in this country, and from the experiments made have reason to hope it will succeed. They have also introduced into this place the art of fineing and spinning of cotton into yarn in a proper manner, a thing hardly if at all known here formerly. In this way a considerable number of people are kept constantly employed, and the yarns made by them have been sold in England to advantage. But the views of the Directors go further by introducing and securing the principles of a manufacture, which when a proper opportunity offers, they may themselves commence vizt of printing cottons, gowns & furniture, Checks, Stripes & Demitys, great quantities whereof are in daily demand for home consumpt.

The Court unanimously declared their satisfaction with the above detail and state of the Company's affairs and not only approved of the same, but ordered their thanks to be given to the Deputy-Governor in particular therefore, and to the Court of Directors in general for their great care in superintending and conducting the affairs of the Company in such a proper and prudent manner.

To William Tod, London

10 April 1755

My Lord Milton desires you would wait on Mr George Ross who is agent for the Earl of Home's and sundry other regiments and make Lord Milton's compliments to him and let him know that if proper samples were fixed upon 'tis believed this Company could supply most of the regiments (at least in time) with their shirting linens and that if Mr Ross thought it fit a trial might be made of supplying Lord Home's regiment which is now in Scotland & if that pleased others might be contracted for herafter. And likewise the Company could engage to supply them with their linen for splatterdashes.[1]

I have declined George Young's at Coupar of Angus his proposal and I think it right to give up with Baron Wolf's as there is not this year one-third of the linens to be bleached there was formerly throughout the country. I have desired Mr Doig to give up with his manufacturing of linens for dyeing as he cannot thereby get the first cost of his yarn and to bleach up all of his yarn that is proper to take a good colour as 'tis probable he may get a better price for these hereafter, tho' if he could get the price quoted for Brunswich yarn of the same weight he would really be a gainer by the sale in that shape.

To William Tod, London

15 April 1755

With regard to sales which you say you do all in your power to promote but that you cannot force a market. The first I always knew and what I can depend on. As for the second the Directors or none of your friends here expect any such thing. But they know and say that no opportunity will be lost, perhaps many found out, while you stay, of disposing of the Company's effects to advantage and introducing them to new customers. My Lord Milton says you should endeavour to stave off the maladie du pays till towards the end of June next when in his opinion you could with less chance of loss to our interest at London return to this place and be in time enough to concert measures for next campaign. With regard to sending goods to Glasgow where you wish us to sell some of Mr Doig's brown Edinburgs for export—I'm very much tired of that place both on the general bad payments and of the too many bankruptcies that have fallen out there to our share. However there [are] some good

1 Gaiters or leggings.

people in it and we have samples there of our own and some are going of Mr Doig's. If I like the terms people offer I will send the parcels wrote for but nothing more in the way of warehouse or chance sales.

To William Tod, London

17 April 1755

It is desired by some of your friends that you would inform yourself particularly as the quantity and as to the quality of the linens that may annually be imported from the Electorate of Hannover into Britain. And in case it were any how eligible to give a preference or favour to them in point of exportation to our colonies, how or in what manner these could be distinguished from other linens of Germany.

It has been talked of at sundry meetings of late of our Court of Directors as a thing that might prove to the public as well as to the Company's private advantage for us to take in goods to our London warehouse upon commission. And on their arrival at London and being such as the chief officer should approve of, the Managers here be allowed to advance the consignor of such linens one-half of the value consigned upon interest until repaid by the value of the goods to be sold. That for this purpose a sum of £20,000 should be alloted and that to such extent the Company's own notes might be circulated. Upon this branch it's apprehended a profit would annually arise of from 15 to 2,000£ betwixt interest and commission. And more if the Company should insure the debts by 1½ per cent. That this might serve to conciliate the minds and interests of sundry linen dealers thro' the Kingdom to that of the Company's from which many of them are not a little estranged.

The Directors therefore desire you may have this under your consideration and write me what objections may occur to the scheme or what alterations should be made so as you and they may be ripe on that subject on meeting.

To David Flint, Board of Trustees

1 May 1755

Your obliging letter of the 21st February duly came to hand desiring that Mr Tod and I should betwixt and the 1st of May inform the Honorable Board what regulations and encouragments appeared to be necessary for the improvement and advancement of the linen manufacture. Mr Tod, as one of the commissioners appointed by the Royal Burghs applied last winter to Parliament in conjunction with some agents likewise named by the Linen Board of Ireland and by the most considerable linen manufacturers in England for sundry regulations and encouragements concerted upon amongst them as proper and necessary for advancing the linen manufacture of Great Britain and Ireland;[1] and as Mr Tod is not yet returned, I must desire you to have me excused to the Honorable Board for not making any explicit reply or answer to your letter until such time as he returns to Edinburgh which I hope may be in about a month from this date.

To Lord Kames

19 May 1755

Ever since this Company has issued notes for the payment of their spinning and weaving and other branches of the manufacture; the officers of the Excise have been in use to take our notes in the revenue payments, and that upon the recommendation of Mr Udny of Udny and Mr Drummond. The Customs have likewise being in use of doing the same thing, and some time ago (I mean the Board of Customs) gave orders to all their ports to accept of no notes in revenue payments excepting those of companies established by public authority, so as to prevent their receiving any Glasgow notes in payment. About a week or two ago, I am told the Board of Excise wrote to all of their collectors a letter of the same import with the Customs, but it seems some of their collectors or perhaps all of them (no doubt it would be just as they were desired) wrote back to the Board for an explanation of their master's letter; and I am assured that their meaning was to accept of the notes of the Old and New Banks, only, in Revenue payments; at least this much I am assured that none of our weavers in Angus or Perth can now utter any of ours because the Officers of Excise refuse to take them.

I must say I think that the three commissioners remaining at Edinburgh have not treated their two absent brethren with much civility or delicacy, seeing that both Mr Udny and Mr Drummond are proprietors of this Company, and this explanation of their letter is not what the Banks, at least what the Royal Bank asked of them. I have reason to believe that all of this proceeds from the spite of one man at that board to a certain gentleman in the Direction here along with your Lordship. However I must beg of you the favour to write to Udny on their affair, and desire him to write or speak to the Collectors of Perth, Angus or where else it may put his conveniency, to take our notes as formerly. It surely can be no advantage to the Revenue the suppressing of the manufacture. I well know Mr Udny's public spirit, and that he understands

1 The Board of Trustees duly prepared the 'States of the Annual Progress of the Linen Manufacture, 1727-1754' (SRO, NG1/114). This has been published with an introduction by R.H. Campbell (Edinburgh, 1964).

things in a different light from Mr Cochran. Mr Udny is at his country seat in Aberdeenshire.

To Alexander Adam, Forfar

29 July 1755

As there's every day a greater probability of a war being declared betwixt this kingdom and France, and insurance having already started upon all goods sent by sea and which will no doubt be still higher when war is actually declared. We therefore think it were better for you to ship all the best pieces of those linens you wrote us about in your letter of the 22nd inst by the first ship for London from Dundee and place the value thereof to this Company's debit and send us as formerly the shipmaster's receipt & invoice in course of post.

To David Campbell, Dunfermline

15 October 1755

One of your weavers called here this day and presented us the enclosed petition as the same time complained of the hardships they suffered by your keeping off part of the wages they thought their due. We hope you'll take into consideration the particulars mentioned in said petition and return the same to us with your answer thereto. Pray endeavour to make everything as easy with them as possible.

To David Campbell, Dunfermline

21 October 1755

We received your letter of the 16th current. But in place of being a particular answer to our query concerning the weavers' memorial, it consists of quite a different subject. As we do not chose to have clamours with any of the people the Company deal with, we should be glad to have that affair put to rights and for that purpose we wish you make a step to this place on Monday first or any day next week when we might converse fully about it.

To George Young, Coupar Angus

31 October 1755

Having the opportunity of the bearer Mr Alex Moubray we send you herewith five hundred pounds stg in our notes which we desire you may circulate in the best manner for this Company's behoof and that you would in return therefore remit us bills on London for which we will pay the current exchange together with a commission of 5 per cent for bills that are either on your own drawing or that shall be endorsed by you to us and in the event of your not readily meeting with London bills we desire you would make a remittance by bank notes or bills on sight at this place. We expect that you'll be able in a fortnight's time to disperse the above quantity.

By our advice from London the prices of linens are by no means upon the rising hand. We have also the disagreeable news that the linens you shipped for us per Captain Mill had met with considerable damage in the voyage.

PS In the event of your sending bank notes care must be taken of either sending them by private hands or by sending large notes only by the post, a copy of the numbers of which you'll keep.

To David Baillie, The Royal Bank, Edinburgh

19 November 1755

By your letter of the 12th, I understand Mr Shairp has been so good as to lay my letter before the Bank with regard to our furnishing them with bills of exchange on London for twelve months from hence to a certain extent quarterly. The same has been agreed to by the Directors of this Company to the amount of £8000 in all conform to the enclosed extract of the minute relative thereto. And if no obstacle remains in point of form with you I shall begin upon this agreement by drawing on London tomorrow or the post thereafter.

To William Forsyth, Cromarty

4 December 1755

We have to acknowledge the receipt of your sundry letters of 6th, 13th & 27th ult., as also your letter to Mr Doig agreeing to pay £42 10/- per ton for the Marienburg flax. We assure you it is much superior to the growth of Drujaner last season, and that at this price we are considerable losers by it; and indeed we are surprised you have taken such a dislike to it, as we do not think it will be to you be an unprofitable bargain. We shall expect the sundry undertakers' receipts for their quantities received stipulating the price of the Marienburg as above. We understand that Alexr Mackenzie & Co have a considerable sum owing them by Mr Doig so that if they please to pay these bills in this place, you'll please to return them. We are obliged to you for allowing no lights to be made use of in your heckling house on account of the Company's flax in your possession, and return you thanks therefore.

To David Campbell, Dunfermline

5 December 1755

We have now got a return from London anent the qualities and quantity of diaper that will be wanted for the ensuing season. Which are Vizt

400 doz 6qrs Table cloths to cost about 21d or 22d per cloth; 1000 doz ditto to cost from 29½ to 2/- such as are generally made of yarn 7 oz warp & 6½

woof; 250 or 300 doz at most of 7 qrs, to cost from 3/- to 3/5d; 130 or 150 at most of $^{8}/_{4}$ table cloths to cost from 3/10 to 4/6d per yd.

That is seventeen hundred and eighty dozen of Table cloths in all, to be made ready betwixt and the first of August next. In part of which we shall reckon those that now are and have been delivering in since last bleaching season was over. We expect you will make the 7 and 8 qr Table cloths of an equal assortment of prices, that is to say, an equal proportion of the highest and lowest prices mentioned. We desire you make the $^{6}/_{4}$ Table cloths that used to cost 21d per cloth of yarn one degree finer for which we are satisfied to allow from $\frac{1}{2}$d to 1d more per cloth. We have not yet heard how the clouting diaper as now altered please at London, but as soon as we hear you shall likewise have an order for it.

To William Forsyth, Cromarty

1 January 1756

We have to reply to yours of the 15th. The bills on Alexander MacKenzie & Co for £162 19/- transmitted you and now returned are placed to your credit. You write us that these gentlemen are still of the opinion to give up their spinning business at Dingwall and propose your brother's settling there. We truly cannot advise you to that just now, for if the bounty shall be renewed as the Ministry have promised, it is more than probable our Directors will think of introducing the manufacture in whole into that place and neighbourhood. And for that purpose probably engage some people here that have been bred to and practised in the arts of sorting, boiling, bleaching and weaving yarns to settle at Dingwall, so that the method may from thence be spread all over the neighbourhood. However nothing can be said about it till we see how the application to Parliament succeeds.

To George Young, Coupar Angus

17 January 1756

With regard to the affairs of the country we can only advise you that the greatest part of the Ministry have signified their intentions of being willing it should be granted and it was to have been in before the house this week but we cannot say anything about it with certainty till the thing is done. There is to be opposition by the Glasgow people joined by a few from this place against the bill unless there is likewise a bounty granted on fine goods altho' we are hopeful it will be to no purpose.[1]

To William Duff, sheriff of Ayr

24 January 1756

There's a fabric of linen in your county that's commonly known by the name of Irvine linen which if a little improved and altered from what is usually brought to the market would in time and especially if the bounty is renewed be of general demand for export to Spain for their West Indies. I have for time past employed Mr Brown the stampmaster at Irvine to buy up the cloth brown which was found fault with abroad on account of its not being equally alike broad and being rather too thin. This year I desired him to employ 6 or 8 looms in making that sort of cloth of yarn well sorted and boiled to be full 29 inches in breadth out of the loom and set a little thicker than the usual run of country cloths which are bought from 9½d to 11d per yard and the Company would take all these looms' produce for one year by way of trial. He has wrote me that he cannot get any of the country people to alter their method. I'm therefore at a loss whom to employ or how to get another proper person to correspond with on that head. I therefore presumed to give you this trouble. I desire you to show this letter to anyone you think proper and if too high profits are not insisted upon, in time that branch might be extended considerably in your country.

To John Brown, Ayr

20 March 1756

Yours of the 10th with three pieces of linen are safe come to hand. We have narrowly inspected them and compared them with some of the common country make and find that they are better made both in point of colour and of the yarn, sorting and weaving. But they are still to be amended both in the thickness of the cloth and making them of equal lengths. They ought to be full 56 yards or 56½ yards after lying some days in a loose manner when out of the loom. The thin setting of the yarn in the reed and the rubbing by the weaver together with the stretching the piece must have in the loom, requiring the cloth to be laid loose so as to return to its true length and breadth. You will

1 One of the problems in the campaign to get the Bounty restored was the inability of the Scots to present a united front: a coalition of Glasgow and Edinburgh fine linen manufacturers argued that it was unfair that the Bounty was only on coarse and medium fabrics, and wanted it extended to cover all linen. See A.J. Durie, 'The fine linen industry in Scotland, 1707-1822', *Textile History*, vii (1976), 43-9.

see by the subjoined note of the lengths of these 3 pieces how much such a precaution is necessary. What goods of the like kinds we have had bought up for us in your neighbourhood have usually been paid for with a discount of 5 per cent for measure. At least we think you should allow the Scots ell brown to hold out the yard when bleached.

As to what you say about contracting with you for 16 looms and our agreeing to give a higher price if yarn shall rise above its present rate, these cannot at present be replied to. For if your magistrates and town of Ayr shall succeed in what they have in their great wisdom thought fit to petition the Parliament for; vizt not to grant a bounty on our own manufacture's exports or to take off the duty on foreign yarn, this Company cannot give you any employment because the allies and friends of your good town who carry on this individual species of manufacture in Silesia and other parts in Germany have a drawback on all their linens exported from Britain. We cannot therefore export them on equal terms without a bounty or the drawback being taken off. And unless our yarns be kept at a price equal with the foreign will that bounty be of any general good to the nation? We say therefore that if your towns of Ayr, Irvine, Glasgow and Paisley shall succeed in their opposition to the linen manufactures of Great Britain in conjunction with the dealers in foreign linen, you can have no contracts made for greater or lesser number of looms.

Court of Directors

8 April 1756

The Managers reported that by the state of the yarn now on hand there was seventy thousand spindles fit for making into cloth of different prices and qualities that would be entitled to bounty, conform to the regulations agreed upon by both houses of parliament. That from the great decrease of looms in and about this place ever since the bounty ceased anno 1754, they were now forced to enquire out and hire looms at such places as could be done with the least expence of carriage. That they had conditionally engaged looms at Dalkeith, Musselburgh, Kirkcaldy, Dundee and Arbroath to the number of 488 in all, for weaving up the above quantity of yarn, all of which were ascertained of work for one month and so to be continue[d] in employment, but at liberty to be free upon one month's premonition on the part of the Company.

The Court ordered the managers to proceed in the manufacture of these goods and how soon the linen bill shall have received the Royal Assent to endeavour the securing of these looms for one year certain, or such time as shall be found necessary to weave up the quantity of yarns on hand.

To David Doig, Perth

1 June 1756

I give you the trouble of receiving from the bearer, John Ross, two paper parcels sealed with the same of this letter containing £200 in this Company's notes. They were intended to have been sent directly to Mr William Sandeman at Perth but having learned with certainty today that a deputation hath gone from the two banks here to the two banking companies at Glasgow to demand a sum in specie from them of no less than £25,000 stg for like value of their notes. This may occasion a suspicion amongst dealers of holding other notes as well as Glasgow ones. It is therefore I would beg of you to enquire how the dealers and traders in general stand affected to the notes from this House before you deliver the notes now sent to Mr Sandieman.

To John Jamieson, Glasgow

5 June 1756

We duly received your obliging letter of the 4th saying you should in the course of 3 months have occasion for about 30 thousand yards of Osnabriggs and other linens and desiring to know how we were sorted in such goods. You will please to observe that we have just now great choice of Edinburgs or Osnaburgs either brown or white from 6¾ to 9½d and 10 per yard, the bounty to be received on exportation being included, as also there are come in sundry parcels of white ⅞ wide linens in the Coleraine fabric from 12 to 18d per yd, bounty included. And as sundry of your city merchants like to have assortments of lower price Osnabrigs than the above prices, we now have in the looms and in a week or two will be able to give you an assortment of such as will not exceed 6d or 6¼d at most with the bounty included.

The gentlemen in the Direction of this Company's affairs do not at present seem inclined to have any other warehouse in Scotland save that here as the expences of an establishment for that purpose have hitherto been rather higher than any extraordinary sales or profits that could or did arise from it. If you are pleased to favour us with your commands at any time, [we] will be answerable for both the qualities and prices at which the goods shall be valued and sent you; tho' it would be still more agreeable to have the pleasure of seeing you here yourself, when such goods as best suited your taste or market they were intended for might be laid by for you.

To Michael Herries, Glasgow

15 June 1756

The reason of our giving you the trouble hereof is to know whether the following report be true, and if so to beg the favour of your laying the case before your friends at Scotstown, and to have their and your advice in the matter. It is asserted here that sundry of your principal merchants have formed a resolution not to deal with or buy any goods from the B.L.Co and for the more effectually carrying their resolves into execution are handing about a paper whereby the subscribers bind themselves under formal penalty or obligation not to buy from or in any shape to deal with this Company. And that because (say they) some of the gentlemen that are in the Direction are likewise Directors of the Banks who lately made a demand on the Banking Companies of Glasgow.[1]

It is true that some of the gentlemen here are likewise directors in one of the banks, but the doings of the bank directors are as much a secret and unknown here as they are at Glasgow until they are public to all the world. And we say the affairs of this Society are just as much unknown and independent of the influence of the other societies as they are of us. We are free to say that this Company had no hand in making any run upon the Banks of Glasgow (and were it of any consequence to give an opinion now that the thing has been done) as little approved of such proceedings as the world in general do here, because we think that every man has a natural right to prosecute any branch of business that the Law approves of and protects him in, and whoever goes about to disturb him in the carrying on of his affairs does not do any friendly office to society in general. Altho' it has been again and again asserted here that such a resolution has been taken and paper handed about for subscriptions at Glasgow, as above mentioned, yet we can hardly give faith to it. For during the several years this Company had a warehouse at Glasgow, we flatter ourselves that none of the merchants has cause of complaint for our being either hard to deal with in point of prices of goods or rigid creditors in demanding payments at the day of becoming due. On the contrary they might appeal to themselves whether our goods do not give as good content as others and that they did frequently prefer persons of less stocks in point of payments to this Company. It cannot therefore redound either to the honour or the interest of such to declare open enmity against a whole society for a supposed fault of some few perhaps included in a majority of others who have no connection with this Company.

1 In what Checkland (*Scottish Banking*, 101) calls the third banks' war, the two Edinburgh banks were engaged in an attempt to crush the new Glasgow banks which had had the temerity to set up agencies in Edinburgh. The campaign caused much resentment in which the British Linen Company was caught up.

To William Sandeman, Perth

22 June 1756

We really do not know what you mean by the Edinburgh spirit against this Company having reached your town. The spirit of Edinburgh in general or the people of character in it must not be estimated by either the life, temper or manners of some few manufacturers who having no business of their own take the liberty to find faults with those they suppose may have. Pray what is the cause of offence now? Is it for the Company's having interested itself to procure the bounty to be established on a sure footing? If your townsmen were enemies to a public encouragement to the linen, why did they not in due time join Mr Hart, Mr Spence, Mr Biggar and the other patriot manufacturers of this place?[1]

William Tod to Ebenezer McCulloch, Glasgow

21 September 1756

My Lord Milton set out for Glasgow early this morning and I doubt not you will have seen him ere you receive this. Since you left this, Watt's ship from Riga arrived in Burntisland harbour and is to come over on this tide. Today we received a letter from Wilkie dated at Elsinore the 13th of this month, advising that he was to sail under convoy of the Rainbow, man of war. This letter came by a ship which was off Fisherrow yesterday afternoon. The shirts you order shall be taken care of as you direct. The large quantity of flax we are importing & other things will undoubtedly require a great deal of cash about the term. As you are now at Glasgow I doubt not you will get all the money you can as well as orders for goods. All your friends here are well and as you are now out, take your own time in returning.

To James Dunlop, Glasgow

16 October 1756

It gives us much pleasure to find that the yellow goods please Mr Rae & you. We have resolved to do all in our power to beat the foreign linens, & if none of these sent Mr Rae had given content we would have been much discouraged. There is just now a man of war expected from London as convoy to the ships from thence to this firth, and there are some ships here, preparing to sail

1 These were three of the leading fine linen manufacturers in Edinburgh who had colluded with their counterparts in Glasgow to block the restoration of the export bounty unless it were extended to fine linen as well.

to London when that man of war returns which they think will be about 8 days hence. With these ships we intend to send a large cargo of our Osnaburgs as we do not know when another convoy may offer. This will prevent us from sending the bales you desire immediately. But we are receiving daily such goods from the weavers, the quantity you mention will be sent soon after the convoy sails. We thank you for your friendly advice and shall take care for the future to send none of the white goods unless desired.

To Captain Robert Wilkie, North Berwick

23 November 1756

Some people of skill here say that it may be yet possible to float the wrecked ship the Planter by nailing rawhides on the bulges made in her sides & in the event of having too little water to float her, to fix empty casks to the sides with ropes and therby raise her and carry into port for being refitted. There is one Captain Cleghorn at Leith said to [be] very skilfull in such matters to whom we have wrote begging him to go down to assist you. It was only on Saturday last that we knew with certainty of your ship being the one that was put a shore, although on the surmise of a wreck we wrote to Mr Hogg to be assisting to the crew in case of need. But we flattered ourselves from what you said when here that the ship was actually in Newcastle. The hemp you had on board if wet must all be washed and wrung out in fair fresh water, or when dry it will go to more dung and rot. You must therefore employ careful people in washing and wringing out the salt water. In case of the worst, that the ship cannot be raised or floated, the state of the wrecked hull must be laid before the Admiral[1] and the same put up to roup and sold to the highest bidder.

Court of Directors

2 December 1756

The Court examined the state of the cash from 13th to the 27th ult as per the Cash Book which they found right. Thereafter the Court having taken into consideration that state of the Company's affairs, how the same should be conducted and carried on to the best advantage, and especially as to the extending the sales under the aid of the late act of Parliament allowing a bounty on linens exported.[2] And having received information from the managers, and

1 The Court of Admiralty was responsible for all maritime cases, including questions of wrecks, salvages and insurance policies.

2 By 19 Geo. II, cap 15, 'An Act for granting a Bounty upon certain species of British Linens exported and taking off the duties on the Importation of Foreigh Raw Linen Yarns made of flax', the bounty had been restored as of 24 June 1756 and guaranteed for a minimum of fourteen years.

particularly from Mr Tod in consequence of the remit to him of the 8th April last, concerning the trade carried on by the linen factors in London. And having enquired into the state and situation of the Company's warehouses both here and at London, and of the Yarn Staplery under the inspection and management of David Doig, and fully considered the same, they were of opinion that the sales of the Company's goods at London should be more particularly attended to and extended, and that it would be for the Company's interest that Mr Tod should in general reside at London and conduct the Company's affairs under the direction of the Court or any of the Proprietors having particular authority for that purpose.

And considering that the present method of sending a state or balance of the transactions and trade of the London warehouse only once a year at the general balance is extremely inconvenient, it is ordered that a book be kept at London, distinguishing under proper heads not only in the particular kinds of linens sent there for sale, but likewise the different values of goods of the same denomination. That on the debit side of this book shall be entered all the linens received, and the credit side all the pieces sold. And that a copy of this book, or the balance of each head be sent here every month for the consideration of the Court; and that Mr Tod shall write his opinion with respect to the several kinds consigned, and the reasons that occur to him why such and such goods do or do not answer at that market, with every other information he may receive with regard to the linen trade in general, so that the Court may the better know how to direct the manufacture and trade of the Company here.

Mr Tod having represented that his living and keeping family in London would be attended with greater expence than all the money he could receive from his share of the eventual premium allowed the managers would support, and that by his contract with the Company he is debarred from trading on his own account and thereby would be even on a worse footing than the present warehouse keeper in London. That therefore it was most reasonable that the Company should indemnify him of the difference of his charges and expences betwixt living here and living at London attending the Company's affairs. Which being considered by the Court, they were of opinion that Mr Tod might be allowed to deal in commission for such things, and to trade in such articles on his own account as this Company did not trade in or could not be concerned with by their charter. But in the event of his trading on his own account, his private books should be open to the inspection of the directors or any of the proprietors of the Company at London appointed by the Court, and that he might lodge in the Company's house at London without being charged with any rent. The Court and Mr Tod both being of opinion that these considerations might not be a proper indemnification to him, and it being uncertain how far the Company's trade at London might be extended to afford a further allowance; it was agreed that Mr Tod should go to London and make trial for one year, after which this affair should be again taken under consideration. And in the mean time he should be vested with every power for the direction of the Company's servants and warehouse at London, which he is hereby vested with.

To Mrs Sutherland, Leith

7 January 1757

We sincerely console with you in the loss of your husband. And as it is hourly necessary to make use of his keys of the Company's warerooms and cellars at Leith, we must beg of you to deliver the keys to the bearer, James Drummond, and that at the same time some proper person would show him the places which each key belongs to.

To George Young, Coupar Angus

8 January 1757

We have to reply to your favours of 4th and 28 ult respecting the prices of yarn and linen and we are now resolved to make trial of three several sorts of linen as aftermentioned. You know the quantity yearly made of our goods is rather more than the London market requires of such a fabric but if you could alter the fabric in imitation of some species of foreign linen we think it would be of service to the country and we therefore shall be assisting to it all in [our] power. There is one kind of foreign linen 27 inches breadth when white which ought to be fully 29 inches when brown and wove in pieces not less than 120 yards in length, of much the same quality and prices with those you sent us last summer. Another species is cloth when white 31 inches wide which we suppose must be between 33 and 34 inches brown and wove in pieces of 104 yards in length. Both these kinds differ little from the fabrics usually made in your country excepting in their breadths and particular lengths but great care must be taken that no gouty or uneven cloth be taken off the weaver's hand, or admitted to pass with you.

The other fabric is of that strong thick cloth we wrote you of in ours of 25th past which was there so fully described that it is needless to say anything further of it but that the breadth must be kept up to full 30 inches when white. Of each of these three species of linens we desire you'll now make or cause make for our account fifty pieces and how soon these 150 pieces in all are got ready you may send them to us by water from Dundee. Or when you have made a sufficient quantity for a cartload you may send them there to be shipped for Leith till the whole is sent off. The Board of Trustees are anxious to promote the last mentioned strong fabric which they are informed is exactly the sort of linen fit for clothing in the army and in order to encourage this branch in the country are to given premiums for three different lots of not less than 20,000 yards each for the best lot £75—for the next lot £50,—for the next £35 premium.[1] If you therefore shall chose to make to the extent of 20,000 yards of this last mentioned species we shall go a half concern in the profit or loss on that quantity as to which you may have your thoughts and write us hereafter.

To William Forsyth, Cromarty

8 January 1757

We have received yours of the 4th enclosing Geo McDonald's receipt for flax. We know of no necessity that should induce the people here to give the prices mentioned to you. We know that if we had three times the quantity we imported this season to Leith we could dispose of it for £5 per cent more than we look for it. Cutt Marienburg of a worse harl than what we imported gives now at London £38 per ton to pay at two months. Complaints and grumbling from the North about prices of flax and challenging of ill made yarns are so frequent and seem to be thought so necessary a part of the correspondence in trade for so long a time past that we neither are nor ought to be surprised at them.

For this reason we are preparing to be as independent as possible by carrying on the spinning nearer our door. We are sorry that the Company's endeavours to extend industry through the country has not pleased the undertakers and we can safely say the Company has no reason to brag of their profits from it, as it requires the nicest management to make the half of their yarns even spun at this day of any use at all. Pray let us know what character Captain Reid gave of the cargo of flax which he brought home for us as we understand by the character of the flax given by him you were induced not to receive any part of that cargo tho' otherwise you would have taken 8 or 10 tons. This man left out no less than odds of 30 tons at Riga to be at more liberty to carry on some private trade of his own; 'tis supposed he gave that bad character of the flax that he might be the sooner dismissed. As to this reply by return of post.

To Captain Thomas Murray of the Wilmington

12 February 1757

Agreable to our communing, we have made up an assortment of white linen men's shirts for sale at Jamaica. We have for a trial caused ruffle some of them

1 The Board of Trustees subsequently scaled down the scheme to lots of 10,000 yards and a top prize of £40, stipulating that the yarn used must be Scottish and the cloth woven within the shires of Perth and Forfar: SRO, NG1/1/14, BOTM 24 June 1757. The first prize that year was taken by another of the Company's client manufacturers, William Sandeman of Perth.

at both hands and breasts and others only at the breast, and the rest are plain. They are charged in the invoice herewith at the prices they cost ourselves, and we leave it entirely to yourself to sell them at such advance as the quality of the goods and the demand of the market will allow of, hoping that such advance will more than pay for freight, insurance, your commission and other hazards of trade. The shirts are packed in four trunks marked CD N1, 2, 3 & 4. We desire that none of them may be left for sale under consignment to any person in the Island of Jamaica, and that all your sales may be for cash so as returns may be had by this ship for what is sold. And if it should happen that any of the goods remain unsold at the time of your returning from Jamaica to Britain we desire that the goods themselves be rather brought back rather than left in Jamaica, but as was agreed on in your former voyages we are to pay no freight on goods unsold. We agree to pay the freight outwards the same as others pay with commission and storage. We have not to add but leave it to you to do everything for us as you would for yourself, and hope that as soon as you arrive in the Island and have made any considerable sales, you'll please advise us. We heartily wish you a good voyage.

To John Watson, Ceres

22 February 1757

We received this day a letter from you without date whereby you propose of going to the Shire of Athol & buying at the fair there 80 or £100 value of yarns for weaving cloth for the Company. As you know we are soon to send you some yarn from hence for that purpose we don't think you need buy any more than 40 or £50 worth there. We therefore herewith enclose you fifty pounds stg in 20/- notes for that purchase, the receipt of which money you'll please acknowledge in due course. The 20/- notes will answer better for you than £5 ones and we hope you'll take the whole sum with you and circulate it in that country. We desire that before you go to Athol, send over the linens you say are ready for us.

Court of Directors

24 March 1757

The Managers informed the Court that it would be necessary to import early this season from the following ports the several quantities of flax undermentioned for supplying the demands of the Company's manufactures vizt:

From the port of Riga ninety tons of flax whereof sixty to be shipped by John Mudie in terms of his agreement with the Company in part payment of the debt due by him and the other thirty tons to be purchased in loco. For which purpose they had entered into charter party with William Cleghorn, shipmaster at Fisherrow and hired his ship the Sally of Leith and had become bound to pay him of freight fourty-five shillings per ton with one shilling and sixpence per ton of port charges in the usual manner. Of which the Court approved.

From the port of Konigsberg 40 or 45 tons of flax and one hundred barrels cashube and about six casks pearl ashes, for which they the Managers were in terms with George Barclay, master of the ship Christian of Dysart who offered to hire his said ship to them for fourty shillings per ton of flax and last of fourty hundred weight of ashes and two thirds of all customary port charges to sail on or before the 15th of April next. And from St Petersburg the quantity of fifty tons of twelve head plescow flax, for the importation of which they, the Managers, were in terms with Messrs Charles and Robert Fall merchants in Dunbar who offered to let out to the Company sufficient portage in their ship the Mally of Dunbar, John Middlemass master, (being about half of her burthen) at the rate of two pounds fifteen shillings stg for each ton of flax with one shilling and sixpence per ton of port charges to sail from Dunbar with all convenient dispatch. With which the Court being satisfied, they directed the Managers to enter into charterparty with the said George Barclay and Charles and Robert Fall for the above purposes and upon the above conditions accordingly.

To William Tod, London

26 May 1757

With respect to your observations concerning carrying on the linen manfacture by small factories or master-weavers possessed of 4 looms rather or so instead of large factories of 40, 50, or greater number of looms, they are certainly right in the main were this country masters of the manufacture and possessed of either tolerable houses or utensils for the purpose but as that is not the case, it becomes necessary to collect them together into larger factories fitted for the purpose and provided with proper utensils. These people we apprehend in a year or two may be branched into different places in the Country and suburbs and employed in the way you propose of master-weavers. The truth of these things we have experienced of late most of the weavers bred up during the bounty deserted this country on its discontinuance and upon our again offering to employ them who remained which were only about 80 or 90 looms within six miles around, we had our coarse linens very ill made owing to their houses and utensils as well as to their want of practice whereas those linens made in large factories with good utensils and under the direction of Mr Neilson or Doig proved not only well made but cheaper than the others. Mr Doig has at Leith factory about 60 looms, Mr Neilson about 45, Alex Flemming at Kirklison has about 20 making in all 125 looms employed in the manufacture of Osnabriggs together with about 80 or 90 looms of Master-weavers mentioned above who are now doing some better. With these we will hold ourselves contented for some time without establshing any more factories on this side of the Forth until we see how trade turn and you approve of the goods manufactured. Mr Doig as we wrote has got a large quantity of yarns from the North which are now sorting into the proper qualities for bleaching and for brown yarns. And during the summer season we intend likewise to have the yarn fit for the brown Osnaburgs milled, beat and prepared for the loom against the winter season so as to be ready to extend in the manufacture of either the one or the other kind, as you shall advise.

To William Tod, London

28 May 1757

As you sometime ago promised to procure us the secret of dyeing yarns an uniform buff colour, if now when we are preparing the yarns for the Winter's weaving, you could favour us with it, it would be of great advantage. We omitted to mention in our last that there were 40 looms employed at Cranston in the manufacture of Edinburgs and Mr Neilson says that instead of the 45 we wrote you of, he will soon have 60 looms employed in the Cannongate in the manufacture of that branch which will make in all 260 looms weaving Osnaburgs.

To James Smith, Brechin

21 July 1757

We have your favours of the 19th with your brother's receipt for 100 pieces of linen. As to the instructions given your stampmaster they are the same which are given to the stampmasters here, who notwithstanding never affix the breadths of the linen they stamped so that he stands in no risk in stamping the lengths of these linens without the breadths, as he has no proper stamp for them. As to the clergy's complaints of your brother's allowing his cloths to lie on the field on Sunday (unless he or his servants wrought there, which is not to be supposed) they are surely altogether groundless, it being the universal custom, but if they should really prosecute him, you will only need to represent the matter fully to the Board of Trustees in a letter to their Secretary Mr Flint, who will take care of him. And your brother may when necessary for his business continue to let it lie out on Sunday with all safety.

To David Campbell, Dunfermline

4 August 1757

We imagine your engagments with your weavers will soon expire, we shall be glad to know as soon as convenient how many hands you have had employed this last season and how many good hands you could now engage for weaving

6, 7 & 8 qrs Table cloths. We think you ought to pick up all the good weavers possible of these kinds of linen, & you may safely engage them for a twelve month from this date. As to which please write us as soon as possible. By the carelessness of the shipmaster by whom the last bales came from you they were every piece very much wet; we hear he laid them open upon deck. This must be adverted to by you for the future. Some months ago you got a pattern table napkin from us, which you'll please return by the carrier next week as the person to whom it belongs has been enquiring for it. The pearl ashes you desire shall be sent you. We have ordered two matts of this years Thesenhausen flax to be sent you for a trial. It came by a ship arrived last night, who has outrun her letters so that we do not yet know the cost.

To William Tod, London

11 August 1757

It would seem to be a very material point to have the possession of a properly situated and large warehouse so as to enable you both to sort and to show your goods to advantage. As well as to render you in a capacity to accept consignments. If anything were to be apprehended from the factors we might for a while make some of those we already deal with a consignment for once or twice of Osnabriggs and Dowlas to cover the real intention of the Company by making everything appear as on your own bottom. For they surely could say nothing against any particular person's doing for himself. The goods making by Mr Neilson in the Cannongate, and at Cranston seem unexceptional and those too by Flemming at Kirkliston. Leith factory is behind both but is on the improving hand. The Dundee people do better than formerly but not comparable with the three first named factories. The worst of all are those made by small master weavers in and about town. In short these think any person and any sort of utensils good enough for making Osnaburgs. Time and punishments can only reclaim such evil doings. You seem afraid of overstocking. We make almost no bleaching linens save Garlix or Silesias or diapers. Osnabriggs are only made from our Highland, Leith and Cranston spinning; if these are too much we must retrench the quantity of flax imported and contracts with the Northern undertakers. The price of weaving the high setts such as 26 porter and upwards must only be attempted when we have weavers to chose upon: at present that is not the case. The national manufactures were by discontinuing the bounty almost lost; by losing our hands we lost our trade like a great ship run aground there is more labour and disagreeable trouble to refloat her than originally to launch her to sea.

To James Robertson, one of the Company's overseers

31 August 1757

In consequence of the conversation we have had with you, we desire that you would immediately set out for England on the plan and for the purpose proposed of recommending the Company's manufactures to the sundry dealers either for exportation or home consumpt for which purpose you have hereto subjoined a note of the sundry articles and prices of them as nearly as can be put in words and likewise your sundry samples or specimens of the linens themselves which may be necessary to show to such as may not know or have any notion of the quality or value of our goods, and to such only we think it would be of use to show them, as samples never can show the goods so well or so fully as the goods themselves. In order to obviate that as much as possible we have made the samples of lawns and carolines larger pieces than the other samples as we wish you would by all means help us off with a parcel of them at what they would bring. This you will best know after trying some two or three of the principal dealers and comparing the prices they offer with what we have marked. Merchant exporters are usuallly indulged with 12 months' credit, those for home sale commonly called drapers from 9 to 10 months.

In all of these places where you shall find any dealers it may not be amiss to ask them to take a glass of punch or ale with you at your quarters, excepting those in the export trade, who may perhaps think themselves above such entertainment and whom it might possibly affront. Or when any man has been singularly useful and obliging, you cannot do less than ask him to a glass of wine or punch, but in this your own judgement and prudence will best direct. We think your route should be Morpeth, Newcastle, Stockton, Durham, York, Hull, Boston, Norwich, Lynn, Cambridge, then return by Leicester, Nottingham, Leeds, Richmond in Yorkshire and Wakefield.

Court of Directors

1 September 1757

The Court being informed that the Managers were now about contracting with the several undertakers for spinning in the North country vizt William Forsyth at Cromarty, Thomas Lindsay at Kirkwall, John Mackay at Cyderhall near Dornoch, Joseph Forsyth at Dingwall, William Anderson at Wick, Harry Munro at Tain, Robert Gordon at Cromarty and Hector Scott at Inverness, for furnishing them with flax as the Company's agents or factors and having the same returned in yarns, and upon the terms mentioned in one of the said contracts with William Forsyth which being already executed was read; the Court approved thereof and ordered the whole of the contracts with the rest of the above persons or such of them as should be willing to engage, to be executed in these or like terms with all convenient dispatch.

The ship Sally, William Cleghorn master, having arrived at Leith from Riga with a cargo of flax for account of the Company, the master informed the Managers that there were 220 matts of L[ithunian] Rakitz flax shipped on board his ship by Mr Mudie for account of Mr George Ouchterlony of London, altho' the ship had been chartered solely for the Company's account; and it being found by letter from Mr Tod at London instead of shipping the whole cargo for account of the Company as was agreed upon to be placed to the credit of his account, he had drawn on Mr Tod for £800 as the value of these 220 matts in favour of George Ouchterlony, and that Mr Ouchterlony by his agent here had demanded the flax to be delivered up to him, or that bill on Mr Tod to be accepted. The Court ordered the Managers to reply, 'That by agreement with Mr Mudie the quantity shipped by the Sally had been paid for by the Company and was put on board at Riga for their account. That had any accident happened to the cargo in the river after loading, such loss would have fallen upon the Company. Mr Mudie, after detaining the ship many days after she was loaded, compelled the Master to sign a bill of loading in favour of Mr Ouchterlony for these 200 matts now claimed, and that Mr Ouchterlony had been already properly informed and intimation given him by Mr Tod not to come under any engagements to advance money in virtue of that bill of loading.'

To William Tod, London

18 October 1757

Enclosed you have the copy of a letter we have this day wrote to Mr Adam at Forfar for the manufacturing of such goods as we apprehend to answer for the low priced Osnabrigs for the Jamaica market and the other sugar islands, which we hope may come to us at about 5¼d yd. If you think the directions given anyhow defective, you'll please to acquaint us and say what quantity it will be proper for us to contract with him and others for. On account of the indifferent made linens at Dundee for some time past, Mr Doig has been in use to have all that were made there brought up to to Edinburgh to be inspected. By this means the fabric is now much improven but an unnecessary expence has been brought of freight insurance, shore dues and lapping about 21d per piece. This we apprehend might now be saved by shipping directly from Dundee to London with such lapping as the stampmasters there usually give them, provided that you at London have a place and time to give such goods an inspection so as to check any frauds that might be practised. We don't know that but it might be an advantage to the good look and sale of the Osnabriggs to have them all sent up in the rough and when arrived at London to be repacked or lapped, because the straining of the ropes so disfigures the pieces and the putting one piece against another so tussles the outside fold, that they really look much worse for the money than they would do, were they sold when newly made up. The price for lapping a piece of Edinburg here is 5d for a piece of 100 yds and 6d for a piece of 120, they finding black twine for tying the piece.

When our E. McCulloch was at Glasgow last week, he made it his business to look into the fabrics of Osnabrigs sold there either home or foreign made, the foreign are considerably dearer than the home made in proportion. The merchant exporters chiefly supply themselves from the furnishing shops or warehouses, with Osnaburgs and every other article for export, except in some particular instances where they have an opinion of and purchase at this house.[1] The owners of these shops are sharers in almost all the shipping adventures, sometimes 1⁄16 or 1⁄32 of the cargo. By this they draw in the trade almost wholly to centre to themselves, such Osnaburgs as we sell at 12 months for 6¾d they are furnished with from Dundee and other places at 6¼ to pay in two months (really 4) of delivery wherefore they can sell on a par with us to the merchant exporters. Therefore we made offer to Mr Glasford and Mr Dunsmore to furnish them with some specimens of our different fabrics of Osnabrigs and agreeable to what they should pitch upon to furnish them in any quantity not less than 20,000 yards per annum at 6¼ 3 months credit or 6¾ in 12 months, 7½ discount etc. To which propositions they seemed to listen and specimens are now making up to go to Glasgow but we cannot hope to make it a very general trade for not only the shopkeepers but the merchants are daily seized by every weaver who can make up six pieces to make a horse load which he hawks from door to door and often sells below what they really ought to be, which tho' to their own prejudice time only and experience will prevent their doing. It has occurred to us here that it would not be improper for you to make such contracts with some of the principal wholesale linen drapers in London as is above hinted. The giving them three months credit from the date of shipping the goods would be equal almost to ready money to us and is an indulgence to them, and we apprehend the abatement in point of price would connect their interest with ours while at the same time a much less stock would be necessary for carrying on our trade than is now absolutely wanted.

1 On the structure of the wholesale trade in linen see J.M. Price, *Capital and Credit in British Overseas Trade: The View from the Chesapeake* (Harvard, 1980), 110-12.

We see you have been advised lately of the cost of manfacturing the Silesias or Garlix at Coupar which is no more than 1¼ and 1½d all charges included above the cost of yarn for winding, weaving, factor's profit etc. The information given is not very exact or business like but Mr Young is not really a manufacturer tho' a good enough judge of linens when made; it is as satisfactory as could have been expected but we still think (after knowing your full sentiments on the alterations necessary in that branch of the manufacture from what you have already seen of this year's make) it will be very proper to send one of our best Cambric weavers there, who we hope might be paid for by the Public and might have 6 or 12 looms employed in that branch with yarns from Mr Young.

To George Young, Coupar Angus

21 October 1757

We have just now been perusing our letter to you of the 8th January last, directing such and such sorts of linen to be made and that most of the linens then and since ordered, have been delivered in from the bleach. We find that many of them are very good for the money, but in general when compared with the foreign they are far short in sorting of yarn and neatness of weaving and exactness of breadths. This we apprehend by some little pains and expence, which we think ought and hope, may be defrayed by the public. For example we would have you set up 10 or 12 looms in a good house and well appointed with good utensils for weaving, get a proper master or foreman who has been bred in the french way of sorting yarns for Lawns & Cambrics and whose exact and neat way of weaving is far superior to those in any other branch of the manufacture and which in our opinion would be very well adapted to your fabric of linens, which are like coarse Cambrics. In this house we would have you take as many journeymen as would fill it, and when they are completely taught and practiced in the habit of neat weaving, boiling and sorting of yarns, let these men be dismissed and another set be taken in and so on for some years until the country is generally instructed. If you shall approve of this proposition, we would have you to make out a plan for that purpose, setting forth the extraordinary expences you would be at, the benefit that would accrue therefrom and thereto subjoined a petition to the Board of Trustees desiring that the same might be defrayed by the public. We apprehend a foreman such is as wanted might be got for from £20 or £30 per annum. The rest you can make out for yourself.[1]

Something we think too should be asked by way of premium for yourself for buying and selling yarns for these and other looms in the country to be sold in warps and wafts ready made up to the weavers. You should likewise propose and if agreed oblige yourself to have such number of good and sufficient reeds and caims to be lent out at some triffling sum per web or per week to weavers when demanded. If, as was said, you shall approve of this, we beg the plan and petition may be made out and delivered in to the Secretary before the middle of next month and if the Board approve (which it is to be hoped they may) they will surely engage with you for at least three years certain.

To James Dunlop, Glasgow

3 January 1758

We are favoured with yours of the 2nd and extremely glad to have your friend's approbation of our goods, and of their superiority to the German. It is our constant care and we flatter ourselves not without success, to make daily improvements. We shall observe the directions you communicate to us, that the linens for that market should be rounder threaded. The Law orders every piece of Scotch linens to be stamped with the yards and forbids any violation or alteration of the stampmaster's mark, but we can mark the German ells on the outside of each piece and put the thistle out of sight, as we have often done to oblige customers in England, and we dare say it will answer as well as putting the ells on the end of the piece. We shall be glad to receive the orders you propose to give against May and we need not assure you that everything in our power shall be done to encourage you and your friends.

To Richard Oswald, Glasgow

11 February 1758

We were duly favoured with yours of the 6th current and shall as you direct make out and send to Mrs Murray of Clardon a contract for four tons flax yearly. What you wrote in her favours we shall look upon as sufficient security. As to your friend Mr William Anderson of Wick, we will renew a contract with him on the same terms as with others. We applied in his favours to the Board of Trustees and procured him just now £36 in cash, wheels and reels.

1 A copy of Young's petition to the Board of Trustees which refers to the lack of properly instructed weavers in the neighbourhood of Coupar Angus is to be found in Lord Milton's papers: NLS, Saltoun MSS, Box 329.

He seems by some of his letters to wish it were all in cash and that he had a salary annexed to his office of stampmaster. We presented a petition from him for the salary but the Trustees do not think that the manufactures in that part of the country are yet so extensive or his troubles so great as to deserve any allowance besides the perquisites of the office. And they always chuse to distribute part of allowance to spinners in wheels and reels. Upon the whole we think Mr Anderson very well off, and at the same time if we can be of any service at that Board he will not want our good wishes.

To George Young, Coupar Angus

7 March 1758

The bearer Mr Dow having now provided part of the utensils and looms for carrying on the intended manufacture of Silesia linens at Coupar, he has shipped you thereof by a vessel now going to Dundee, and along with the looms has sent an experienced journeyman to be employed in weaving these goods for some weeks who we thought would be of use in Mr Dow's absence from the men, both as an example of neat workmanship and as a check to bad practices in such as are new brought in and unskilled in the trade. For it is not possible for him to be, while sorting, cleaning or perhaps buying yarns, so close with the journeymen at first as it would require him or someone else to be. Mr Dow has directed the other looms and utensils, when ready, to be sent by water to Dundee. This Company will readily take the produce of your manufacture off your hands at a reasonable rate. But we apprehend till you have for some little time made trial of your cost and charges and therupon calculated a profit, you should be entitled to from experience, you cannot so well fix any rate or we on the Company's part make you any just offers. In the meantime we have wrote to London for the exact lengths and breadths these goods ought to be made into. We apprehend it would be for your and Mr Dow's mutual advantage to allow him a share in the profit or loss of the manufacture upon his bringing a stock proportional thereto to be embarked in the business, because it will more interest him in the care of it, will leave you more at liberty for carrying on your other branches of trade, and if due care is taken of the business there will be room enough for employing almost any sum of money you could find either separately or jointly to employ therein. The cloth last wove by Mr Dow pleases us very much both as to the scale of setting and weaving.

To David Campbell, Dunfermline

4 April 1758

In the beginning of winter we sent you some patterns of foreign diaper table cloths. We wish you would take a look at these particularly as to their ends,

Mr Tod having wrote us this post that all such of our 8 qr table cloths as cost above 4/- or 4/2 green should be bordered at both ends and have no fringes and only a small division left for cutting between each cloth because the foreign at and above these prices are all made so and better liked at London. We therefore desire you would look at these goods as abovementioned and follow their method in what you shall hereafter weave at and above these prices and breadths. In making the clouting diaper it were best to do off two different prices, and of the 6qrs whereof you will henceforth have this season 40 looms employed (20 to be employed in cloutings) you will please employ 10 looms or so in weaving 6qr diaper in the piece without any division in the piece.

Court of Directors

27 April 1758

The Court being informed that with respect to insurance from Bergen in Norway to Leith on the cargo of the Elizabeth, Captain Ringrose, formerly mentioned (tho' that cargo should be repurchased) the same cannot be got done in this place under from 5 to 6 guineas per cent, and the policy in case of not purchasing, not to be vacated under ½ per cent, and that the Managers had wrote to Mr Tod to desire Mr Alexander of North Bergen to give him timeous notice of the shipping said cargo, in case the same should be purchased for the Company's behoof, so as he might insure the same upon the easiest terms possible. They likewise ordered a letter to be wrote to Captain Ringrose of the said ship Elizabeth of Hull, desiring to know of him the condition of his cargo when taken by the enemy, and likewise desiring Messrs Sill, Bridges and Blount of Hull to get the Captain's affidavit relating to the capture of his ship, that the same might be sent to Mr Tod at London as a document for ordering insurance etc. And they delayed giving orders further concerning the purchase of flax from Konigsberg until the receipt of Mr Tod's letter as to his concluding a bargain with Messrs Shairp & Maister or not.

The Court being informed that Mr Tod by his letters again advised the pushing the sales of the Company's goods at Glasgow, by reason sundry articles would sell there to profit which were not so well adapted for the London market. That the Glasgow merchants generally do not like to give orders as they rather chose to see the goods before purchasing. That the Company's sales there before the discontinuance of the bounty amounted to 5 to £8000 stg per annum and at present the orders from thence for these two years past have not exceeded £2500 p. annum. But that when the Company had a warehouse there formerly, for the last two years of that time the payments were very dilatory, some in 16, 18 or 20 months, occasioned by their trade with America turning out very indifferently, and credit being sometimes being given out indiscriminately to supercargoes and other adventurers to America, beside that

James Johnson who had the superintendency of the sales there had stopped payment. And all these reasons and accidents had hitherto occasioned the declining to re-establish a warehouse there on the Company's account. The Court desired Mr McCulloch, one of the Managers, as soon as convenient to set out for Glasgow and inquire into the state of trade there, and whether it would be prudent for the Company to think of re-establishing another warehouse in that place, or to continue for some time the present way of receiving orders for goods, to be supplied from their warehouse here, and of consigning goods now and then to a correspondent for sale, and to report the same.

Court of Directors

4 May 1758

In consequence of the minute of Court 27th ult, Mr McCulloch one of the Managers having gone to Glasgow as there directed, he reported to the Court that by what he could learn of the merchants concerned in foreign trade, it would be very acceptable to them for the Company to establish a warehouse again at Glasgow, as thereby they would have far greater choice of linen goods to suit their demands; but that such a measure would entirely clash with the interests of such merchants there as kept general warehouses (called furnishing warehouses) for assorting exporters with all sorts of goods as well as linen for exportation. That two of the most considerable of the wholesale dealers had spoke to him while at Glasgow and proposed to make trial of Osnaburgs and other linens from the Company, whose goods they recommended as preferable to others they had seen. And said that this ensuing autumn they would begin by an order of 1000 or 1500£ value of different kinds of linen to be paid for in 2 or 3 months thereafter, and leaving it to the Company to charge for these as they could afford; from which trial a judgement might be formed on both sides if it were for their mutual interest to continue.

The Court were of opinion that considering the certain charge attending the re-establishment of a warehouse, the almost unlimited credits formerly given there by the warehouse keeper and even to persons residing out of Britain, and that several of the most eminent exporters did now give their orders in writing by post to the Company's office at Edinburgh for parcels of goods; and that the establishing of a house would prevent the chance of sales to the furnishing merchants, it were better for the Company to be at the charge of sending one of the Managers to Glasgow as occasion should require to cultivate a correspondence and trade with the merchants than to establish a warehouse at present.

To George Young, Coupar Angus

11 July 1758

You have herewith William Bell's receipt for one trusse as per note subjoined of what you call factory linens returned for insufficiency in the workmanship such as being too thin, unequally wove, broken selvages etc. We have taken in a good many of these linens which justly speaking ought to have been refused in hopes you will soon amend, though at the same time we cannot approve of the hazards you yourselves run and consequently make others do of giving out yarns to such numbers of weavers who surely cannot as yet have in anyways benefitted of your factory methods, or have got any instruction from thence either in theory or practice. We therefore remark this day anew that no surprise or complaints may be had if we prove stricter in examining your linens for the future. Of the last entry of your factory's linens there are two pieces lost; the rest are all entered though none are up to the standard Mr Dow can bring them and we hope he'll exert himself.

Court of Directors

3 August 1758

The Managers proposed that James Robertson, who was employed last year by the Company in a journey through England, and who made sales there of the Company's goods to new customers to the amount of £755 at the expence of £23 for charges, should now make another trial in that way this year. The Court ordered the said James Robertson to set out for England in the manner as last year, and likewise to go to Manchester, Wigan etc with samples of the yarns the Company have to dispose of, and attempt the sales therof at these places or any others where he shall see a prospect of success.

Mr Richard Neilson, who is presently employed by the Company in the manufacturing of Edinburgs, Dowlas etc, having intimated to the Managers that he could not propose to engage further with the Company in that way, unless he could be assured of their employment for a space of years together. The Court did not think it proper at present to enter into any engagement with him for that purpose further than for one year.

To William Tod, London

12 September 1758

You say in freighting ships to bring home our flax we should consider where it would be most our interest to unload the cargoes. Leith in our humble opinion is the properest place because few or no purchasers in this country exceeds 5 or at most 10 tons, at a time by any one person, almost none that we can find out will buy without seeing their purchase. We think it is better to have the command of our flax here as there is access to almost all the places of sale (except Glasgow) by water. With regard to the spinning in the North, instead of reducing them to one-half, or paying them any penalty for not implementing our contracts, we apprehend it were more eligible to spin the cargo per Fair Trader, Main into yarns from 16 to 24 cutts per lb to which grists by its character that flax is well adapted and the increase will be more to the Company's advantage, seeing you observe the finer grists of yarn must now rise in price. To this purpose we have wrote the undertakers and have confined their spinning of waft yarn solely to the braiden and undrawn tow of that flax. With regard to our spinning here, it is to be in hempen yarns and in a small quantity of Dutch flax spun into yarns from 2 to 4 hanks per lb for supplying our manufacture of linen in the Irish fabric. There will be no flaxen yarn for Osnaburgs spun for some time. What you say of the quantity of Osnaburgs we have on hand and are to be made, enough to serve for two years sale, we hope will prove otherwise; you certainly were of different opinion last spring and winter and we cannot yet see why there should be less reason now than formerly to fear the want of demand for that article. However that may be; we have not increased any looms, on the contrary ever since your advice that 300 might be enough, we have kept rather fewer employed.

With regard to selling goods at Bristol, Liverpool and Whitehaven, the expence of carriage on these goods from this distant situation either by land or water is a great bar to extensive sales. There was a considerable draper from Liverpool here last summer (one Mr Lightbody) who liked our manufactures and to whom we wrote. We know no person at Bristol but Mr Gordon to whom we sometime ago transmitted a letter under your cover, but have not had a reply. We have lately sent a bale of our Osnaburgs to Hull but as yet have got no account how they are liked. The Newcastle drapers decline buying any, saying there is little or no vent for them, we have however wrote to a merchant there and shall advise you when he gives us his reply.

We have this day a letter from Mr Whyte of Kirkcaldy in which he offers us the best goods (ie Checks) made there at 6d per yd ready money and to leave one fourth of the value to be paid in our flax when it shall arrive. We have desired him to condescend on the quantity he would impose of on these terms and told him we would give him a reply in course of post from London, and have asked him whether he would chose to go a half concern with the Company in consignment of the parcel to your house. You'll please therefore write your opinion. A gentleman from Mansfield told us here the other day that about 14,000 weavers had given over working at Manchester and its neighbourhood and (as he said) these were chiefly those in the check trade. If this be true it should surely increase the demand for Scotch checks.

To William Forsyth, Cromarty

12 September 1758

We are just now favoured with yours of the 7th transmitting the accounts of the delivery of the cargo of flax per Main. By it we see it has intaked about 19 cwt of the original purchase weights. We are glad however it has proved of such good quality. We indeed directed our friend at Riga not to hesitate on a dollar extraordinary to lay in the best qualities, and accordingly he has always bought up the best parcels with an allowance of picking the same which makes what they call best Lithuania or Thesenhausen Rakitz. This cargo we apprehend must be altered in its manufacture from our original intention on contract. It is too good to make into the ordinary run of common Edinburgs and must therefore be wholly spun up into yarns wet spun and well twisted and the grists it will best put to from each respective dressing into yarns from 3 to 2 lib per spindle or in other words from 16 to 24 cuts per pound and then let the braids only or the tow undrawn be spun up into 10 and 12 cut yarns.

But besides the above reason of applying this Thesenhausen so as to fine yarns only, there is another most unfortunate cause has happened. Two of our ships outwards for the Baltic were sometime ago taken by the enemy. To supply these we hired two other ships here; one of them was then at Copenhagen, and her owners here agreed for her freight to Kirkwall and Cromarty as the ship was only going upon chance freight to Riga. However the master thought fit to counteract our agreement and took in a cargo of wood; we have got a protest and will recover damages but that will not replace our loss or lay down our flax with you and at Kirkwall. They at Riga are in some distant hopes of getting a ship and say they are endeavouring to provide one, which prevents our attempting the thing here for fear of paying waste freights and ship's insurance. And therefore we have to request you may spin up your yarns to the grists abovementioned which will keep your people employed till the next spring that [when?] we can with certainty provide you with flax for the lower kinds. It's possible that a ship may be yet got to go to Kirkwall and to Cromarty but we by no means can bid you depend on it. At any rate this alteration will prevent you from complaints and give you as full employment and profit as if spun in the other way.

To William Tod, London

14 September 1758

I am sorry to see you are still throwing out reflections as if I or anyone here wantonly or without judgement was laying in quantities of goods to occasion a loss by a dead stock. You say 'If you stop the spinning, the yarn may in time be sold off, but as to your Hollands, I can only repeat what I have said these many years that the fabric of these goods are out of fashion, and if you would sink 20 per cent I could not sell any great quantity of them. I am sorry any has been made for these three years but I shall do all I can to get off with these and the yarns. The Arbroath and Dundee people carry on their trade like merchants and men of judgement, attending to the value of goods they can sell in a year, spinning as much yarn as will make these goods and importing as much flax as will make that yarn. In this manner they have no dead stock. I am not against people's importing more flax than they spin if they can sell it; nay I am pretty sure that more money can be made by dealing in the materials of manufacture than following it through all its stages, and selling at last on long credit tho' at an extravagant profit.'

First with regard to the Hollands, there has none been made these last three years but what were absolutely necessary to assort and help of the others on hand, and these too in very small quantities and just as they were needed. As to the enlarging in that article at all in the first instance, I neither particularly advised it or made any particular bargain with any one maker of the goods that were made. I know that confined to the office here at home, I often complained, as it appeared to me, of the conduct of our affairs at London. I was in every year put in hopes of better doings. At last I said (and I still think) there was no way of knowing what is fit to be done below or any surety for our affairs being well conducted at London but by your residing and taking the charge of them there. The truth is that at that period when we laid in so many fine linens, we made and bought up these in hopes of a market in the only branch of the linen manufacture that was then tolerably understood or known in this Country. Mr Child was of no use in their sale and you was otherwise employed. By this means the Company came to be possessed of quantities and at the same time deprived of sales in due time. Why then should the blame if any is due be laid at my door? With respect to the yarns the Company you know resolved even when the bounty was discontinued to keep up the spinning introduced in the North. This was no doubt more of a patriot than a mercantile resolution as we have therby been loaded with an unnecessary dead stock of from 6 to 8000£ value per annum for near these two years bygone. Many of those yarns were ill-spun and others of a staple different from what you found to be the proper kinds for the manufactures chiefly wanted at London. Of these improper grists there are still great quantities on hand. In summer 1757 when our contracts were to be given up or renewed for spinning, I transmitted the plan both as to quantity, quality and price to you. That was approved of. Our other spinning was at Leith as had formerly been practised there for supplying that particular manufacture and as a check to the manner and price of spinning in the North. In January last Mr Doig wrote you that there was then on hand fully as much yarns as would keep their looms at work and to spin up more would be but losing interest; but if it were in your opinion more to the Company's interest to go on, he should do it. Your reply was to go on with the spinning of the coarse grists for wafts which was accordingly done. You desired some time ago that the numbers of looms for Osnaburgs should be confined to 300. I have ever since done so, and at this present there are not above 220 employed. This general rule of restriction I understood to be very prudent until such time from our acquiring better hands and skill in the manufacture and your knowing the particular qualitites of goods wanted we should be enabled with safety to extend. You no doubt expected to vend more of that article on account of the German war and the improvements we may have made in the manufacture than you now seem to hope for, having lately wrote that you had on hand sufficient to serve for 9 months sale. But from your writing last winter to continue the spinning of coarse yarns at Leith besides what came from the North, you certainly hoped for better and more enlarged sales, and we hope you may still do better than your present expectation. Now, if in this affair I have given a true state of the case, why should I be accused of carrying on trade unlike a merchant or without judgment? It surely cannot be a fault to obey the Company's resolutions, and where I can obtain your advice to act accordingly.

With regard to the third affair mentioned, as to the nature of our future trade, I in general so far agree with you that a small profit on raw materials is better than an apparent large one upon goods at long credit, but must add thereto by saying that in order to establish with certainty the Company's profits and these in their employ and in order to render the Company's stock more generally useful to the country and its manufacture, it were to be wished the Company resolve to take in goods to sell on commission at London, agree to advance to all such as required it to the extent of one-half of the value so consigned, and upon sales being made to advance if required perhaps one-quarter more upon interest.

To the Company there would be a sure laying out of their stock and a more general acceptation and circle of their notes than at present. To the owners would accrue the advantages of safety, the advance of cash if necessary, and as good sales it's to be presumed as any other would make without these favours. On the whole I should think where a person acts honestly and in concert with others he should bear no more blame than he may have incurred by deviation from these principles, and as it is our interest as well as duty to conduct our affairs honestly and carefully and with mutual trust and harmony, I shall hope for your more favourable construction of my doings, And where anything seems doubtful, you will for the future at least enquire of me or others before you give judgement.

To Robert Whyte, Kirkcaldy

26 September 1758

From what we can learn there will be but few goods exported this year to America. If therefore the quantity of checks made in or about your place, or that you expect will be made this autumn and winter be as large or possibly a greater quantity than was made the last or preceeding years, that article must still fall in price. The highest price such goods now give at London sold to exporters on 12 or 14 months is only 6¾d per yd, which after deducting freight, insurance, commission and interest of money earns no great return premium for one's risk and trouble, if indeed anything at all. It would appear absolutely necessary before we adventured further in the purchasing of that article, [to know] what quantity are usually made at your place and what of these are commonly sold to Glasgow and particularly what has been done this year by sales to that place. As also to know what quantities have gone by this fleet to London consigned to factors, and what are still on hand in your place undisposed of. In short if there are not many gone to London into the hands of factors and a small quantity only as yet exported to Glasgow, it might turn to your and our mutual advantage to be masters of the market by buying the quantity in hand at the rate of 6d the best and 5¾ or 5$^{10}/_{12}$ for the more inferior kinds, and the money payable in 2 or 3 months for ⅔rds of the value and one-third in flax. By having the command of the market at London it's not improbable we might draw 7d but if there are quantities parcelled out in factors hands there, we should perhaps not even reach to the parcel already sent up 6¾. If you shall therefore think well of it, we will go a half concern with you on the above mentioned linens, in the purchase of what may now be at your place of 3 qr wide checks, besides those of your own you made us an offer of being about 13,000 yards 3 qr wide and 2000 ⅞ wide provided as we have said there has been few sent to London or Glasgow as in proportion to their former quantities. We would chose to have as few ⅞ wide as possible. Before the next fleet sails for London one may make what sales they can to Glasgow, in proportion to the price they may bear at London; what is unsold may be sent in the same way of this last parcel consigned to Mr Tod, who as we have said, he has the command of the markets, may draw us better profits.

Court of Directors

28 September 1758

The Managers also represented that in consequence of the advice given them by the Court, Mr Tod had by means of Al. Anderson at London (to whom a commission of 1 per cent only was to be paid) had sold off part of the Company's superfluous stock of yarns presently on hand vizt 3000 spindles of

12 cutt at 8½d per pound, and 7000 spindles @ 8¾ per pound, the first at 3 the other at 6 months credit of which the Court likewise approved.

There having been shipped of the Company's goods consigned to Mr Tod and sundry others for sale on account of the Company to the value of about £3900 besides about 3000 spindles of yarn on board the fleet which sailed from the road of Leith on Monday the 25th current under convoy of His Majesty's ships Falmouth of 50, Sapphire of 32 and Jamaica sloop of 14 guns, and insurance having been ordered to be made by the Court on the Company's property with the underwriters here, the Managers reported that they referred that matter entirely to Mr Tod and wrote him on the 23rd current that in case he should think it proper to make insurance on the value of the Company's goods on board said fleet, he should do the same at London in what proportion he should think proper, as the Court had left it to him to do therein as his prudence should determine or as circumstances may require, either from bad weather, or his being long in hearing of the arrival of the fleet in or near the Thames.

To William Tod, London

30 September 1758

After discounting the 10,000 spindles of 12 cutt yarns sold, there remains just now in the warehouse 4238 spindles of that grist, and of the 14 cutt there are in all 9046 sps, as will more fully appear by the enclosed state taken the 27th inst. by which you'll see the general state of all the yarns presently on hand; if we are to accept of your offer for 3 or 4000 sps more of 12 cutt for Messrs Neilson & Co you see that grist will be almost entirely exhausted, unless there shall be still yet more of it to come up from the North.

We have just now received a letter from James Robertson dated from Manchester the 25th by which we learn he has made but very little progress in the sale of yarns at present, his orders being but for 400 sps in all from 16 to 10 cutt yarn. But by the enclosed letter you will see he gives a pretty accurate account of the trade there, and 'tis to be hoped from the correspondence he has opened betwixt Messrs Hart & Bolton and this Company something considerable may be done in that branch, as the prices noted by these gentlemen are not unfavourable.

To William Tod, London

10 October 1758

By the samples sent you of dyeing linen, you will best judge whether the 10 or 12 cutt yarn is best for wafting these goods with, we certainly can make this or any other branch of the Osnaburg manufacture here as cheap and as well as in any other part of the Kingdom, provided any regard is to be had for the honesty of the fabric, which we are sorry to say is not the case almost anywhere else. We have occasion to see parcels made in Angus of our own yarns for the Company as well as parcels brought here for others. There are two or three yards on one end of the piece made well, the rest generally from 10 to 20 per cent less work. By the outside fold they are judged good and sold accordingly, the merchant's apprehending he has a great pennyworth but in the event it must ruin the trade of the Kingdom, for they who make use of them once, never will again. We no doubt labour under some disadvantages here at present being obliged to have our goods made in factories for want of choice of master-weavers; that is now seemingly in a way of being ammended as is also our method of stating the cost by allowing a full 10 per cent profit on the yarns, which makes it both appear to you and us more expensive than from others. This we proposed to have had amended at the last balance and to have an advance of 4 per cent only on the yarns, but this Mr Doig strenuously opposes until he has conversation with you in order to the adjusting some matters that lie, he says, betwixt you and him chiefly to clear up; however these and sundry other things we hope to have adjusted when you come down which you propose should be sometime this month.

To Robert Whyte, Kirkcaldy

12 October 1758

I have this night letters from Mr Wm Tod advising his having sold the whole of the parcel of checks consigned him on your and this Company's account by last fleet but the price he has obtained is very moderate, being no more than 6¾ per yard to pay in twelve months and he to be at the charge of upmaking and cylendring which is not less than ¼d per yard. It is true the outcome measure will in part indemnify that expence, being in general about two yards on the 100 so that it is properly speaking about 6⅝ per yard or thereby. The advantage is chiefly a quick sale and together.

To the Publishers of the Edinburgh Evening Courant

23 October 1758

These are to give notice to such master weavers in or near the City of Edinburgh, who incline to weave plain linen of different breadths and setts from a 5 to 12 hundred warp on the breadth, that William Hill at the British Linen Company's warehouse in Edinburgh, gives out yarns ready prepared for the loom with reeds and caims where wanted, and will contract with the said master weavers to employ them for a time certain at such prices as are usually paid for weaving these different setts of linen. Such as incline to be employed must apply soon, and bring with them proper certificates of their honesty and knowledge in their business.

Please insert the above advertisement in the Edinburgh Evening Courant Thursday first for account of the British Linen Company.

To William Tod, London

24 October 1758

We are glad to see you approve of the proposed consignment of yarns to Hart & Bolton. These goods are now making up and part of them will be forwarded this week. There will in about 4 or 5 weeks hence a ship sail from Glasgow for Liverpool by which these yarns will be sent. From what you write of Messrs Neilson & Co in your letter of the 19th curr. the yarns are now ordered to be delivered to their friend at Glasgow. Mr Richard Neilson tells us that almost all of his weavers at Cranston left their employ during the harvest and that very few of the tow wafted goods are made. Such of the weavers as are returned are now putting them in the loom. We are extremely glad to see you have got a warehouse in some degree to your liking.

The trade from Glasgow has met with several severe checks this year, the short crop of tobaccos in Virginia and the high price of the small quantity coming home will prevent their sending almost any goods there and the capture of 8 or 9 of their ships for the West Indies (tho' insured) has deprived them of proper ships and masters for carrying on that trade at least so far, from all which we expect but small sales to that place this season.

Court of Directors

16 November 1758

Mr Tod having advised that he had sold all the chequered linen sent him on the joint account of the Company and Robert Whyte at 6¾d per yard, and that if betwixt and Christmas (when the fleet for America was expected to sail) there could be sent him from Leith 20,000 yards more of these goods, he could dispose of them in the same manner. The Managers informed the Court that they had wrote to Mr Whyte to procure and ship by next convoy for London of about 30,000 yards of chequered linen at the rate of 6d per yard. Of which the Court approved.

Mr Tod having likewise advised by his letter of the 17th Oct that by reason of the great inconveniency and expence of being obliged to keep great quantities of the Company's goods at different wharfs for want of room in the Company's warehouse, he had hired other warehouses to that purpose which he hoped would accommodate the Company sufficiently and keep all their goods for which he had agreed to pay £75 per annum.

Court of Directors

30 November 1758

The Managers represented that in obedience to the order of the Court of date 8 April 1756 they had used all possible diligence in getting the yarns then on hand and what have since been produced in consequence of the contracts for spinning, to be wove up into cloth. That the quantities of yarn had proved larger than could be got manufactured by at least a surplus quantity of £5000 value yearly. That on mentioning this to the Court sometime ago, it had been resolved to dispose of such quantities as were not immediately necessary, in consequence whereof there had been sold since last balance about 35,000 spindles. And rather as keep such a quantity on hand a price was accepted of much about 5 per cent below the cost. And that in consequence of sundry advices from the Company's correspondents at Liverpool, Manchester, Preston and Warrington there were now made up ready to send thither by way of Glasgow the number of 10,827 spindles which it was hoped would come to a tolerable good market. And that agreeable to the desire of the Court, they the Managers had stopped the sending up of any more yarns from the North to Leith, and therby the freight and insurance would be saved and the yarns shipped from thence at a cheaper rate for Hull, London or Liverpool etc as markets should offer.

Mr Tod further represented that the present state of the trade at London and the manufacture here differed greatly from the time when the Company introduced and carried on the coarse linen manufacture solely on their own account and risk from the raw materials to the sale of exportation, several fabrics hardly known some years ago having now become staple articles, in so much that they can be purchased when occasion requires as cheap as when manufactured. And not only in Scotland but in England & Ireland large quantities in imitation of Osnaburgs and Dowlas have been made and brought to the London market for sale. Which had not only retarded the sales of the Company's goods but had likewise reduced the price from too great quantities being brought to market. The above was likewise the state of the diaper manufacture, a very considerable quantity having been sent up last year to London for sale from the town of Dunfermline alone in competition with what the Company manufactured. That as to fine plain white linens, the quantity on hand was still more than the expected demand would consume for some time, tho' a considerable value of these goods had been sold lately. That there were several species of low priced linens called Soldiers' Shirting and those made in imitation of foreign Silesias, Garlix and Irish linen which had been attempted lately and promised success both with respect to the country and the Company. These goods were mostly made by common manufacturers, tho' some of them were made in and about Edinburgh. That an exact book was now kept of the several sorts of linen the Company deal in, which the Managers craved leave to refer to, as by that book the quantity on hand of each species at the warehouse here would appear. A particular note of the yarns on hand distinguishing the state and condition in which the yarns are was likewise made out and submitted to the consideration of the Court.

The Court having considered the above representation with the several accounts referred to did find that there were 39,586 spindles of Osnaburg or coarse yarn now upon hand already prepared by boiling, milling or bleaching, and by that means in such a state that it could only be manufactured. They therefore ordered that the said quantity be wove up into Edinburgs, Dowlas, Sheetings or such goods as these goods were most adapted for, and recommended that the same be done gradually and in such manner as to keep only the best of the weavers, already engaged, employed for some time. And that the rather so that the low priced or Osnaburgs may now be purchased with more advantage to the Company than they can be manufactured. As to the green or brown yarns (as was formerly ordered) they again desired the same might be sold off to best advantage.

The Court likewise considering that there were now a considerable quantity of diapers on hand, and as such goods could now be purchased they were of opinion no more of that article should be manufactured for some time unless it were the yarns already in David Campbell's hands at Dunfermline which should be wove up, and about 1300 spindles of the 14 cutt yarn in Mr Doig's hands already prepared which they were advised might be wove into toweling to more advantage than any other fabric. The Court were still of opinion that no more fine linens or Hollands should be manufactured until those on hand should mostly be sold off.

The Managers further informed that agreeable to the desire of the Court the 9099 yds Soldiers' Shirting linen formerly offered by Alexr Adam of Forfar and Partners to be consigned to Mr Tod for sale on their account had been purchased by the Company, as also above 4000 yards of the same kind of linen from one Richardson in Perth. It was likewise proposed that the Company betwixt and April next should contract for next year's quantities of Soldiers' Shirting with Sandeman and Richardson of Perth each 10,000 yards together 20,000 yards; with Adam of Forfar and Smith of Brechin each 10,000 yards, being 20,000 yards. And that there should be manufactured here of the Company's yarns 10,000 yds of that kind of linen of ¾ and ⅞ wide linens in the Irish fabric (for the making of which the country around Kilsyth seemed very proper) 400 to £500 value to be contracted for with Mr Hector McLean, and a like quantity with Wm Sandeman at Perth; and the remainder of the £1200 value of these linens formerly mentioned to be manufactured in and about Edinburgh. That the chief bar to the making of good linens was the want of proper utensils, particularly reeds and caims.

Court of Directors

4 January 1759

That William Sandeman and James Richardson of Perth had both made proposals for delivering Soldiers Shirting, but for the aforesaid reason of the rise of materials and the smaller chance they may next year have for a premium than formerly they required not only 9d per yd for such linen but money in advance to enable them to manufacture the same, without paying interest for the same on which terms Sandeman would contract for 12 to 15,000 yards upon the Company's advancing him £400, and the balance to be payable on the delivery of the goods. If the goods should not please, he to repay the cash advanced with interest from the time of remitting. And Mr Richardson proposed to furnish 10,000 yards of said linen upon the Company's advancing him £300 in the above terms.

The Court approved of the Managers agreeing with the above named manufacturers in the terms aforesaid upon their finding sufficient security for the money advanced and for their punctual fulfilling of the above contract.

The Court were further informed that Mr Tod by his letter 19th ult advised his having contracted for 30,000 yards best Osnaburgs, 28 inches wide, at 8½d per yd for the use of the Navy, deliverable in 4 or at most 5 months from that time. And that the Managers had given orders to have the same quantity made as quickly as possible, which they were in hopes to complete before the time prescribed. And that they having made an agreement with Mr Hector McLean, writer to the Signet by their letter of the 23 ult concerning the making of linens after the Irish fabric at Kilsyth on the conditions and conform to the regulations mentioned in the said letter which was laid before the Board. They approved thereof.

To John Henderson, Riga

9 January 1759

Our last to you was of the 5th October, since which we have had sundry of your favours and note the contents. You will ere this have learned the misfortunes that have happened to the ships of Captain Main and Captain Glassford. By these disappointments we shall be under a necessity of having two cargoes of flax ready to be shipped first open water from your river, and this therefore serves to desire you will purchase for the Company sixty not exceeding 65 tons of flax at such times as shall seem to you most proper, to be shipped by a vessel to be sent from hence as soon as you shall advise she can get into the river of Riga. The kinds of flax we wish this cargo to consist of are one half to be of Lith[uania] Rak[itzer], one fourth of Druj[uania] Rak[itzer], and a fourth part of Cutt Marienburg or Bad[stub] Paternoster as the quantity and price shall direct you. We do not mean to confine you entirely to the above quantities, but wish to have them pretty agreeable thereto. For the purchase of this cargo, you will when necessary value on Messrs George Clifford & Sons of Amsterdam, whom we have desired to honour your current account of this Company to the amount of £2000 stg, which credit he will no doubt confirm to you. We hope it is needless to recommend to you the utmost care and attention to this order from the Company as the best means of securing their future favours. You will advise us from time to time of the contracts and purchases you make, as also of the state of your market and occurences in trade.

To William Tod, London

11 January 1759

With regard to the Navy linens, Mr Doig has the patterns of the foreign Ticklenburgs lodged with the foremen of the different shops as a rule for the weaving off these linens for the Navy. Those that were last made and sent up (as formerly pointed out to you) had no objection as to the colour; we imagine the mixture of white and brown yarns will no ways disfigure the goods. Those sent having been made from brown warp and white wafts and to our fancy looked very well. As to Mr Campbell's imagining that he can contract for linens for the Army it is perhaps possible, but we do not know a weaver capable to do them or fit to be trusted with money other than those mentioned to you already to be engaged for the Company, and we believe if we were to engage them to do any more it would only have the effect to produce dearer and worse goods and thereby affect the character and trade of the country. You may be assured that we will spin no more yarns till necessity require it.

Court of Directors

18 January 1759

The Managers informed the Court that they having received advice of the failure of the house of Messrs Sill, Bridges and Blount of Hull who had an assortment of the Company's goods sent them for sale on the Company's account, and to show the manufactures to the various dealers in that place, they had wrote to Mr James Hamilton of Hull to appear as the Company's attorney and claim the goods consigned to Sill, Bridges and Blount as the Company's property, together with all debts arising from any part of the said linens which had been sold for the Company's behoof. As likewise they were to write to David Denholm who acted as clerk to the above house to be assisting in having the affairs of the Company with them cleared up, and so distinguished as not to interfere with their property or debts.

To William Tod, London

1 February 1759

We yesterday laid your proposition before the Court of Directors anent the consigning of a 100 p[iece]s of the Company's hollands to the Messrs Hallidays who you say have a house in each of the West Indies Islands, and that you had prevailed with the eldest brother now at London to accept of that quantity upon commission. The Court resolved that upon the recommendation of Mr Tod the consignment should be made providing that he shall think there is a reasonable prospect of sale there and that the elder brother will become security to account for the proceeds in Britain.

The narrowness of the Trustees' funds prevents their doing many things they are satisfied would be of great use to the linen manufacture. Their best fund of £3000 per annum you know is confined to the Highlands and therefore little or nothing can be done for Fife or any of the low countries. At the same time the Highland plans hitherto followed do by no means either answer the expence laid out on the ends intended. For instance the Highland stations stand them in and about £1200 per annum and last year these produced in all about 3000 spindles of yarn. The Board are now resolved to to alter their plan and after some conversations with our E. M[cCulloch] on the subject of this Company taking the care of the spinning and its increase upon them it seems now to be understood betwixt parties and may be resolved on as follows. The Company to have the command of the undertakers at Lochbroom, Loch Carron & Glenmoriston and be conveyed into the Board's security from these men for their fidelity, to have 1000 wheels & reels to distribute, together with 13 spinning mistresses to teach such as may be ignorant, to have £50 per annum for each undertaker, £5 per annum for each spinning mistress, and 5/- for each woman taught together with 6d per spindle for each sp[indle] of yarn spun in these countries for the term of 3 years. The Company being bound to supply those stations with as much dressed flax as shall be called for, to be there spun up into yarns not heavier than 3, and not less than 1 lb. per spindle and over and above the price of 10d per sp[indle] to the spinner, shall allow the undertaker 1d per sp[indle] for each sufficient sp[indle] of yarn.

If this agreement take place we propose (at least for the first year) to heckle all the flax at Leith so that we may be as little hurt by waste or ignorance of heckling or by a dead stock of tow on hand. There is a probability that at the end of the second year this spinning may amount to from 50 to 60,000 sp[indle]s of yarn and you see the Trustees by knocking off so many useless salaries have a reasonable prospect of getting the government's intention executed and we hope the Company thereby made no losers.

Lady Milton desires if the things she wanted you to send her down are not already sent that you would put them on board the Concord, Robt McKenzie master, for Prestonpans; she lies at Hoare's wharf.

Meeting of the Court of Proprietors

19 February 1759

Present, the honorable Lord Milton, Deputy Governor, and sundry others of the Proprietors.

The Court of Directors having (in course of post) received Mr Tod's letter of date 4th January last, resigning his office as one of the Managers of the Company, did in consequence cause this General Meeting of the Proprietors to be called in order to lay the said letter before them, together with the opinion of the Directors thereupon, which is as follows; 'That this measure of Mr Tod's resigning his office as Manager, and thereby being at liberty to folow out any other branch of trade, from which by his agreement with the Company he is now prohibited, will be attended with no inconveniency, and appears to the Court to be for the Company's interest in regard his premium qua Manager, and his additional allowance for extraordinary expence on account of his being obliged to reside in London, will be saved and likewise by reason Mr Tod can still in this way be of as much use to the Company as formerly; as to which he has already made offer of his services.

'That on taking the average for ten years bypast, of the charge of keeping up a warehouse at London and paying Mr Tod as Manager, the same does more than double the expence it would cost the Company to pay him even the usual commission as a factor. That the Company have hitherto been obliged to have a large stock of goods over and above what were sold annually, being much about £8400 value on an average, which for the future, it is hoped, will in a great measure be saved. That for these reasons the Court had given up their warehouses at London and proposed to make trial by employing Messrs Tod and Anderson at London as their factors, and to allow them such charge for commission as may be agreed upon.

'The Court had further to remark to the General Meeting, that by Mr Tod's resignation of his office,[1] the contract between the Company and the Managers

1 NLS, Saltoun MSS, Box 62, Tod to Lord Milton, 2 Jan. 1759: 'A friend has offered to drop his commission business in my favour which brings him £800 p.a. This offer, my Lord, required no hesitation on my part. I have been acting for some years without a premium and my name as a manager without power and at 400 miles from the place where things are conducted.'

is now at an end, and therefore it will be necessary that accounts be settled with both for preceedings, and that a new agreement be made with Mr McCulloch for the future. Also that the collective firm or subscription of McCulloch & Tod be from and after the first of March next in disuse, and that all the deeds, notes, bills, letters and all other writings concerning the affairs of the Company be thenceforward executed in name by Ebenezer McCulloch only, as sole Manager for that purpose.'

The abovementioned letter from Mr William Tod to the Company resigning his office as Manager for them, being read in presence of this general Court, they were satisfied and accepted of said resignation. The Court having likewise considered the foregoing report and opinion of the Court of Directors, they did approve thereof, and empowered them to settle with the Managers in relation to the preceeding accounts, to agree with Messrs Tod and Anderson of London for negotiating the Company's affairs there on as easy terms as possible, and to contract with Mr Ebenezer McCulloch for the management of the Company's business in time coming, in such manner as they shall judge proper.

To William Tod, London

20 February 1759

We duly received yours of the 15th by which we see the ships the Reward and the Leith Packet are safe arrived. We are glad to see you have made a contract with Mr Brodie for 35,000 yards Soldiers' Shirting at 10d which we can easily fulfill, having since we formerly wrote you anent the quantities engaged for agreed to a further 15,000 yards more, besides a parcel now making for us in Angus under Wm Coupar's care chiefly of our own yarns 20 and 18 cutts which we hope will come about 8⅔d only per yard; the quantity Coupar may produce is uncertain, but in all besides his parcel we have now people engaged for the making of 50,000 yards. Great care is promised to prevent the thin goods being run at the bleaching or as you call it frayed, the error was in rubbing these indiscriminately with the strong made goods. When you have closed an agreement with Mr Brodie as to these Silesias it will be proper to write both as to price and quality; as to the quantity in our opinion it would not be proper to contract with Mr Brodie for any greater quantity at present of these soldiers' shirting until the terms of delivery and payment are known, with what charges may further attend the sales besides the freight and insurance to which you'll please write us.

Yesterday the General Court of Proprietors accepted of your demission as Manager and agreed to the report of the Directors for employing Mr Anderson and you as their factors.

Court of Directors

1 March 1759

The Court having further taken into consideration the insurance of the Company's goods from Leith and Dundee to London, and being informed that from May 1747 to February last, there had been shipped from these ports on the Company's account and risk to the value of £132,819 which at the lowest average for insurance being 1¼% amounted to £1660 4/9, they agreed therefore for the future that the Company should run the risk to the amount of £300 on each bottom from Leith to London without insuring, when the ships shall happen to sail with convoy and desired Mr Tod might be certified thereof.

In consequence of advice received from Mr Tod, Mr McCulloch informed the Court that he had given orders to David Campbell and David Hart, both manufacturers at Dunfermline, to manufacture and purchase for the Company to the extent of about £500 value each of Diapers of the qualities desired by Mr Tod, deliverable at the Company's warehouse betwixt and the month of August next on the terms mentioned in Mr McCulloch's letters to them of the 16 and 20th current. Of which the Court approved.

Court of Directors

29 March 1759

The Court having this day taken into consideration the remit to the honorable Lord Milton to correspond with Mr Tod concerning an agreement with him and Mr Alex Anderson his partner for managing and transacting the Company's affairs at London by commission; His Lordship reported that he had corresponded with Mr Tod thereanent who he understood would accept of the following terms vizt 'That they Messrs Tod and Anderson shall be allowed at the rate of 2½ per cent commission and ½ per cent of warehouse rent on all goods sold for the Company, deliverable at London while the amount of such sales does not exceed £15000 per annum, and while they are under that sum to have no allowance for paying or receiving moneys for the Company or for making insurances or getting losses made good for them. But if the sales shall exceed £15000 per annum they are to abate ½ per cent of the commission, but in that event to have ¼ per cent on all bills negotiated for the Company other than for goods sold by them and ⅛ per cent on all insurances transacted other than for goods consigned to themselves, together with 1¼ per cent for making up all average of general losses with insurers. That there shall be a set of books kept purposely for the Company's business and trade in their care, and all the sales made in the Company's name as their factors, and that the securities shall be taken in their name for the behoof of the Company.'

The Court having considered the above proposal, and being fully convinced of Mr Tod's ability to serve the Company in all the affairs they have to transact at London, they agree to the same.

To Wale & Fraser, Riga

17 April 1759

I wrote you 13th ult by the Europa of Dysart, James Normand, chartered for bringing the cargo of flax ordered from your house by this Company by post of 31st ult. To both which letters I beg leave to refer you. I am now favoured with yours of the 10th March (OS)[1] and have duly noted the contents. As I see thereby that the ship's charter will be necessary to protect her from being impressed into the Russian service, and as the owners live at too great a distance to learn from them timeously if or not the master took his copy in the ship, I thought it proper to send you herewith one of said charter parties to prevent all accidents. Said ship will probably be now arrived at your port as we have advice of a vessel that sailed in company with her from this firth being safe at Copenhagen on the 25th past (NS).

I am glad to learn that this year's crop of flax turns out well and hope you have purchased the remainder of the order given you on more favourable terms than noted. As this flax is to be employed in the Company's manufactures at some distance, I beg the favour you will carefully inspect this cargo distinguishing the qualities both in the invoice and the bills of lading, marking on the packages of the of the best Lithuania Rak[itzer] TP, the more ordinary of that kind R., the best of the Drujaner TxDxR, the other DR. and in the same way distinguishing the better kinds of the Cutt Marienburg or Babstip Paternoster. And if any matts should be already shipped, pray note their quality on the bills of lading tho' the marks cannot be put on the packages.

To Dr William Horsburgh, New Providence

24 July 1759

Your kind favours to the Company of 29th Nov. and 2nd Feb. last came to hand in the end of April, and yours of the 23rd April brought me on the 1st current a copy of your letter of the 27th July 1758, the original of which never appeared. I am glad to see that the goods last sent you were safe arrived; I hope

1 Old Style, i.e. Julian calendar. This was still in use in Russia and some Baltic states, although Britain had adopted the Gregorian calendar ('New Style'), then 11 days ahead, in Sept. 1752.

the damage on the Edinburgs was not considerable. You mention that the Edinrs are too good for your market; if therefore you will be so good as to point out kinds that would answer, they can be provided you by this Company on as reasonable terms as any can be afforded. On the other side you have a note of the payments made on your last goods by which you will see there is still £40 14/11 due besides interest. Concerning this Mr Russel will write you particularly.

In obedience to your obliging orders, I looked out and packed up the goods you desired, but no convoy has since sailed for London till last week, when I shipped the 2 trunks marked WxH No.1 and 6 on board the Edinburgh, John Hay master. On the other side you have invoice of same net amount £133 13/-. I have desired Messrs Tod & Anderson at London to ship these goods by first convoy for South Carolina and to consign them to the care of Messrs Dewar and Mann there, writing them to forward them to you at New Providence at first opportunity. Messrs Tod & Anderson are directed to insure these goods from Leith to London, from London to South Carolina and from thence to New Providence as formerly in such way as to cover the invoice's value, premium and abatement in case of loss.

To Lady Strathnaver

24 July 1759

My not having the honour of being known to your Ladyship's son the Earl of Sutherland makes me take this liberty of addressing your Ladyship. In the first place I beg leave to congratulate you on His Majesty's commissioning My Lord to the command of a regiment.[1] And then would beg you would let my Lord know that this Company (in which we have the honour of your Ladyship for a Proprietor) can provide my Lord with clothing for his regiment on better terms than any else in the Kingdom. I have the pleasure to acquaint your Ladyship that our linens are now demanded at London preferable to the foreign. In so much that there is now in this house an order from one contractor only at London for 50,000 yards Soldiers' Shirting. If my Lord Sutherland please I can provide him on the same terms with these contractors who therafter furnish the different regiments. This much I thought was my duty to acquaint Your Ladyship with, being what I apprehend both for the Earl's and the Company's advantage.

1 A commission had been given to William, 17th earl of Sutherland, to raise a Highland regiment.

To Joseph Forsyth, Dingwall

28 July 1759

There is no doubt every person would chose to have as little trouble and as great profit on his business as possible, but that may be drove too far as the undertakers for the Trustees' stations are likely to experience. The Board of Trustees are now heartily tired of house building and giving salaries in the Highlands. It will therefore be unnecessary to make me any proposals for building houses or giving salaries other than what a premium for executing the work will bring in proportion to the extent of the spinning. The present year is merely a trial at what rate of expence the business can be carried on, for this purpose the Trustees will allow 2d per spindle above the price paid the spinner and pay all charges of transport to and again. This you know is double the rate it can be done for in this country. The method Mr Scott takes is to cause erect houses made of turf with a ditch thrown round to keep out ground dampness, and to employ a woman both to teach the ignorant and give out his lint and receive in his yarns. By this method he will get business done on cheaper terms than the way you propose and I hope make something to himself. Against another year I propose to deliver him the flax rough and receive the yarns when spun upon a price stipulated, as is now done with the white flax for coarse grists. But the Trustees must first know the charge of transport before a fair and honest allowance can be made on that account. If you are pleased upon these terms to make a trial I shall order so much flax to be delivered you. If not, I am sorry for it but can propose no other terms than what Mr Scott asked when here, and Mr Mackay has since approved of and accepted himself.

To Hector Scott, Inverness

21 August 1759

I come now to reply more particularly to your letter of the 15th. I agree with you that the wheels and reels should be inspected, marked and numbered as quickly as they are made so that they may be distributed early in the season to the spinners and for that purpose you should get some of the magistrates to direct the inspection of the wheels and reels and to attest them by 50 or even half of that number. With regard to Mr Shaw's refusing you access to your own house, you may be certain he will use every method in his power to disappoint one he imagines will supplant him and therefore if you cannot force him to quit his possession, you must do the best in your power without him.

I dare say you will find difficulties (as must happen in all new undertakings) in establishing colonies of spinners in the different parts but these you must endeavour to surmount. If you yourself think it proper to carry on a spinning at Lochaber, do so and let me know the name of the distributing places, as I must get it marked in the Trustees' books. And from what you say about the Governor of Fort Augustus, I suppose Lochaber must come in the room of Fort Augustus for a spinning station. I apprehend the behaviour of the Governor to be owing to his connection with Mr Shaw; however you may do without them. Only let me know the whole particulars in a letter such as may be shown. As I have an entire confidence in your integrity and application to business I have no difficulty to assure you that I shall take my hazard of being reimbursed, and thereby agree to allow you for this year upon any extraordinary expences for house building or spinning mistresses' fees that has not hitherto been allowed for in your agreement and proposals to the amount of £20 stg more upon your instructing such to be really necessary. I hope there will now nothing happen to retard your going on with spirit. I desire you may write me from time to time as to your success therein. I hope you will not lose time in fighting with Shaw or the Governor but cultivate a friendship with the McDonalds and Frazers and establish yourself there on a firm footing. Mr Mackay of Tordarroch who carries on the spinning on the same footing with you at the head of Lochurchqull [sic] and Assynt assures me of this year of 5000 sp[indle]s of yarn.

To George Young, Coupar Angus

4 September 1759

I have yours of the 1st curr covering invoices of bales 85, 86 which I fear will arrive too late to be bleached this season and therefore I desire you may send no more till further orders. During the winter you should employ none but the best hands and take only the very best goods. By advice from London I find that your Silesias of 31 inch wide linens would answer better if made half an inch narrower and to cut in pieces of not more than 35 yards. This you will please advert to in all you make for the future; the lessening of the breadth will have a considerable effect on the price, and the reeds should be ordered in conformity from the above.

It was not at all meant to exclude you from the distribution of the utensils to be given by the public; very far from it. I recommended your servant Mr Dow for that purpose, as I dare say he will act entirely by your directions. And it was better to have that matter in his name than in yours who had already otherwise a considerable allowance from the Board.[1]

1 George Young had, for instance, received £80 for a school at Coupar Angus for 'instructing and perfecting the country weavers and journeymen in the most proper methods of sorting and preparing their yarns': SRO, NG1/1/14, BOTM 9 Dec. 1757.

To Joseph Angus, Glasgow

29 September 1759

As to the sheetings in your former parcel which you say will not answer your market, I shall receive them very readily on your paying the carriage. We have a much greater demand for these sorts of sheeting than any other, they are chiefly asked indeed in England for what they call footmen or servants' sheeting. The kind you want, I see, is finer for the money but in these goods the London drapers say that strength is greater excellence than either fine colour or fine thread. If you should incline I could send you linen 36 inches wide much finer and fairer for the money.

To James Robertson, Edinburgh

3 October 1759

I herewith deliver you a state of the sundry accounts due this Company in England for goods furnished in consequence of orders delivered you, as you are now to set out again for England. It will not be at all necessary for you to [go] into the West of England but just make as speedy a journey through those places where money is due. From the many losses sustained by those who upon your recommendation had goods from the Company, I desire you will be much on your guard to recommend none but such as are of undoubtedly great credit, and such gentlemen you are to endeavour to persuade trials of this Company's manufacture of which to that purpose you have herewith a list in which are noted the different qualities and prices. The only conveyance by which goods can be forwarded from here to most places in the East of England is by sea to Newcastle or by the weekly waggon.

I had a few posts ago a letter from Mr Hancock, attorney at law in Whitby, informing me that James Stewart, linen draper there, who you see owes this Company £49 6/- has stopped payment, that his creditors had obtained a commission of bankruptcy against him, but he proposed to deliver up his effects which however it was not thought would amount to 7/6 per pound. This affair has the appearance of a notorious fraud, and unless Mr Stewart can instruct very great losses since the furnishing of these linens he is entitled to no favour. As to this inquire respectfully from the creditors and others in the place and do in it what shall then seem to you for the Company's interest.

To Thomas Junor, Kirkcaldy

30 October 1759

Your letter of the 16th and 29th are both before me. I really do not know what reply further to make you now anent Provost Whyte's proposals of hiring you into his service than what I told you when in this place last time. Vizt that I should be far from standing in the way of your being better provided but that if you chose to continue in this Company's employment as their agent, I apprehend their business would neither increase or decrease but that no doubt would greatly depend on your own care in either making purchases when ordered or weaving up the goods properly that were entrusted to your care. If therefore you chose to rely on the Company's employment, I shall assure you of as much business as you can execute well and they have occasion to carry on with you. You may have any reasonable quantity of yarns just now, to be given out to the weaving either warped or not sorted and warped as you shall see best. But in the meantime I think it were proper that you come over yourself to this place and looked over the yarns wanted. You have herewith bill Andrew Davidson for £11 7/- which I desire you'll do the necessary for procurring payment. I thought to have sent you some warped webs by Mr Connochie but Mr Hill has such daily demands on him just now that there is not a piece ready prepared so you must come yourself and take such as will suit your weavers.

To Richard Neilson, Edinburgh

3 November 1759

In consequence of the sundry conversations we have had on the subject of carrying on the trade of selling flax and purchasing linens at the towns of Dundee and Cupar of Fife for the account of this Company, I herewith subjoin the heads of several terms and conditions condescended upon mutually by us, which it is agreed on to be put into the form of a contract upon stamped paper after a trial of three or four months' practice. Not that by any such delay it is intended that either party shall have it in their option to resile or draw back from the Dundee plan or intention of this document. And as in pursuance of said plan you now propose to go over to Dundee to make a beginning therein.

With regard to purchases of linen manufacturing, I can at present encourage only your contracting for Soldiers' Shirting, that is to say linens of the breadh of 30½ inches when brown, having 6/100 warp of the breadth and made of yarns of 2½, 2¾ lb per spindle, and of 6½ hundred warp, 2¼ and 2½ lb per sp[indle] on the same breadth whereof you may buy up betwixt and June 1st to the amount of 60,000 yards. With regard to the other sort called Pomeranias, they are linens wove in reed 31 inches in breadth. Of these you may purchase to the extent of 40 or 50,000 yards. It is needless to say that such or any other goods must be upon as reasonable terms as the nature of this thing and the market will allow.

[Enclosed] Conditions of establishing a house at Dundee and Coupar Fife for promoting the linen manufacture and the sale of flax in conjunction with the British Linen Company.

No.1 This correspondent should in the first place be possessed of £1000 capital stock of the B.L.Co as a pledge for his fidelity.

2nd That he be concerned with no other person in the making or purchasing of linens but the Co solely for the space of 5 or 7 years or such time as shall be agreed upon. And that he will sell flax or hemp for no other persons but solely on commission from the Company.

3rd. That all the trade for London market be on joint account of profit and loss. The Co bound to advance for this branch to the amount of £5000 or £6000 per annum to be laid out on manufactures at such times as Mr Tod shall advise or the Co shall see most from the joint advantage.

The Co's ½ share of the purchase of goods to be burdened with a commission of 1 per cent to their correspondent, and at each shipping of goods, the account of purchases to be settled and his draft taken for the ½ of the amount shipped upon the factor the goods are consigned to, payable to the managers for the Linen Co at 6 months thereafter. The Co being allowed discount of 4¾ per cent per annum for the time such bill has to run. NB. The practice at Dundee, Perth etc is for the merchants who draw such bills to allow their banks 5 per cent per annum for 5 months of the six to run and 10 per cent more for negotiating.

4th. Many of the Glasgow shopkeepers being furnished with low priced Osnaburgs from Dundee, which are paid for in about 3 months at soonest in 2 months, it is proposed that whatever business is procurred in this way should be executed on a commission of 2½ per cent whereof 1 per cent to be allowed the resident and 1½ to belong to the Company, to indemnify them the advance of money and the troubles of securing payment.

5th That whatever goods are wanted for the Edinburgh warehouse such should be bought up on a commission of 1 per cent, the Co. always furnishing him with notes for effectuating the purchases.

6th That for all bills of exchange on London or Holland bought for the Co he to be allowed 2/6 per cent commission.

7th That he be allowed 1 per cent on the sale of flax or hemp or 2 per cent, the correspondent running the hazard or as it is called standing del credere of the outstanding debts.

8th That with regard to what goods may be purchased at Coupar they shall be on the same footing as those bought at Dundee.

To Adam Beglie, Saltoun

30 November 1759

Your son who is just now here tells me that your spinners are leaving you on account that others are giving a higher price for spinning than what you are allowed to give. This I very well believe, and therefore I hereby on the part of this Company agree to allow you 11½d per spindle, the spinners' price, your own premium and carriage included, or 11d per sp[indle], the Company paying the charges of carriage for all yarns spun by your means from 16 to 24 cutt per lb of flax from and after this date and to continue so until altered.

To George Young, Coupar Angus

6 December 1759

I come now to reply to your letter of the 31st ult respecting this Company's employing Mr David Wilson who you say would willingly settle at Falkland for the manufacturing and purchasing of linens there. You may be assured that any recommendation of yours will have great influence with this Company. But you'll please know that for some time past Mr David Walker of Strathmiglo, about a mile distant from Falkland, has been employed by this Company for the above purpose; he has a son who was bred to the weaving business who carries on his affairs. This last year the Trustees have given him a present of reeds and caims at our recommendation and it would therefore be hurting the business to employ two persons so contiguous to one another, to the detriment of themselves and the Company.

If this gentleman would set up at Kilsyth, considerable things might be done there, and I believe that there might be little difficulty in getting him the countenance of the proprietor, Mr Campbell of Shawfield and of this Company for a purchaser. It's a fine country for flax. There are just now in and about 160 to 200 looms employed very indifferently and that could with some little attention be turned into a useful manufacture.

PS I have mentioned your scheme of giving premiums to such as I thought would bring it to bear and I am promised your request shall be granted.

To James Bolton, Preston

6 December 1759

My last to you was of the 20th ult., to which refer. In conformity thereto I have now to acquaint you that this Company have resolved to employ your good self as their sole agent at Preston and its neighbourhood, and that none other by any commission or authority from the Company shall interfere with you in any manner of way in the sale of yarns. The Company reckon that about this time there may be 60 or possibly 64 bales of linen yarn arrived at Liverpool, and in the hand of Messrs Crosbie and Traffords which quantity or whatever part thereof may be in their custody. They have this night desired may be delivered you, or to any having an order from you to receive the goods, you'll please call on Messrs Crosbie & Traffords or give an order to any to call on them for whatever bales of linen yarn may be in their hands belonging to this Company, and I shall hereafter furnish you with a proper inventory of the contents. Please give orders that inspection be made as to the safety of the packages so that one may know where the blame of damage lies. I hope you will lose no time in doing this which will be adding to the favours you have already done the British Linen Company.

To John Henderson, Riga

20 December 1759

Mr William Weir, lately of your city, now merchant of this place, being considerably indebted, at least there are considerable sums of money and transactions intrusted to his care for which I have not been able as yet to get him to account for to this Company, I have been obliged redress by legal methods. On Tuesday last I arrested a cargo of goods entered by him in the customshouse from Riga on board the Sally, Captain Andrew Duncan; he has since found security to the Admiralty court for the value of these goods in case he shall be found liable to pay the claims I have made upon him. In the course of progress, it will possibly be necessary to ask from the Admiral Court a power or commission to the magistrates or any one of them at Riga to examine upon the oath the person who furnished or shipped these goods to declare what quantities, qualities and value of goods were shipped by him for Mr Weir and in whose name the bills of lading were taken. This will no doubt be attended with considerable charges and might be prevented if the person who shipped the goods put the affair into writing and submit it. As upon seeing Mr Weir would not possibly give any further trouble, when it could only serve to heap up expences, and probably the judge might say that if Mr Weir did not rest satisfied thereanent, he should pay the charges of formal examination himself in the event there was no difference between the factor's written account of the matter and the one he himself might give upon oath. I would therefore beg of you to apply to one Mr Thirmigh of your city who it's said was the gentleman who shipped the goods for Mr Weir, and beg of him to put down in writing the quality and quantity as above of the goods sent per the Sally to Mr Weir, and in whose names the bills of loading were taken, their date and when transmitted to Mr Weir; that so we may be able as soon and at as little charge as possible to put an end to this lawsuit.

To David Sandeman, Dundee

20 December 1759

Your letter to me of the 19th I received with great pleasure as I should upon all occasion be glad to render you or any of your friends any acceptable service in my power. In answer you'll please know that this Company cannot consistent with their rules lend money or issue notes upon interest upon any security whatever. That is properly the business of the bank, and you may be assured that were it in their power they would with pleasure serve your friends. But tho' I cannot directly serve you for this Company, if you will allow me to be your agent in the matter and send a note or proposal of the security to be taken, I shall propose it to the Royal Bank and I would gladly flatter myself that I would not then be without success and if it should be unsuccessfull there I can then apply to private hands.

This Company is no doubt much obliged to you and many other friends in Dundee for the ready acceptance of their notes in payments or indeed any one else in the linen trade, for if we would but look to the quantities wanted at Market, and the qualities, it will be found that there can never be any rivalship amongst ourselves. There may indeed be among Germany, Russia and this country, but not even between this Kingdom, Ireland excepting, as to that of excelling in point of goodness in fabric of the linens manufactured. I know it is generally thought that this Company by means of their notes can afford to undercut private traders. But if gentlemen will consider the expences they must pay in factorage and carriage above what a private trader does, besides the losses by introducing new branches into different parts of the Kingdom, they will find that they have no advantage above a private trader—at least I have found it so by some years' experience.

I likewise freely own to you that the Company cannot lend money upon bill, bond or cash account in the way of a bank, but there's nothing in their charter to prohibit their extending their circulation to extend the manufactures, and if you or any good man will point out a way in which such a thing could be done I should think such an undertaking might be carried on to the advantage of these gentlemen and the Company. Supposing the Company for instance were to advance the money, charge the partner a moderate interest and divide the profit on the sales some such thing I say might possibly be of mutual advantage tho' not done in the way of a loan as to which I shall be glad to have your thoughts. Bills on London are this day got up to the extravagant price of 7/6d premium for 60 days and so for others in proportion. I shall be glad to have your answer.

To David Flint, Secretary to the Board of Trustees, Edinburgh

2 January 1760

I herewith transmit you two abstracts of the amount of yarns bought and brought up from sundry counties in the North from 1st November 1758 to 1st November 1759 amounting in all to the number of 75,207 sp[indle]s received partly by Mr Doig and partly by myself; which with the reasons for doing so will appear from the abstracts and dockets. And I have now to observe that if the Honrbl Board shall be of opinion that the yarns for the future shall be received and accounted for by Mr Doig, it shall so be done. What was done this year by mutual agreement was in a great measure executed before receipt of your said letter of 29th August. However I am hopeful that the receiving the yarns by either of us will be no obstacle in the way of the Board's either now or afterwards granting the proposed bounty of one penny per spl proposed for any quantity not under 55,000 and not exceeding 75,000 spindles of yarn.[1]

To David Flint, Edinburgh

11 January 1760

In consequence of the letters I had wrote to the sundry agents employed by this Company for promoting the spinning of linen yarns in the several stations of Loch Broom, Loch Carron and Glenmoriston, I was in hopes that before this time I should have received an exact state of the charges attending the spinning, together with a note of what wheels and reels would be annually wanted with the premiums to be paid for teaching the ignorant and prize money to the best spinners, but as yet I have received no answer from them. By what I have hitherto been able to learn concerning the expence of land carriage etc for spinning in the interior parts of the Highlands, I am persuaded that nothing less than 5d per spindle will prove to be a saving bargain with anyone who contracts with the Honorable Board. This seemingly extravagant demand arises from the high charge of land transport, and that the first undertakers of those stations having begun and their continuing to give the price of 10d per spl to the spinner, being the same that is given in the Lothians where expence of living is higher and almost no risk or charge attends the trade whereas for the same grists of yarns spun in Orkney, the sea coasts of Sutherland, Caithness, Cromarty, Ross and Inverness shires no more is paid the spinner than 8d per sp[indle] and out of the difference which is 2d per sp[indle] the undertaker has a handsome reward for his trouble and is enabled to furnish his employer with yarns in quantities upon reasonable terms.

If therefore the Honorable Board shall think it proper I shall adventure on behalf of the British Linen Company to contract for the spinning of 100,000 and not less than 60,000 spindles linen yarns to be performed in the space of four or five years from this date, to be spun in the above stations of Lochbroom, Lochcarron, Glenmoriston Sutherland towards the Bay of Tongue and other interior parts of the Highlands and in the Isle of Skye at the rate of 5d per spl amounting in the highest to £2083 6/8 of 100,000 spindles and for 60,000 to the sum of £1250. It being always understood the Board will allow the

1 The Board of Trustees duly allowed £2 per 1000 spindles: SRO, NG1/1/15, BOTM 11 Jan. 1760.

necessary sums for teaching, for prize money and for wheels and reels. And I hereby pledge myself that if any thing lower can be done how soon I have received the final answers from the agents employed in the spinning in these parts, I shall communicate it to the Board and deduct accordingly from my proposition of 5d per sp[indle]. But I apprehend it were prudent for the Board as well as the Company to know what shall be further done in those Highland stations, that so the necessary provisions on both sides may be prepared in time for executing what may be agreed on. By my last accounts from the agent employed for carrying on the spinning in Assynt, and to the head of Strathurehill in consequence of my agreement with the Board last year, I was made to hope for 5000 sp[indles] of yarn against next May or June, and from Stratherrick, Beauly, Laggan, Auchindrame etc. I am told above 100 girls have been taught that never saw such a machine as a spinning wheel before, and a demand is made for liberty to teach more and desiring I would allow him for these 5/- per head as well as for those stipulated in our agreement.

To John Anderson, Perth

24 January 1760

One Mr Richard Neilson from this place, a very knowing and experienced manufacturer having lately gone to Dundee to settle there, he is now employing many hands in the county about in some new branches of the linen manufacture. This it seems, and an opinion that Company are to deprive them of their trade as the man comes from Edinburgh and is a near relation of Mr Tod at London, has exasperated the merchants so much that they are trying to stop the progress of the Company's notes there and at Coupar Angus, and I dare say everywhere else. I must therefore beg of you to aid the Company in this matter by satisfying the ignorant and showing others the bad consequences of hurting the credit of particulars and the trade of the Nation.

It's a pity that the people in Dundee did not see farther into things. While there is two million stg. of foreign linens annually imported, it must surely be a blessing to the Company to employ our own poor rather than Germans or French. No man can say his trade is diminished since the commencement of the Company. If these things are true can a man of skills settling in a place be a hurt to it in particular, or could it be a hurt supposing this Company had settled him there as their agent? On the contrary I think the place and country about are greatly obliged. I shall detain you no longer, only to beg you would write any of your friends at Dundee to befriend Mr Neilson instead of distressing him and to show the error of attempting to hurt the Company's circulation.

To Richard Neilson, Dundee

28 January 1760

With regard to this Baillie Ramsay, who you are told is collecting a parcel of our notes to send over hither, I think it would come very properly from Collector Clerk[1] to send to him or to ask him if the report be true that he is employed in gathering up the Company's notes, because he may by applying to him save himself of the trouble and risk of sending the notes to Edinburgh in so far as he has cash. And consequently desire Ramsay to say how many, that is to what value, he is possessed of them. If after all Ramsay shall chose to send over to Edinburgh, it is no other matter than my paying them here and sending them out as occasion offers again.

I do not imagine George Young had any part in this matter, but on the contrary meantime I have wrote him what is given out as to him as to telling my author, by which I shall more nearly come at the truth. In his last letter to me he says that he now sees his proposal of the Company's taking his weavers' debts in another light and owns I am in the right not to take them but with recourse in case of non-payment, but his proposition was caused by his own knowledge of the goodness of the people, and further says that if you and he can settle as to prices there will be no other difficulty remain. You will therefore transact with him in so far as you will see it for your interest, in which you may be sure I shall rest satisfied and confirm accordingly.

To Thomas Boyes, Dudhope, Dundee

2 February 1760

The intention of the British Linen Company in settling Mr Richard Neilson at Dundee is thro' his means to introduce and establish in the country several branches of the linen manufacture, not yet practised or known in it and particularly just now a species of linen called Pomerania, not so fine as linen made for Soldiers' Shirting (which this Co. introduced about two years ago) and not so coarse as Osnabrigg of either of which sorts of linen the consumpt is almost treble to that of the Osnabrigg manufacture introduced 10 or 12 years ago, with this additional circumstance in preference to the Osnabriggs, that all the Soldiers' Shirting and Pomeranias are sold white, which employs a number of more hands in bleaching. If now during this war when German linens are difficult to be had and consequently dear, the people in trade would introduce these foreign fabrics and show the London drapers and merchants that such goods could be introduced at home, in time of peace their trade might be

1 Clerk to the Board of Excise.

maintained seeing that besides the bounty upon exportation there was last year a duty of 5 per cent more laid on all foreign linens imported.

As nobody seems to attend or to understand these things or possibly are afraid to begin, it becomes the duty of this Company to point out to the Kingdom the proper articles of manufacture. It is now with pleasure that I can assure you that by an establishment made at Coupar Angus about three years ago under the conduct of George Young for introducing three branches of the linen manufacture, vizt Silesias, Garlix and Britannias, their weaving is now brought to that degree of neatness and so much in conformity to the foreign that these articles alone last year amounted to 180,000 yards. Of about 85,000 yards of Soldiers' Shirting I had contracted for last year to be made and bleached in Angus and at Perth, there was not above 35,000 yards I could call good linen; the 50,000 yards of ordinary cloth was owing to carelessness, bad utensils or the weavers chosing improper yarns, and sometimes to all three faults together.

To remedy these faults and for the purpose abovementioned of introducing new fabrics as may be of service to the country, this Company has pitched on Mr Neilson for his skill, integrity and substance to settle at Dundee and its neighbourhood. I find it from many hands that this establishment at Dundee gives great offence to many of the merchants there. Were this matter explained to them and they willing to understand it, this would surely not be the case. For an increase of trade and manufactures must surely be a blessing to any place, or the merchants of a place; this they at Dundee have experienced in the Osnabrigg trade, introduced by this Company, and I wish those complaining would look at their stampmasters' books for the annual produce now, and what it was in the year 1749 when the trade began; by the return to the Board of Trustees it was anno 1749 817,416½ and this last year 1,275,689 yards. Is this addition of trade any hurt to them in particular? Any loss to the landed interest? Or any prejudice done the spinner or weaver? But, say they, this Company import their own flax and issue notes for the payment of work whereby they hurt our trade and buy or make goods cheaper than we private folks can do. I answer that the Company or no private trader will buy at second hand to carry on his trade with, and as to the Co's using their privilege of paying with their own notes, the saving there does not pay for the commission they must give to a factor or agent to do their business for them, which I aver is more than compensated for to the private merchant or manufacturer residing on the spot where his goods are made, who by being his own agent or factor saves that commission the Company is to pay.

By all of which you may judge of the purity of the Company's intentions, which the Court of Directors hope will meet of your approbation.

To William Dalrymple, London

5 February 1760

I was duly favoured with two letters from your new copartnership of Coutts Brothers, Dalrymple of date the 1st and 29th ult to which society, from the personal knowledge of the gentlemen who compose it, I most sincerely wish all manner of success. With regard to the order for goods intended to be shipped for your house at Cadiz, they are not near as yet got up, owing to an almost constant hurry in making up goods for the American markets; the brown and white Silesias are put up, and in my apprehension are most neatly finished off. Altho' I have not allowed one piece of Pistol Lawns to go out of the house since you favoured me with your orders of the 5th December last, yet I am afraid I shall not be able to make up the whole quantity of 600 p[iece]s because of the injunction not to make up any one number unless the total quantity of 200 p[iece]s for one box was complete, and before the receipt of your order I had sold off a large quantity to Glasgow. I shall however take care that what can be sent shall be conformable.

I have often in my mind thought of some method for getting a share of that large sum of money the Spaniards give to other countries for linen, and of which from what you have seen here I flatter myself you are satisfied a large share might in time be brought to Scotland. The capital stock subscribed to this Company can go little further, unless it were to lay aside its present, and I may say its established trade of making goods for the American market. But with the King's charter, and privileges therein granted, £40,000 might yet be subscribed, and we have a liberty of issuing notes to the extent of our capital stock already subscribed to this Company which now circulate the same as banknotes. With these advantages I should be of opinion that an additional subscription for the present but £10,000 and 7/10ths thereof to be paid in against November and February next when the money might be wanted to pay for the goods intended for Spain, I could with the help of our notes easily produce from £20 to £25,000 value of proper goods against August and November thereafter, and so yearly in proportion thereafter until the whole was exhausted. This new subscription might either be received with the old, or kept in books by itself as to its progess and success. One thing I am sure of that in either way a great saving might be had. The same directors, officers or clerks, house rent and taxes would do the business, at least with very little addition, this country would be greatly benefitted, the particular adventurers profited and the business of your house increased.

To me the only thing and the chief thing wanted is the subscribers. But even in this too I am not without a scheme. I have reason to believe that you are well known to many of the most considerable Jewish gentlemen who carry on large trade with Spain. I flatter myself these gentlemen would draw no inconsiderable gain from such a plan under such advantages as this Company would convey to them. Pray then could not a Gideon be induced to bring about such a thing? All I know is that if your good character and experience in trade with the joint advantages of Sir Hew Dalrymple and yourself does not bring it about, I shall despair of seeing it succeed. If this looks feasible, pray be so good to advise with Sir Hew about it and let me have the favour of your opinions thereanent. I have not mentioned it to anyone here, and will not further it unless it meet your approbation and resolution to endeavour to bringing it about.

To Alex[ander] Forrest, Saltoun

26 February 1760

Finding that the prices of spinning linen yarns are considerably increased throughout the country; in order to maintain the Company's spinning with you, it will be necessary to augment the rates. I therefore agree to give you 12d stg for each spindle of yarn spun for the Company below half spindle in the pound and not coarser than 3lb in the spindles, and to give you 13d per spindle for all yarns that are 2 lb in the spindle, you delivering the yarns to me at Edinburgh for these prices.

As the factory at Cranston is about to be given up, I hereby make offer of employing you in weaving Osnaburgs, Pomeranias or Soldiers' Shirting cloth at the rate of 3/6d per piece Osnaburg from 114 to 120 yards in length and so in proportion for other goods over and above the prices paid the journeyman weaver, and that in full of house rent, use of utensils and your own labour, the number of looms to be any most convenient for yourself, not exceeding thirty in all.

Salton Bleachfield Journal

29 February 1760

Account of Materials expended d[ebtor] to sundries

		£479 12 11
White soap	32cwt 3lb	79 - 9
Starch	1241 lb	23 6 4
Cashub ashes	6 casks	14 3 4
Pale soap	23 firkins	27 12 6
Pearl ashes	76 cwt 1qr 2lb	139 11 6
Coals	1390 loads	20 6 9
Polish weed ashes	2 casks	29 - 11
Konigsberg ditto	5 casks	53 5 9
Smalts	1178 lb	76 16 7

Muscovy ashes	1 cask	9 9 -
Bran	35¼ bolls	4 17 6
Milk	96 gallons	1 12 -
Profit and Loss (for the year)		
D[ebtor] to sundries		£1004 14/7
Tear and wear of bedding	£10 per cent	3 7 6
Ditto of utensils		43 5 4
James Armstrong		25 - -
Latching		12 18 11
Pins[1]		6 16 11
Incidents		57 7 3
David Mackie		20 - -
Robt Lithgow		15 - -
Wages		267 17 -
Mrs Armstrong		8 16 -
Materials used as per act		479 12 11
The British Linen Co for interest on money advanced		12 19 -
Cartage		52 3 7
		£1004 14 7

To George Young, Coupar Angus

4 April 1760

I am just now favoured with yours of the 5th covering invoice of linens delivered to Andrew Skirven at Baldovie, for which when examined you shall be credited; the bleacher's receipt should mention the yards delivered them as well as the pieces—send me bleachfield receipts for the linens formerly delivered. I observe in the last invoice you charge no less than £1 13/- for carriage to the bleachfield which ought to be paid by Mr Skirven, as all bleachers take out and return linens at their own charge.[2] I observe you charge one penny per piece for thread and marking these linens whereas here (where wages and everything is greatly higher) we pay only a penny per p[iece], and in your place it should only be ¾d at most. What 3qr linens will not cut into the regular lengths prescribed you, must cut as nearly thereto as may be. And if your people are fully supplied with what they can bleach you may send over

1 These pins were used to peg out the cloth on the drying field.

2 This was indeed standard practice. The cost of bringing and returning the cloth to and from the network of agents of the bleachfield was a charge on the bleachers, not the customers, which enabled them to tap quite a wide catchment area. Hugh McVeagh's field at Huntly, for example, had agents in 1760 at Inverness, Nairn, Forres, Banff and Aberdeen.

the rest to Leith for Dundee as formerly, tho' I would wish to give your country bleachers encouragement and employment, providing they bleach as well and as regularly as here. I'm glad what you write as to the improvement in your fabrics and wish it may make up for the high prices you pay. I observe your demand for money but no opportunity at present offers, and I have not ready a sufficient quantity of notes worth dispatching a person from hence. On Thursday afternoon I propose sending off one of the clerks to Dundee, if no private hand occurs sooner.

To John Henderson, Riga

19 April 1760

I am truly sorry that what with your own impatience and the looking on Mr Goldie's friendship to you as a drawback and hurt to your interest, the plan I had formed for establishing you at Riga must now be laid aside. The Directors will by no means agree to employ you without a security's being given that the money entrusted to your management shall be employed in the way and manner directed. This Mr Goldie was willing to give the Company upon an equitable consideration from you but the repeated complaints you have made for him being allowed any proportion of your commission and (as he tells me) a letter from yourself saying that unless the Company gave you the whole of their business without any distinction you would that instant leave Riga. For these reasons he will no longer be looked upon as any hurt or hindrance to your interest and therefore declines being security as formerly for your fidelity. For even by this last letter of 19th March you transmit no obligation to him to communicate any share of the profits or any letter to take off the force of the former saying you were to leave Riga, if any diminution was to be made. Upon Mr Goldie's declining I applied to Mr Gentle your brother in law, and desired he would state the case to Mr Crichton and your other friends, to see if they could give the Company that letter of credit wanted. But this they will tell you has been declined.

In this situation I have nothing left me but to try what can be done through the means of Mr Zuckerbecker for this season only, and in order to help forward with the payment of your necessary expences at Riga, for the doing of which I have by the enclosed letter given you a credit upon him for the payment of 120 tons flax to be shipped for this Company this ensuing season conform to the directions now and hereafter to be given, provided you shall think proper to do. Mr Zuckerbecker I dare say will use you gently and I can assure him his so doing will not hurt his interest with this Company.

To James Armstrong, Salton Bleachfield

23 April 1760

Since I last saw you, I have had an opportunity of talking with my Lord Milton on the subject of erecting the Beetling machines on a place by themselves without being (as at present) a hindrance to the other works at the field. My Lord seems to like well enough the place you mentioned to me for situating the intended house and machines, vizt that place Megrie farm near to where the lime kiln stood as it is out of the view of the house of Salton in the road from the field to Edinburgh. His Lordship says there must be a stone canal built across the river to force up the water and a leader to the intended mill be taken off from it on the Meagrie side of the river, a calculation of the expence of which must be made out.

The things which I apprehend to be necessary for the Company are two sets of beetles and beams proportioned, and to move if necessary at the same time and with the same outer wheel, these beetles made to stroke perpendicularly or straightways on the cloth and not aslant as at present. A Dutch Callander or Cylinder of wood consisting of five rollers (like the one Mr Meikle made for me at Edinburgh) and capable of dressing cloth fully 45 inches in breadth and to move likewise by the same outer wheel. Besides room for these I should also want room for a press and for two tables for men to take and make up cloth at, of from 8 to 10 feet in length each. From what is above said you can get Mr Meikle to make a calculation of the whole expence and to form a plan to be laid before Lord Milton and which I beg will be done with all possible dispatch, because how soon it is made out, orders will be given for its erection.

Court of Directors

26 April 1760

That as all the advices from London seemed uncertain as to the sailing of a British fleet up the Baltic or what effect such an event might have on the prices of flax, and it becomes necessary to order flax to supply our north country spinners and other demands, the Manager had on the 26th April written to Riga, ordering Messrs Thomas Zuckerbecker, widow & son, and Mr John Henderson each to purchase 120 tons of flax, in all 240 tons, and as Mr Zuckerbecker is a foreigner in whose hands the Company's property would be safe in case of a war between Britain and Russia, he had lodged a credit in his name for £7000 stg (for payment of the whole quantity of flax ordered from him and Mr Henderson) with Messrs George Clifford & Sons of Amsterdam, as the said letters in the foreign letter book fully bear.

Agreeable to the orders of this court 26th April 1759 a policy was taken out from the Sun Fire Office at London on £8000 value of goods belonging to this Company in the warehouses of Messrs Tod & Anderson. That policy was by these gentlemen's desire lately returned them and a new policy is now taken out, N. 175626 on the same value of £8000 lodged in the warehouses and at the wharfs of Hoare, and Hargreave & Charlton (as per particulars in the Insurance Register apart); premium £10 5/- payable annually on the 19th May at London. This policy was by order of the Court delivered to the Lord Provost to be lodged (as he had already been so good to lodge N 174,923) in the Charter chest of the City of Edinburgh.

To Mr Thomas Zuckerbecker, Riga

15 May 1760

I am sorry to see by your letter of 24th March and 19th April that flax has risen so much in price as to be by the last of these no less than 22 R[ix] D[ollars] for Lithuanian and so for others. This rise will prove a heavy loss for the Company seeing 12 head St Petersburg is bought at 20 RDs per Barquet and the exchange at 40 stuivers per RD. I should therefore be of opinion it were better to wait purchasing at the present prices at Riga. The probability is that they must conform to the other markets in some degree, at least it is reasonable to chance the prices cannot be higher than 22 RD. But this I must leave to your better judgement both as to your own and best advice to Mr Henderson for what he may purchase for the Company. I have now chartered the ship the Cathcart of Alloa for home bringing 60 and 70 tons flax to be unloaded at Cromarty; the ship will depart in about 15 days hence, and is to lie at Riga for thirty working days for intaking the cargo. I am in terms about hiring another ship to hold from 70 to 80 tons but this vessel if I do hire her will not sail from hence the month to come, so I will not straiten you so as time of purchasing the other part of the cargo wanted as I formerly wrote; it will not be sent for till next July or August next.

To David Wilson & Co, Coupar Angus

23 May 1760

Aggreeable to what I wrote you last post I herewith send you £150 stg in this Company's notes at your debit. You will be careful in circulating the £5 notes, for unless they are carefully dissipated, I may expect them back here in a week or two which is a loss to the Company as franked covers cannot just now be easily procured for remitting them to the country again.

To Alex[ander] Gray, Glasgow

7 June 1760

I am told by James Drummond that he has this day a letter from you saying that you wait my call for coming to Salton Bleachfield in order to your taking up, dressing and lapping linens there, and instructing such other persons as I shall present for instruction at that place. I desire you may be at Salton field at Thursday next at furthest, tho' I would rather have you there a day or two sooner as I am to be at the Bleachfield on Friday forenoon, and should be glad to know then what things you should want for your business, other than what I have already provided, because in my opinion it will take a day or two to judge what things will be wanted.

James Drummond tells me you and he agreed on £20 stg per annum of wages with two guineas for each person taught. These terms on account of the character given you I approve of, & agree to pay. And besides if you shall act so as to deserve the Company's thanks, I agree to make you a present for the first year of either a free lodging or five guineas in money as you shall like best, and if your business should require you to return to Glasgow at six month's end, I shall agree to pay in proportion. You may call here for a line to Mr Armstrong, the Bleacher at Salton.

To Richard Neilson, Dundee

23 June 1760

The Shirting for London must all be packed in the waterfold and it will be proper they be in bales of 100 pieces each. The Petersburg flax is much superior to the Narva. In a short time I shall know the lowest price it can be delivered of at Dundee and Messrs Speid and Craufurd and any other of your friends may keep themselves disengaged till then. Freight, Insurance and sundry charges attend flax delivered at Hull before it is delivered at Dundee which they should calculate. There is no doubt that Osnabrigs will be in demand both here and at London in harvest, and I much approve of your pushing off the coarse flax by giving the weavers assurances of employing them in that article, but do this prudently.

As to the bills on London I shall explain that matter to you on meeting. I imagine you have sold some flax and delivered some in part payment of the Edinbrigs you have bought in. There is some bales of foreign yarn here belonging to Mr Tod, fit as he says for Osnabrigs. The Invoice is just now come to hand, how soon they are examined, part will be sent you for an experiment.

To William Dalrymple, Cadiz

26 June 1760

I duly received your esteemed favours of the 19th April, signifying you were to send me a box with 30 samples of linens and accordingly I had lately a letter from Mr Tod at London, saying he had received a box of samples of such foreign linens as are in demand at Cadiz from you, which he proposed to send me by first fleet bound for Leith, from which amongst other favours I stand bound to you. I beg leave to return my most sincere thanks. These samples are not yet come to hand. How soon they do, I shall make it my study to copy after them. This rupture between the French and Hamburghers, I am apt to imagine might be made to turn to the advantage of this country by now introducing our linens on more favourable terms to Spain than if the old trade was under less embarass. This Company is possessed of a considerable stock of linens fit for making up into Platillos, Britannias, and double Silesias, all of which are in demand for the London market, but in different lengths, packaging and uptaking from the bleachfield. If you shall therefore think of doing any thing with us this year considerably, I would put off our demands from London in a good measure to keep provision for you, which if known in time, the goods could be more properly adapted and taken up for the Spanish market from thence, than it's possible to do afterwards. I pray your answer hereto with your first convenience.

To Alex[ander] Speirs, Glasgow

26 June 1760

I write you this by Robert Simpson carter with two bales of Osnaburgs Nos 4 & 8 and as these complete your order and the post does not go till Saturday, you have the other side the amount of the whole, amounting to £381 18/7 at your debit with this Company. I flatter myself the goods will meet with approbation from you and your friends, being all extremely good. You mentioned that at this time you would probably order a parcel of the linens of the Company's make in the Irish fabric. I now presume to remind you thereof and assure you that all regard shall be had to your interest in the chosing of them; and were you to make a trial of our other white linens, both coarse and fine, I really hope any prejudices you and your friends may have conceived in favour of the foreign linens may be removed, at least there is great reason to think so from the ready sale they meet with at London, and several foreign markets where the linens are. However as you were so good as to promise me the favour of a visit this summer with one of your Virginia partners I shall then show you the goods, and you can judge what is your interest. Our cambrics and lawns will, I hope, merit your attention. I return you my most sincere acknowledgement.

To David Flint, Board of Trustees, [Edinburgh]

14 July 1760

Having lately received sundry letters complaining of the undertakers for the stations of Glenmoriston and Lochbroom from Hector Scott at Inverness who I had employed to introduce and carry on the spinning of flax at Lagan, Auchindrome, Stratherrick, Strathglass, Beauly etc as also from Mr John Mckay at Cyderhall who I had employed to do the same at Strathorde, Assynt etc. In consequence of the agreement made with the Honorable Board of date the 30th of March 1759 I hereby transmit you one of these letters from Mr McKay dated the 17th of May last, together with one from Mr Mcleod of Ledmore to him for your perusal; from which, and from what Mr Scott the bearer can vouch, you will be convinced of the unfair dealings of these undertakers and of the impossibility of a frugal scheme's succeeding at the same time, and in competition with one by much more liberal in its appointments. Mr Scott by living at Inverness, where wheelwrights are at hand, by his knowledge of the country and the language, got his part of the scheme in a great measure executed before Mr Shaw had time to counteract him, and in fact has taught 100 girls to spin in these parts, who were ignorant of that art. The part Mr Shaw had then to act, was only that of giving more money to the people employed which indeed he has done to the extent of no less than 2d per spindle, over and above the high price formerly paid of 10d per spyl. In this extravagant folly of Mr Shaw's, I have been obliged to follow him by giving the same rate for spinning, because otherwise I must have given up the plan, after all the flax was sent there and the people employed to carry it on. And in this way Mr Scott has spun up about 2000 spindles of yarn, whereof 930 spindles have been delivered me of very well made yarn considering the short time the spinners have had to learn the art. Of these yarns 395 spindles were spun at Stratherrick, 225 at Laggan & Auchindrome, & 310 at Beauly. Mr Mckay at Cyderhall in Sutherland, at the date of writing me his letter as above, sent up 1521 spindles of yarn which are now all examined, and found to be every way as well done as those by Mr Scott.

The cause of Mr Mckay's not having taught many more hands the art of spinning in the mountainous, and more interior parts of Sutherlands is that in winter these countries are inaccessible, and when he set about, early in this summer, he was prevented in the manner set furth in his and Mr McLeod's letter, and besides the fault of throwing away the public money in unnecessary expences for teaching spinning, Mr Ross at Lochbroom had added another of giving away wheels and reels to those already instructed and that have long been in the employment of the said Mr Mckay, thinking by that means to hurt him, and by such unfair methods to make a figure in the eyes of the Board by thus increasing the quantity of yarns made at his station, tho' in fact far distant from Lochbroom, and instead of raising new hands, he is only decoying the old experienced spinners with the public's utensils and money.

All of which I beg you will please to lay before the Honorable Board of Trustees and when considered you will be so good as to let me know what shall be done with the flax I have already prepared conform to agreement in March 1759, that can now be got spun up with the agents, and their spinning mistresses engaged, and with the wheels and reels not disposed of.

To James Wright, Lawton

16 July 1760

I am this day favoured with yours of the 14th curr enquiring whether we are to make our insurances for London by this fleet at London or Edinburgh, and the rate or premium asked at Edinburgh. This Company always prefers the Edinburgh underwriters on equal terms but at present they take no less than 6 guineas per cent, to return three for convoy; so that I imagine we shall order all our insurances at London. The insurers here have met with some severe checks lately which makes them more cautious and makes them ask higher premiums than formerly. At any rate I would advise you insuring; as to the place you may judge for yourself. At London it will cost a commission of 5 per cent but I dare say that will be gained on the premium tho' I have no advice lately from thence on that head. If you desire it I shall order the insurance for you as you shall direct. I observe you advise that the yard wide linens are but few in quantity this season. I thought there had been considerable parcels made of these linens. The quantities however that is made with you will not much influence the price at the London market, where I heartily wish our joint adventure success.

To David Doig, Edinburgh[1]

19 July 1760

Why does Smith ask for money here? Why no money from Mr Doig these 3 weeks? Is there no cash of the Staplery in his hands? Has any intimation been

1 The copartnership bewteen the Company and David Doig in the Edinburgh Yarn Staplery established in 1751 was about to dissolve in acrimonious circumstances; McCulloch's anger at Doig here led him to write in the third person. See letters of 2 Feb. 1761 and 20 Mar. 1761, below, pp. 143 and 144, to John Tait, writer in Edinburgh, and David Doig respectively. Not until 1766, however, was it possible to close the Staplery's books after the last of the yarn had been finally disposed of.

made the Company of want of money, or how Mr D. wishes to have the bleaching carried on? What way has been or is the cart and horses there to be employed? Do such belong to the Staplery or the Leith Factory? On what footing is this yarn bleaching carried on ? What's the rent of the grounds, to whom these belong? Are there any tacks and to whom granted, and for how long? What are Smith's wages and how long engaged? The bearer William Smith having again and again called on me for money to carry on his business of bleaching yarns, and as I cannot take any charge on me that belongs to another without his knowledge and consent; and at the same time it being quite necessary that the Company's affairs must be looked after and their work people paid. I must beg you to furnish me with some answer to the above queries by write or word of mouth, and shall be most suitable to your own liking that so business may be carried on without prejudice to those who have put the trust of it in your hands. If not agreeable to you to do so, let me know so much, and I shall have the business carried on as it should be.

To Buchanan & Simpson, Glasgow

6 August 1760

With regard to the Garlix not being liked in the West Indies I should be glad to know the particular cause of not liking them. I know that till this year I have laboured unsuccessfully to get these and other thin made goods taken up without being run in the bleach or as the English term is fraying. But now a method is fallen upon of taking them up from the field as evenly and neat as the foreign. I have likewise got our Coleraine linens to be much finer threaded for the money than formerly and would therefore beg your allowance for sending a few pieces of each sort before you lay in any quantity that so if ours please you would be so good as to let this Company serve you with Scotch instead of Irish cloth or foreign linens. Upon looking through our quantity of Osnabriggs on hand I find there are only 500 yards of the best kinds can be sent you just now and if this does not suit you, I am sorry for it as I can not otherwise serve your orders.

To Alex Gray, lapper at Salton Bleachfield

9 August 1760

I had this day sent me in from one Mr Nisbet's Bleachfield at Paisley a parcel of clear lawns, the best taken up and the evenest of the thread that I ever saw in my life and I think better then any foreign I have seen. I would therefore take as a favour if your father in law or any other of your friends about Glasgow could procure one or two hands practised in that trade as well skilled as those servants of Mr Nisbet's to come to Saltonfield this season in order to show the method they have of doing up fine thin goods, because whatever is absolutely necessary for these fine clear lawns being taken up without ruining the threads will be of great advantage for Silesias and Garlix, and especially also as there is just now some Cambrics to be taken up.

I would not wish your friends at Glasgow to hire other people's servants or inveigle anyone away by giving higher wages, or without their master's knowledge. But I think it is possible to get one or two servants either men or women to come for the season or for a few days either upon day's wages or a piece of money as shall be agreed upon, and such folks too as may either be unengaged now or have leave for eight to ten days for that purpose from their master. Show this to Mr Armstrong, and let your letter be wrote and sent in here on Monday before six at night to go by the post then. And I dare say your friend will be careful to get the people wanted upon as reasonable terms as possible. But in such a case as this I do not think he should stand for a triffle of money providing he has a good character of the folks wanted. If your friend cannot get two, let him hire one person. I shall allow your friend a consideration.

To David Neilson, Dundee

23 August 1760

This chiefly serves to advise that Mr Tod has received your goods (I mean the Osnabriggs) by last fleet. He thinks them equally good with others but seems afraid of going deep in purchasing even at these prices till the market are proved and therefore says you should be just going on without launching deep until he writes. This I thought proper to write tho' I doubt not his letter to yourself by this post may say as much. Be so good as to forward these Osnaburgs for this house per first occasion to Leith together with the linens for bleaching. I yesterday talked with some of the Commissioners of the Customs as to what you wrote about orders given for not unloading more than one ship at Dundee at once. And they say no such orders came from the board. On the contrary the Tide Surveyor at Ferry Port on Craig has orders to remove to Dundee and to serve the office of land surveyor or land waiter as occasion may require and the Collector direct.

To Thomas Junor, Kirkcaldy

16 September 1760

I have received yours of this date with invoice of 6 pieces checks which are received per Kemmel and shall be entered to your credit. I cannot afford to allow you to pay such high prices for checks and must therefore want [i.e. do without] them as they will bring no profit to the Company. You need not therefore buy any more till further orders unless they can be had as usual @ 8d per yd for the broad and 7d for the narrow. Or at most and one shilling more per piece for the very best. But for such poor rascally goods as those last sent no price can be given nor are you to accept of any of such a mean fabric and bad colour on any account. N268 be ill dyed with logwood. The goods which were sometime ago bought by you are returned by the purchaser for being poor and thin and in no respect equal to the Manchester of which you got patterns.

In place of imitating these patterns the weavers you employ have debased this fabric to a mere rag, even inferior in quality and colour to their ¾qr wide. This Company will not bring their character into disrepute by vending such stuff. You are much to blame to receive any such and your stampmaster for passing them. If your weavers will not regard their own interests and make such goods as can be sold with honour and credit we cannot accept of any other nor will any yarns be delivered them from hence to be misused as these are.

To Thomas Zuckerbecker, Riga

25 September 1760

The Anne & Katie, Captain Kenny is safe arrived at Cromarty, the Christian, Captain Rutherford at Leith and I hope Captain Buchanan of the Cathcart is by this time at Cromarty having sailed from the Sound with Capt Rutherford; of these last two cargoes the invoices are not yet come to hand. The Betsey, Captain Ramage, by which you were desired to find 35 tons of flax, was navigated by Thos Smith and was taken in her passage outwards off the coast of Norway; she was afterwards retaken by the Gosport man of war Captain Ellison who came convoy to the fleet from the Baltic by which John Henderson returned to Britain. Mr Henderson wrote me that he forwarded by way of Elsinore the letters Captain Smith of the Betsy had for you. We were for some time assured by the owners of this ship that after settling accounts with the captain of the man of war she would immediately then proceed for Riga. But I now find that they (afraid of being brought into trouble about the recapture if that ship should go up the Sound) are resolved to dispose of her by sale here. This their resolution at so late a season of the year when no other vessel can be had to go out to Riga is a considerable disappointment. If you have not already shipped that flax destined for this ship which I observe by your last letters you had bought up and cannot procure a vessel to bring it to Britain you must dispose of it to best advantage for the Company as they do not chose it should lie over year at Riga. As prices are extremely high there at present it is to be hoped at least there will be no loss by reselling it and they have no doubt of your doing the best for their interest. They would much rather sell it at Riga than send it to any other port in Britain except it can be sent either to Leith, Montrose, Arbroath or Dundee.

To Patrick Craufurd of Auchenames, Ayr

4 October 1760

Since I did myself the pleasure of waiting on you at Errol I have had an opportunity of seeing some of your Errol linen Manufactures at Mr Richard Neilson's at Dundee. And I have the satisfaction to say that from the nature of the flax and the goodness of the yarns it will be practicable to make it a very valuable manufacture and I think too with no great charge. The cloth is spoiled with the bad utensils used in weaving by the weavers and not boiling their yarns with ashes and sorting them before they are put into the loom and by not keeping their pieces to such lengths and breadths as are fit for sale or for use. To remedy these evils it is proposed to give the weavers new reeds adapted to their size of yarns and to the market breadths; for Mr Neilson to give money only for such as have been made from well boiled and sorted yarn at the same time allowing the the weavers for the charge of boiling and to spirit up the weavers to an emulation in excelling each other in neatness of weaving by giving small prizes to the best and second best made pieces upon a comparison once every fortnight from the 1st of November to the 1st of June that so while the weaving is strongest during the year. This plan with Mr Neilson's directions and now and then particular inspection being continued for one or two years will I am hopeful put your people and the neighbourhood on a lasting good footing.

I took the liberty to mention your name and the above plan to my Lord Milton who seemed very well pleased with it, and on my saying that on your estate only was not less than 150 weavers, he said that he should be of opinion the Trustees would give 30 or £40 per annum for a year or two in such utensils as Mr Neilson should direct provided the laird who was both able and willing would approve thereof and give a fourth, a third or or half of what given by the public because in that way the Board will always be sure that the premium asked is proper and will be duly applied. If therefore, sir, you shall approve of the above plan, be as good as to write to my Lord Milton desiring him to propose the thing to the Board or to allow me in your name to do so and by all means to get the allowance to Mr Neilson to provide reeds and other utensils to the value the Board gives that so the affair may not be delayed but that the weavers early provided with utensils this very season.

To George Swan, Perth

6 October 1760

I cannot agree with you that Messrs Tod & Anderson would groundlessly make complaint and specially so as they know nothing of the persons who bleached the linens complained of. My seeing a single piece or two and approving of those does not answer for a whole cargo. Besides, what I saw and approved of at Perth, is not yet come to their hands. By last post these gentlemen write me that all of your parcel must be callendered, pressed and folded up with the best outerfold the goods will admit of and then after all that charge and arts used to hide the dreying (or running) as they term it, the goods will not bring so much by ¾d per yard as those of the same quality and cost sent from this and sold without charge for lapping in what the drapers call the waterfold.

What I should think even for your interest to do would be to get a friend to look at the goods and compare them with others of the same quality and price in your hands from this Company and let Mr Anderson and your friend thereafter determine what amends should be made, or if any be due for your part, because if such a thing be not done it will not only hurt your interest with this Company but with others. All men are liable to mistakes (your good friend the Pope excepted) and it is no hurt to your character that such a thing has happened. The Company will not insist on retribution to the utmost part. But surely if the thing is so as Messrs Tod & Anderson represent you should with cheerfulness make some amends and in my humble opinion the above method is the best.

To David Sandieman, Dundee

30 October 1760

I had the pleasure of writing you last night and refer you thereto. Since that time I have been looking into the quantity of goods this Company will at present have to ship for London and find they will be about and not under 40,000 yards. You advise that Mr Anderson and you will have 55,000 yards; I compute that Mr Neilson may have about 20,000 but as to this you will learn from his servant Mr Coupar, in all about 120,000 yards. If these with what may be got from others at Dundee will be a sufficient inducement for Capt Caithness to proceed immediately on the usual terms freight per 100 yards, I would think it best that he be immediately hired or agreed with and that no time be lost in putting on board the goods from Perth and Dundee reserving about ten tons to be taken in in Leith harbour. Otherwise I expect all the linens will be taken on board by the corn ships from Leith of which I wrote you in my last.

To Richard Neilson, Dundee

13 November 1760

I am extremely glad to learn from yourself that you are got safe back to Dundee from your highland expedition. I am glad to find Patullo will proceed directly. This house will give him twenty bales brown and if cloth comes in possibly sundry bales more. But he must come here and take in his goods and be ready to proceed wind and water serving in ten or twelve days from Leith by reason the West India (I should have said Jamaica) fleet is to leave London in less than three weeks. For the supplying of which market it is that it can prove to our interest to send the ship without convoy at the charge of 1 per cent more and possibly the paying of some more freight. If therefore Captain Patullo can be engaged on any reasonable terms to proceed from Leith after taking in at Dundee in 10 or 12 days I shall be well pleased to pay freight as you do and if demanded and you think it reasonable some consideration for coming to Leith. But as I hope to put 30 bales on board, I presume that of paying additional freight will not be thought of or asked. No time must be lost agreeing with Patullo or on his proceeding as above said as to which please write me in course. The underwriters on the cargo of the Good Infant have agreed to abate of their premium if not sent as first designed to Cromarty at this season of the year, provided the master likewise settles with the Company. I must therefore beg of you jointly with Mr Halliburton to whom I also write this night to try at what discount Mr Jordan the master will agree to be freed from going to Cromarty firth now with his cargo and be allowed to proceed directly on what other voyage may cast up. The unloading of flax in Cromarty firth at this season of the year in open boats is attended with more risk than either shipmaster, underwriters or owners of the cargo should run. I can delay sending flax there till next April provided I am to be allowed the charges of sending it there then which will be at least from 12 to 15/- per ton. But if Mr Jordan insists on unloading and landing his flax there I no doubt will hold him to it seeing the insurers and he are both bound. But in truth I think it for the interest of neither party.

Of this however you and Mr Haliburton will write me after conversing him. Until that matter is settled I can give no orders about selling any flax excepting what was formerly in your custody. I really don't know the terms of your declaration anent prizes but whatever Mr William Sandeman does, I think you may safely do the same. Mr Tod went this morning for Perth and will be at Dundee with you soon. You must be positive with Patullo about the time of proceeding or it will not do for us and therefore take him bound in writing, that is by letter or charter party. Let all of your own and these goods from James Smith be sent by him.

To David Flint, Board of Trustees, Edinburgh

26 November 1760

You will be pleased herewith to receive an abstract of the yarns bought and brought up from the North Highlands since the 1st of November 1759 to the 1st instant amounting to no more than 60,506 spindles linen yarns. The decrease in the quantity is owing to the low price of grain; and not to any want of consumpt or demand for the goods, the poor people there, as in most other countries, decline working for any more than what will barely subsist them, so that in cheap years little is manufactured, and what is done is paid for at a higher rate.[1] In this account nothing is included of what was spun from dressed flax sent to the more interior parts of the Highlands such as Lagan, Auchendrome, Stratherrick etc, all the accounts of which are kept by themselves and are distinct from the above.

To George Swan, Perth

3 December 1760

I have seen Mr Tod since he was with you. He tells me your cloth is a very good colour and the only fault is not beetling enough and putting it up crested which he mentioned to you. You need not therefore delay shipping the goods one morning for the coming of any one to inspect them but let all that can be sent [be] packed up and shipped for London by the convoy about to sail.

To Richard Neilson, Dundee

24 December 1760

This Company having advised with Mr Tod of London as to the quantity of sundry branches of the linen manufacture to be provided for next year's sale, he is of opinion that the low priced soldiers' shirting now made in and about Dundee may meet with a ready sale at the London markets and with profit. He apprehends that of the sorts made 28 inches wide when white there may be wanted 5000 say five thousand pieces of 25 yards per piece to sell at from 10½ to 11d per yd. at London. Such goods I apprehend may be bought at Dundee at from 9 to 9¼d per yd. for the very best, when brown, with the usual allowance of 10 per cent for measure. Messrs Tod & Anderson also write that the last Osnaburgs sent by you to London on your and the Company's joint account have sold at 7¾ to 8d per yd. I should therefore incline that you go on purchasing in as prudent a way as may be with such goods, still keeping a correspondence with that house and this Company and so you may be timeously apprized of the rates at London or of any changes at that market. By which you must regulate your doings at Dundee.

1 This was a common phenomenon. G. Frame [Sir James Stewart], in his *Considerations on the Interest of the County of Lanark in Scotland* (Glasgow, 1769), 38, commented that 'Necessity alone forces people to labour. Every hour over and above what is absolutely necssary for gaining a livelihood will be spent in idleness.'

Mr Tod mentions that a quantity of yard wide Dundee browns may be wanted for sale at London. This article you say you do not deal in or well understand. I wish therefore you would think of a proper person at Dundee both as to good character and capital that this Company might correspond with there anent, the purchase and sales to be on the same terms with yourself vizt the Company advancing what cash may be necessary on the usual rate of interest and paying him for what share belongs to the Company at the rate of 1½ per cent commission, the goods when shipped to be consigned to Messrs Tod & Anderson of London and the the bill of loading and invoice to be transmitted and the profits or loss to be equally divided.

To David Flint, Board of Trustees, Edinburgh

3 January 1761

You'll herewith be pleased to receive an account of what yarns have been spun up by this Company in the more interior parts of the highlands in consequence of the agreement with the honorable Board of date the 3rd August 1759. There is a considerable parcel of yarns lying in the north that cannot be got up to Leith owing to bad weather and the disappointment of vessels coming from the Moray Firth as usual. There is also a considerable parcel of dressed flax in the hands of the Company's agents which has not yet been spun up so the account will not show the whole of what has been done in these interior parts of the highlands. Yet I thought it my duty to lay before the honorable Board a state of what has been effectuated amounting to 4859½ spindles value £553 11/- as also an account herewith sent of the charges incurred for wheels, reels, instructing spinners, together with the premium due for the quantity actually spun amounting in all to £187 11/5 which account if found right and approved of you will please to obtain an order for the payment thereof to the Company. In the next account there may be yet some further charges, having had no account from Hector Scott of any prizes he has distributed amongst his spinners or from John Mackay of some incidental charges he has already incurred for transporting of wheels etc. But these with what others may be incurred shall in due time be laid before the honorable board.[1]

I have likewise enclosed for your perusal a note of the charges incurred in summer 1759 for finding out the method used in Ireland for putting up their linens together with the expence of making a set of mould or frames for that

1 The missing information was shortly afterwards forwarded to the Board of Trustees. McCulloch claimed that he had purchased in all 425 wheels and 116 reels, and that in the Assynt area alone 120 women had already been taught to spin: SRO, NG1/1/16, BOTM 21 Jan. 1761.

purpose which frames were by the Board's order delivered to Mr Wright's lapper in Leith Wynd, the said account amounting to £9 8/9 stg.

To Mr John Tait, writer in Edinburgh

2 February 1761

In obedience to the intimation made me by you as clerk to the arbiters in the submission entered into between the British Linen Company and Mr David Doig I have now to observe to you, that I cannot lodge any exact claim or demand till such time as the books of the Staplery have been seen and examined and therefore I must pray you obtain an order from the arbiters for the whole of the books of account, vouchers of cash and letters with the letter books or correspondence being put into my hands to be examined. In the meantime you will please know that the capital stock paid by the Company to the Yarn Staplery under Mr Doig's management was originally £5000 stg in November 1750 and whereof no part has been paid back and further there is due by bills to this Company by said David Doig and Company to the amount £10,050 8/6 stg of principal and £1,817 11/- of interest and there is at credit of the said Doig and Company in account current with the Company £8,046 3/-, interest included thereon to this date. But as I have said, until these books of account are cleared up no exact charge or demand can be made out. In the mean time and until these books are examined which shall be done with all the dispatch in my power when once delivered, I hope the arbiters will order all the outstanding debts to be got in and if necessary pursued for at law. And that all cash received by Mr Doig to be paid into the Company to the extent of five-sixth parts, being their proportion of the stock of the Staplery.

To Alex[ander] Flemming, Kirkliston

4 February 1761

Upon enquiry I find the rent of Leith factory and the two other weaving houses in the Cable wynd that hold in all about 96 to 100 looms to be £47 15/8d p.ann., included a dwelling house and garden well worth £8 or £10 p.a, a heckling house in Cables' wynd valued at £7 p.a. and besides there are great conveniences above the weaving shop in the great factory for sorting & warping yarns, and other warehouses. Upon the whole I should think it much your interest to take the whole immediately so as to enter at next Whitsunday.

To James Dunlop, Glasgow

21 February 1761

I do assure you that I am very much obliged for the sending over those samples of Irish linen whose method of finishing and upmaking their linens is much better than ours. I had some bleachers to view them and it's apprehended from the Company's with their own doings here that these bleachers have discovered the ingredients and manner in which the Irish are finished off and I am to have with the first fair and open weather sundry specimens done up for me in imitation of them and for a further satisfaction I should like to have 3 pieces of Irish at different prices from 8d or 10d to 2/- of the same fabric, bleach and upmarking with those you sent me in order to judge how near we can imitate them and which three pieces I beg you may buy and send me. At the same time I allow these Irish goods to be neater and better done up than our own. I am satisfied they are cheaper for the money. It seems odd but it is certainly true that all last year when goods were dearer in Germany and in Scotland too, yet the Irish kept cheap. This I am told is not now the case, their low priced brown linens for the ensuing bleach having risen in price from 15 to 20 per cent.

I observe you are fitting out the Nelly for Virginia and the Peggy for St Kitts and Barbadoes. I hope you will favour us in time with what orders you think proper that so the goods may be packed up for you at leisure. I must also beg the favour of your recommendation of this Company to Mr John Gray who I see is fitting out the ship the Hawke for Jamaica. I can furnish you or your friends with great choice of Garlix and Silesias for these markets as also with platillos and Britannias for Jamaica of which last the Spaniards are in use to buy in quantities.

To David Doig, Edinburgh

20 March 1761

The Directors of this Company have resolved either to sell or let out their utensils for bleaching and weaving of yarns, as they can find proper undertakers for the work. And instead of keeping so many servants upon days wages, and factories on rents certain whether occupied or not, to pay the several persons employed a rate certain per the spindle for bleaching and by the piece for cloth for weaving. In order to this it will be necessary you deliver up conform to an inventory such utensils, looms, bleaching grounds and houses as have been under your direction and management together with an assignation to such leases as you may have entered into for carrying on these branches of the Company's business while under your care.

To David Neilson, Dundee

1 April 1761

I am sorry to find your flax sales so slow, I wish they could be pushed as the interest on a cargo cuts deep. If I have occasion for any of the flax in your hands, I shall write you but I would rather have it sold where it is laid down, and supply our demand from abroad as transporting the flax from port to port is very chargeable and dangerous. If you can form a judgement of what you can sell I wish you to advise me. I imagine you might pay most of your weavers a great part with flax. William Coupar seems extremely dilatory in all his actions; let him send me the invoice of these Osnaburgs sent to Leith in course of post, with an account of the yarns and cloths in his hands. The hotch potch way of sending these bales of Mr Young's should be remedied. I find some bales of last year's linens N200 and upwards are still unsent, and the only regular rule Mr Coupar seems to observe is to send the last numbers first. I wish you to look into and adjust this matter.

To George Goldie, merchant in Edinburgh

14 April 1761

The ship Wolf whereof Alex Alexander is master, bound for Quebec, belonging to Patrick Miller, John Walker, William Gibson and others merchants in Edinburgh being now about to proceed for these parts, I herewith, as was agreed by the Court of Directors, consign to you and to be included in your account of consignments to these gentlemen sundry cases containing men's linen shirts as per invoice amounting to £516 15/- stg. The which goods I desire you will instruct these gentlemen or their supercargo Mr George Lindsay to sell to the best account such goods will bring and in everything to do therein as if the goods were their own, returning the proceeds in bills of exchange on Great Britain rather as by produce of the country, being articles whose values are very fluctuating, and I desire you may caution them as to the clear or rather the striped lawns, that these be not sold as sound goods, (many of them having got damage by water, rats and by wind tears in bleaching) but that they be sold by venue; these goods truly cost about 8d to 10d per yd more of prime cost, but are valued at what their present worth is estimated to be here, the other goods I flatter myself will bring a handsome profit.

Court of Directors

23 April 1761

Messrs Drummond and Tod reported that on the 9th current Mr McCulloch having represented to them that being obliged to be absent from this office for ten or fourteen days he proposed to leave a letter of procuration to George Goldie, Secretary to the Company, to act as Manager during his absence, they had approved thereof and desired that Mr Goldie should keep an account of his intromissions with cash to be cleared with the Manager on his return.

To John Anderson & Son, Perth

27 April 1761

I return you thanks for your obliging letter of the 27th advising me of the malevolent intentions of some people with regard to the Company on the melancholy event of the death of the Duke of Argyll.[1] It is true, and ought ever to be remembered with gratitude that his Grace had a principal hand in the formation of this Company, but it does not thence follow that by his or any other proprietor's death the stock or trade of this Company are to be at a stand. If Court interest or influence is any how necessary, I can assure you (and that from the best authority) that the same will not be wanting; as my Lord Bute has desired my Lord Milton to signify to all his uncle's friends that his (the late Duke's) friends and measures are to be adopted by him and protected the same as when their patron was living. I this day showed your letter to Lord Milton who returns you thanks for your friendship to this Company and desires me to communicate the above to you.

To Tod & Anderson, London

9 May 1761

The Company wants an insurance against fire to be made on linen goods to the amount of £4000 say four thousand pounds sterling that may be lodged or housed occasionally in one or other of the following houses at their bleachfield near Salton in the county of Haddington.[2] There is no fixing a precise value that may be lodged in any one place at a time as you know these goods in the course of bleaching may be carried from house to house to be boiled, bucked, sowered, rubbed, dried or beetled and that (save the last operation) frequently repeated. And supposing the above value at any one time in the bleacher's hands, they will be divided into layers or courses of cloth of four or five different situations of that property at the same time for which cause I think the insurance should not be so high, where the situation of property fluctuates and shifts so much as when it is lodged in one fixed place. It is true it might happen to be lodged all at one place, but that by accident and what could very rarely happen, if at all. It might for instance happen at the beginning of the season when lodged in a warehouse (over the head of James

1 The 79-year-old duke had died 'sitting in his chair at dinner in London, at five in the afternoon' on 15 Apr. 1761. J.B. Paul (ed.), *The Scots Peerage*, 9 vols. (Edinburgh, 1904-14), i, 380.

2 The risk of fire to textile undertakings was very real. Flemming's linen factory at Kirkliston was burnt to the ground on 8 Sept. 1768, with the loss of all his flax, yarn and other goods which 'we hear are insured in the London Sun Fire Office': *Edinburgh Advertiser*, 9 Sept. 1768.

Armstrong's apartments) up one pair of stairs where cloth is laid in at first, in order to be latched and marked, and it might possibly happen at the end of the season or the finishing the bleaching of the first or so the successive laying down of layers of cloth when, after bleaching they are taken to the drying house to be dried and thereafter lodged in the ground floor of said drying house to wait the opportunity of being sent hither.

The houses are, first a stone and tiled or slated house in the one end of which is a water mill for washing or rubbing linen cloth and in the other a division with four places for boiling, this house in the lower part of the field. Next to it, but not adjoining is a stone and tiled or slated house, where the master bleacher resides, in the first floor of which cloth is lodged for latching and marking, to the garret of which house is a tofall or shade, stone and tiled where linens are put into sour. In the upper part of the field is another washing mill with fire places as described in the first mentioned house and next to this is an additional shade or building wherein is placed a beetling machine that goes by water. On the rising ground above, commonly known by the name of the dry field, is situated a large house of two storeys, the first storey of stone, the second storey or dry house part has a wall of brick pillars and many apertures of wood that move up and down to give air or shut it out, the roof of tile or slated. The ground storey or floor of which house (100 feet in length) is divided thus, to the one end a place for laying up cloth when finished, in the middle a place for four horses and a waggon and on the other end two apartments for men with fire places. Last of all, is a house adjacent but not joining to the dry house of two storeys in height and covered with tile. The first storey is built with stone, the second of stone pillars with large doors of wood that move at pleasure up and down for admitting air to turn two beetling machines.

I say that on goods that may be lodged for bleaching in one or all of these houses as above described I would have £4000 value insured, and on the houses themselves to the amount of £1500 say one thousand five hundred pounds stg in the following manner vizt three hundred pounds on both of the wash houses, that is £150 for each; three hundred pounds on James Armstrong's or the master bleacher's house and sour house, six hundred pounds on the drying house and three hundred pounds on the house and machinery adjacent to the dry house in which there are no fire places and used for beetling making in all £1500 on the houses and machinery. If the lodging horses and as much hay as will feed them for a night at any time under the dry house is any impropriety or will heighten the insurance, they shall be removed.

To William Tod, London

16 July 1761

I come now to reply to your letter of the 8th current and I approve very much of your writing freely every thing that occurs as necessary or useful for the general interest of the Company. What you say as respecting the different fabrics of linen that they have all shamefully degenerated of late I can only reply that it is without my knowledge. Excepting a few brown and white Osnabrigs made here, all linens that are intended for the London market you know are purchased by different people on their and the Company's joint account, the greatest part of which I can have no access to see. What in my humble opinion should be done, you should send to the different people samples of such kinds of foreign linens (brown) as you judge they can the nearest imitate, for example let a piece of Garlix and a piece or two of best brown Silesias be sent to George Young or rather the one half to him and the other to me and so to others patterns (that is pieces) of brown Irish or of Pomeranias, Ticklenburgs and Osnaburgs to Neilson, Pearson, Walker and others who act for the Company.

There are some few patterns here of white linens such as Platillos, Taridems, and fine white Silesia or Irish linen but it would be of infinite more use to the makers to see the goods brown from the loom. That this or any country can hit all fabrics I look upon to be a thing impossible. At present one must take such fabric only as their yarns and method of weaving will the nearest resemble and may the easiest be made to imitate the foreign, for it's with the greatest reluctance any one weaver will be persuaded to use foreign yarns, how good soever they may be or how proper soever for making into the fabrics wanted, and until this is worn out, the Manchester manufacturers will have the advantages you mention, seeing nobody will import foreign yarns that cannot be sold off but with loss as this Company has again and again experienced.

With regard to the Osnaburg sorts whether white or brown or those broad kinds called Navy linen, I do not think you in general have any cause to complain of fabrics at least of what are now out of the looms and beside me. I truly think so. The poor prices given at your market for these goods last year determined me to lessen the consignments of these articles upon which no profits were made—7½ to 8d for white Osnabrigs and 8½ for Navy linens—being the prices and at which nothing was made even to defray interest of money. Thereafter your prices augmented and for the Navy linens we got ninepence and the circumstance of using white wafts even disposed of, which was another saving, but then I could not speedily replace the kinds of yarns fit for these branches. And what was worse by the supine neglect or rather worse of Mr Doig who had the charge of the looms, two-thirds of the weavers left the business. I am now getting these evils somehow amended, having by interest with the Commanding Officer of the Regiment here got an order for 60 weavers who are all at work and doing generally very well.

One thing is to be noticed that our colours of white and brown will always differ from the foreign and though the white may be made a tolerable colour at some expence yet from no method hitherto found out is it practicable to give the agreeable colour to ours that the foreign brown linens have. There are just now in the warehouse some 18 or 20 pieces Navy linen as good as any I have seen, some of which are all brown, other half brown and white. I shall endeavour to make up the quantities wrote for on the 11th by your house to 30 p[ieces] to go by first convoy and if these should not please, they may be returned as it is a thing of no difficulty here to sell some parcels of half bleached at from 9½ to 10d per yd. There are just now a considerable quantity of white Osnabrigs in the looms which will be ready to go likewise. With regard to your selling off the ¾qr wide linen and some diaper at loss, I can give no opinion as I know not what you are offered for them in proportion to their cost. But this I know, that bleached diapers are in the country as dear as ever and the white linen markets not much if anything reduced.

Court of Directors

27 August 1761

Hector Scott, merchant in Inverness, (who had contracted to spin up six tons of flax annually for the Company for three years from and after the 5th day of August 1760), having represented by his letter of the 26th current that the high prices of spinning and scarcity of spinners in that country rendered it impossible for him to execute his engagements with the Company and begged therefore that he might be relieved therefrom as he had in view being employed by some merchants in Inverness in conducting their affairs and had procurred from these gentlemen an order for some tons of flax to be bought from the Company. The Court in consideration of the long and faithful service of Mr Scott agreed to his proposal and ordered the Manager to discharge and deliver him up his contract with the Company.

Court of Directors

17 September 1761

Messrs John Walker, James Seaton, Scott & Clerk, John Tod, Ebenezer McCulloch and George Goldie, all merchants in Edinburgh and Messrs Bewick, Timberman and Hodge of Cadiz, having proposed to carry on a trade to Cadiz in the exportation of sundry species of linen,[1] the manufacture of this Kingdom on a joint venture of profit and loss. The amount of each exportation to be divided into six shares and paid for respectively by each stock holder accordingly and not by any joint stock or copartnership. The goods to be furnished by the British Linen Company agreeable to orders to be lodged here on or before the first day of January annually for five years to come and to be delivered at this warehouse at two periods in the year to wit in August and November and apayable in twelve months thereafter at the rate of the neat cost to the Company including the charges of bleaching, dressing and packages, and upon the sum total of which the Company are to charge eleven per cent in full for profits and interest of money till payable as above, the goods to be bleached dressed and be made up in imitation of the foreign and not to exceed two thousand pounds stg of amount annually.

The Court taking the above proposal under consideration think it greatly for the interest of this Company and of the country to encourage this exportation of Scotch linens to Spain and agree to furnish what linens shall be ordered by these gentlemen on the terms proposed.

To David Denham, Hull

6 January 1762

I shall be glad that you remit me the balance in your hands and let it be by a bill on London as you propose. Pray what is done in the affairs of Messrs Sill, Bridges & Blount? Mrs Dixson, Miss Cravend, Mr Wright should really pay interest or at least the charges of negotiation for they well knew that this was the plan of payment of the goods, nay some if not all of them promised very long ago to remit me. The tedious payments, and trouble attending the triffling sums that were due in your neighbourhood and other small towns in England entirely discourage the Company from continuing any further dealings there tho' they much wished that the linen manufactures of this country had been known and introduced with you as they can at all times supply them on the very best terms. But the experiments they have made have cost them dear. And they find full vent for their goods here, at London and Glasgow and elsewhere. I am however obliged to you for your offers of service and where I can serve the interest of you or your friends here, it will be very agreeable.

1 This scheme had been in the making for some time. Samples of the kinds of linen in demand in Spain, for which the Board of Trustees had been persuaded to pay, had been sent by Dalrymple to Edinburgh in the previous year: SRO, NG1/1/16, BOTM 21 Jan. 1761.

To William Dalrymple, Cadiz[1]

6 March 1762

On the other side I transmit you invoice of those linens your Mr Dalrymple purchased from the British Linen Company in Febry 1761 on account of the joint concern of the house at Cadiz amounting to £825 4/5 certain, and in the event of their bringing at Cadiz a sum beyond cost and charges, the Company to be paid £36 10/11 more making in that event in all £861 15/4. This additional price is vouched by the following paragraph in Mr D[alrymple]'s letter to me dated 7th May 1761, 'I am sorry that it is absolutely necessary for me to accept the deduction of 1d per yd but without that circumstance my house must inevitably be great losers and even with it I dont expect to clear any more but prime cost and charges, which if I do I shall think my labour well employed. If any more should arise on them I will make good the half penny per yd as per our agreement.' And by another letter 7th Nov 1761, he writes 'The last 20 boxes of Britannias got safe to market and I believe are sold, I have desired my house to send home the accounts that I may communicate it to you.' The proceeds of the purchase have not yet been communicated to me so must refer this matter to yourselves. The cause of my commencing a correspondence to you jointly is the late misfortunes that has attended Mr Dalrymple in his private concerns which renders it absolutely necessary for this Company to apply to you for payment, lest by any mistake for giving credit for the goods in your books you be brought to pay twice. And this likewise I have intimated D[alrymple] at London that he may conduct himself accordingly with his personal creditors. The goods purchased in February 1761 were sent by agreement to London, difficulties were made by Mr D[alrymple] as to the price charged. And it happened that until May thereafter the goods were not shipped for Spain, from which the credit runs of 12 months.

And I now beg that you will against May next, be pleased to order the payments as aforementioned of £825 4/5 certain or in the event of their having been sold to better account (which I flatter myself has been the case) you will order the payment of £861 15/4 and advise me to whom I shall approach for the payment in Britain, or if that you will remit me here. Give me leave from my acquaintance with Mr Dalrymple to regret his ill success and the misfortunes he has met with and to assure you that if anything in my power were

1 Forwarded to the care of Mr Duff at Gibraltar per the Friendship, Captain Passmore.

possible to serve your house or himself separately, I should with pleasure embrace every opportunity given me.

To Tod & Anderson, London

8 March 1762

I notice what you say respecting the breadths of common Silesias which shall again be communicated to our friends northward. I believe this year, however low-priced now and in how little demand linen goods may be with you there will not be one half of the quantity made this year in Scotland that there was last, so that surely some time hence they must bear a better price at market.

Be pleased to send me a small pattern of about 3 or 4 inches square of such blue linens as are dyed at London and exported. Our dyers here ask 3d or 4d a yard but say that if [it] is done cheaper at London they can come up to it and from the sample we can judge of the materials used in dyeing to cheapen it. When I mentioned on the other side that the sales in company with Young and Pearson were good, I meant those of the brown goods. But for the white there is surely a very great loss. And it is therefore to be considered on one is to conduct themselves [sic] now with what is on hand of last year's buying. If it be so that this country will not produce nearly so large a quantity as in former years, it is presumable that the value of the goods must rise, as to which I pray you'll favour me with your sentiments.

To Tod & Anderson, London

15 March 1762

I wrote you last post to which refer. This serves chiefly to advise that I this day drew upon you by first and 2nd bills for £280 in favours of William Aitkins at 7 days and to which I beg you'll give due honour on account of this Co[mpany]. This is one of these numberless troops of riders for orders that infest this country by picking up notes and demanding gold at the banks and this office. And to save specie we sometimes get them to accept of bills on London. Money is now become so scarce a commodity that the Banks have published a resolution today of accepting of loans in specie or even their own notes upon interest.[1] If payable to the lender upon demand they are to pay £4 if to pay in 6 months certain £5 percent. By this it is projected to stop the

1 The financial crisis of 1762 is well described in H. Hamilton, *An Economic History of Scotland in the Eighteenth Century* (Oxford, 1963), 308-11. The Edinburgh banks had instituted a strict policy of deflation, reducing cash credit advances by a quarter in Jan. 1762, and two months later raising interest rates on deposits as McCulloch here describes; the effect was to restore equilibrium in the balance of payments with England.

credit of the dealers in bills of exchange, who constantly (it is said) run upon the banks for specie, send it to London at a small charge, and draw for the same Cash again at 3 to 3 ½ per cent exchange. And in this way the demands are at the banks to the amount of £18,000 per week. How the proposed remedy will work no one knows. In the meantime credit, trade etc are much hurt in this country.

To Tod & Anderson, London

18 March 1762

I have communicated your letter of the 13th respecting the manufactures to Mr Neilson (now here). He is of opinion the sundry fabrics of coarse linens could with advantage be promoted at Dundee, but that the chief obstacle is their yarns are made generally from ill-heckled and stapled flax and consequently the yarns made very unevenly. To remedy this I have proposed furnishing some of the principal weavers there annually for 3 years with 20 or 30,000 spindles of our north country yarns at about 2d to 3d per spl less than theirs now cost them, of which he approves and has accordingly transmitted my proposal to Dundee to some of the most considerable weavers there. If this takes place he has only to keep the weavers strictly to the weave neatly and close and to buy such goods only as are well done. With respect to the ⅞ cheques of which you say the colours are good but refused for being thin, I have to remark that some two or three months ago I had an inspection of them made by some folks from Manchester who said that the weaving was rather preferable to theirs but that the goods before being offered to sale should be dressed up as theirs are vizt first callendered with the horse callender and then put through a hot cylinder.

To George Clifford and Sons, Amsterdam

29 April 1762

You will please to receive two letters the one for the house of Thomas Zuckerbecker Widow & Sons of Riga to whom I have given orders for the providing a cargo of flax and have given them leave to value on you for the amount which may be as the prices shall rule and the ship contain from £1800 to £2000 and to which last amount you will please to honour their bills and for your reimbursement draw as formerly upon Messrs Tod & Anderson of London. The which credit to Messrs Zuckerbecker widow and sons you will please confirm along with our said inclosed letters. The other letter now enclosed and which you will please to forward is for Madam, the widow of David Barclay of Koningsberg. This lady has often sollicited the Company for employment, the same as in her husband's time, says she has a large family, and by her servants and connections in that place can render the same service as her late husband. This letter goes to know the present rates of goods at Konigsburg and if from your goodselves the Company is in safety to put the trust of 2 to £3000 in her hands, I believe the Company may be induced on account of her widowed state to give her commission and if well executed to continue her in their correspondence.

To Tod & Anderson, London

24 June 1762

I am sorry to see by your letter to Mr Neilson that trade continues still so very dull with you. We have just now 16 looms employed in the Navy linen and by next ship you shall have what is ready. I flatter myself the shirtings now taking up at Saltonfield will please. ¾ checks are bought now at $5^{10}/_{12}$, the very best @ 6d, but even at these prices I dare not go any length in buying, tho' done jointly with Andrew Cowan, as our notes are daily picked up and brought in here for specie, and this commodity is extremely scarce here on account of the high exchange now and formerly to London. I am particularly at a loss to know how to defend myself at this present time. The old Bank have for some time made use of the privilege in their notes of making them to pay in 6 months thereafter with interest.[1] This threw all the riders and others wanting cash for notes upon the Royal Bank. They have now issued the same kind of optional notes with the other Bank, and indeed all of the Glasgow banks; so that this Company only at present issue notes absolutely on demand. The Directors have ordered optional notes to be made and issued for the Company likewise, but in the course of preparing plates and printing etc it will be yet a month ere any can be issued so that in the meantime I have the run to stand, at least much more than usual demands to answer.

Court of Directors

5 July 1762

Memorial offered to the consideration of the Court of Directors by George Drummond and Patrick Lindsay.

In order to give the Directors of this Company a clear view of their affairs, and to show them to what accidents it is owing that they are in the situation they are in at present, we think it necessary to begin with laying before you the state of the linen manufacture in Scotland in the year 1746, when the Company was constituted by charter.

1 The so-called optional clause, to be outlawed by the Bank Act of 1765: 5 Geo. III, c. 49.

In the year 17[42][1] the legislature settled a bounty to be paid on exportation of home made coarse linens, to continue until the year 1754. But unhappily until this Company was constituted, there was nobody in Scotland in a capacity to profit by our being entitled to it, owing to their being altogether ignorant of the fabrics of linen wanted, or of a market for them when made, and consequently there was no such thing as a warehouse in this country where a purchaser could be supplied with any assortment of British made linens, either for home sale or foreign consumpt.

The inhabitants of the Northern parts of Scotland had just then given a melancholy proof upon how precarious footing the quiet of the rest of the Island stood, while these people's poverty and total ignorance of every branch of industry by which they might better their circumstances, disposed them to be fondly subservient to the ambitious views of their chiefs, and to join readily in insurrections and rebellions against the government.

To enable this country to avail themselves of the bounty of the government to us which they confidently expected would not be withdrawn while the infant state of our manufactures required this encouragement, and to secure the quiet of the rest of the Island from the insurrections of the highlanders by the introducing industry and manufactures among them, and thereby making their circumstances easy and comfortable at home were the generous and noble motives which brought the British Linen Company together, and made them set about the introducing the fabrics of linen in demand in our American colonies as well as those fit for the consumpt of England, both of which were great objects.

In the execution of this good design, they had very many difficulties to struggle with, yet so far they succeeded that in the course of the first five or 6 years, it appears from their books that they brought their annual sales to amount to about £30,000. But while they were going on in this successfully, they met with an unhappy check in the year 1754 by a fatality of public measures, and altogether unexpectedly the bounty was withdrawn and there was almost a thorough stop put to their progress in the trade.

In order to make their commendable schemes effective, the Company found it absolutely necessary to begin with the foundation material, and to carry on the whole process of the manufacture upon their own account and risk, from the importation of flax from abroad, and getting it spun into yarn, to its being woven into the different fabrics, whitened, drest and actually sold for

1 15 & 16 Geo. II: 'An Act for granting to His Majesty an additional duty on foreign Cambrics: and for allowing thereout a bounty upon certain species of British and Irish linens exported.'

exportation. For this purpose amongst other undertakings they sent flax, hecklers, spinning mistresses and utensils to Inverness, and all the countries northwards and even to the Orkneys. In these countries the Company have at great expence introduced the art of spinning and heckling flax with so much success that in year 1754 when the bounty was withdrawn, these islands and their other northern colonies yielded them annually towards 50,000 spindles of yarns, which were brought to Leith and manufactured into the species of linens in demand.

By the proper representations which were made to Mr Pelham, who was then at the head of the Treasury, immediately upon the discontinuing of the bounty, by the late Duke of Argyll, at the head of the whole Scots representation in Parliament, he regretted the step that had been taken, owned that he was thoroughly convinced that the continuance of the bounty was an absolutely necessary measure to save the manufacture from ruin and gave the strongest assurances, that immediately upon the opening of the next session of Parliament that matter should be brought in and set to rights. But, his death, and the hurry of other public business, prevented a bill's passing for the renewing of the bounty any sooner than towards the end of the second session, so that till the third year after discontinuance thereof, the trade did not feel any of the good effects of it. Yet during all that time, the Company, depending on Mr Pelham's promises, that we should not be above a few months without the bounty, made no interruption in their promoting of spinning in the North, tho' the yarn could neither be wove up with profit, nor be sold with any advantage while the damp on trade by the withdrawing the bounty continued. And thereby they became possessed of a very great quantity of unprofitable yarns, the price whereof became loaded with the addition of the interest incurred while it remained on hand unused, which brought a burden on the stock which they have never again been able to replace.

But this, however great, was not the only loss which the Company have sustained by the discontinuance of the bounty. For the manufacturers or weavers, who had set up looms, hired servants and got credit from the Company and others, for flax and yarn to carry on their trade with, finding a certain charge unavoidable growing on them for living and wages to their servants, but no sale for their work, became bankrupt, and fled their country whereby it was justly computed that full 2000 looms were thrown idle in Scotland, and by these manufacturers becoming bankrupt, the Company lost considerably.

Soon after the Company commenced, they found it impossible to carry on their trade in competition with foreigners, or with the Irish, on account of the high prices paid for bleaching, at this time there being only two or three fields in any reputation where Hollands were bleached in the Dutch way, at the rate of 6d. per yd and one or two fields where bleaching was carried on in the Irish way at 4d. They therefore found it necessary to have a field laid out and proper buildings erected upon it, and they accordingly set it on foot at Salton. They procurred the best masters they could and hired servants but for the first 2 or 3 years the Company suffered much from their ignorance and unskilful way of handling the cloth, and this was succeeded by the almost total stop of the trade while the bounty was discontinued, and thereby the Company suffered considerably.

Besides these particular losses, the Company have for a number of years had all the disadvantages which every such new undertaking must lay their account they have to grapple with when they first set out; their project was to introduce a new branch of trade into their country of bringing many fabrics of linen to market which the Irish and foreigners by long practice had brought to perfection before we entered on business, and they had thereby established a reputation to themselves in a trade, in which they were to be rivalled by no more formidable antagonist than a Company ignorant themselves of the trade which they were to carry on, by hands no less so, weavers quite inexperienced in weaving these fabrics and therefore our cloths were not at all to be compared in point of quality for a great while either with Irish or foreign, and of course the Company's profit on these goods could not be adequate to the trouble, outlay of money and risk of reputation. In order to extend their commerce, the Company established a warehouse of their own in London and Glasgow, but as they found they did not answer, both are discontinued some years ago.

Upon a careful examination into the list of bad and doubtful debts, it appears to us that the chief part of the Company's losses that way, have been incurred several years ago by the distress which the trade was laid under while the bounty was withdrawn, and by the double risks they were obliged to run at their first setting out, first by the spinners and weavers, and thereafter by the purchasers. Their losses since have arisen from transactions, which were reasonable when they were entered into and consequently unforeseen and such as all trade is liable to.

The Company have now, happily, almost weathered all the difficulties they had to get the better of. They have got the weavers in many places of the country so well instructed that Osnabriggs, Dowlasses, Pomeranias, Military Shirting, Silesias, Garlix, Britannias and linens in the Irish fabrics are now become staple articles of commerce to this Kingdom. They have also brought the Diaper to come near the foreign, and in many respects to equal it, and they have brought our manufacture of coarse chequered linen to be equal to the Manchester checks.

The trade of the Company, and indeed of this Country, in general is on a much better footing then it was formerly and it is daily approaching nearer to the practice of other nations. For instead of being under a necessity of employing people to heckle, spin and weave for us, and to be subjected to the losses arising from the mistakes and even dishonesty of the persons entrusted with our affairs, as we were under a necessity to do in the infancy of our trade, the Company can now safely buy up the quantities of the above mentioned fabrics, which they find there is a demand for, ready made, for which they pay the current market prices here at the time, and that they may be ascertained of having these goods in their quality, and bought for them on the lowest terms. The persons they now employ to purchase linens are skillful manufacturers themselves and a half concerned with the Company in all the goods they purchase and pay interest to them for their advance on their half of the venture, till the advance comes to be repaid out of the subject itself when disposed of, and as there are now bleachfields laid out, which are put under the direction of skilful bleachers who were educated to that trade in the Company's own bleaching field at Salton, they can be in no difficulty to get the excressent quantity which cannot be whitened at their own field in time enough for the market, whitened at one or other of these new fields.

The fabrics brought to market by the Company are arrived at such a pitch of reputation that it has greatly increased the number of our established customers in so much that our sales already amount to between 40 and £50,000 per annum. And the success of the British arms in America and the West Indies, of which we already feel some good effect, encourages us to hope (we think with reason) for a much greater advance in them.

We must observe, and we do it with concern, that the impatience of the Proprietors to have dividends annually paid to them while the Company was in its infancy, struggling with all the aforementioned difficulties in establishing their trade, and before any sum was earned and laid up to answer losses, and their continuing to make such dividends even after the withdrawing of the bounty had greatly hurt the linen trade in the country, is another great cause of the difficulties which our affairs now labour under. For upon a subscription, on which the whole of the calls paid in by the Proprietors amounted to only to £46,885, annual dividends have been made to the amount of £22,932.

In the year 1752 the necessity of reserving a fund to answer losses appeared in so strong a light to the Proprietors that they agreed to reduce their dividends from 5 to 4 per cent on the capital advanced. And the Managers, to contribute to the establishing so prudent a measure, tho' they could much less afford it, did also cheerfully agree to lessen their premiums one-fifth. But the discontinuance of the Bounty in the year 1754 and the Company's continuing to make annual dividends rendered these concessions of the Proprietors and Managers of little or no avail as the profits thereafter till last year, were scarcely able to pay the dividends of 4 per cent and the charges of management, tho' the Managers for their part instead of drawing the 4/5 or 16 sh[illings] per cent on the amount of the sales, to which they restricted themselves in the year 1752 accepted of 2070£ in full of payment thereof instead of about £3070, which their restricted demand amounted to from the time that the restriction took place till the year 1758.

That from the year 1752 the Directors have given their labour to the Company without insisting on any reward of it.

Having now gone through this irksome history of the sources of the Company's losses, from its first erection, till now, we will proceed to lay before the Court the state of the different branches of the Company's trade as they appear to us. To enable you to judge in what manner it is best to carry on in time coming.

[A detailed and extensive analysis of the Company's trade in linen, flax, yarn and ashes is then given.]

We now come in the last place to offer our opinion to the Court of Directors in what manner it will be most for the Company's trade in time coming, in order to repair the losses we have already made, and we hope the observations we have already laid before you, makes this neither a difficult nor a very different matter.

The branch of trade which requires the most deliberate consideration is our trade with London. What offers to us on this subject we shall lay before you.

The London market is the greatest in Europe, and is supplied from all places where linens are made. The prices there rise or fall, as chance brings more or less quantities to it. Scotland is but yet getting to suit our cloths to the foreign fabrics, and to the demand, and on a comparison with them we often fall short both in quality and dress, which lowers our price.

Our trade with London is in two branches; vizt brown fabric bought on speculation, to be afterwards whitened here, and then sent up. The outlay of money on these goods from the time they are bought here, whitened and sent up, the time they must lie before they are sold, and the long credit the buyer there has before he pays for them, and the small profit, which by experience, we find arises from them at last makes us of opinion that our dealing in this branch if not discontinued should be very much retrenched, at least on the Company's proper account, diapers excepted, on which we have generally got a very reasonable profit. It may be proper however to send up small parcels of such goods, sometimes, just to keep us acquainted with the state of that market for them.

The other branch of our trade with London consists of such goods as are sold just as they come from the loom without bleaching. These may be dealt in by the Company with a reasonable certainty of yielding a profit for we can purchase them here at a price proportioned to what we are advised they will sell for in London on their arrival. These fabrics are Osnabrigs for dyeing, Pomeranias, Navy linens, White Osnabrigs, checks of 3 qr, 7/8 and yard wide, Tick[lenburg]s of these breadths, brown linens for buckrams and brown Silesias.

We have said so much here already on the subject of our Bleachfield at Salton that it will be obvious to you that if we continue to trade at all, it is in the Company's interest to rent it. Yet, if we do, in order to ascertain ourselves that the materials used there are managed with the greatest frugality and that every part of the expence of it is governed with the best economy, it may be proper to assume the present overseer of the field to be a partner for a small share of it. His present appointments are £25 of salary from the Company, £25 of the £50 allowed us by the Trustees of Manufactures for instructing apprentices, coal and candle, and a free house.

The scheme of assuming Richard Neilson, George Young, William Sandeman, etc who are employed by the Company to purchase linens for them, to a half concern with them in the goods they purchase was a prudent measure. The net profit arising to the Company last year from these transactions in partnership with them amounted to £532 16/8 and we are of opinion it should be continued and extended. The proposition was made to us by our Manager tho' it evidently lessens his own appointments, and we cannot upon this occasion omit doing him the justice to say that the more we have looked into the Company's affairs we are the more thoroughly convinced that he has conducted himself in every part of his management capably, zealously and with indefatigible applications to their interests. While we are upon this subject, give us leave to suggest that the concerns of this Company entrusted to his care, are of too great importance to be suffered to rest on the life of one man.

Was Mr McCulloch to drop, what an interruption and perplexity in them, must his death create to us. It becomes the Court therefore prudently to provide against such an event. And happily we can do it satisfyingly. We have in the office a young gentleman who serves his time to us, and has well recommended himself to all of us by his capacity, prudent behaviour and zeal for the Company's interest. He is now acting in the office of our secretary, and is very well qualified for that of an assistant Manager. And if we join him with Mr McCulloch, we are of opinion he would be much more usefully employed in that station than in the one where he now is. While Mr McCulloch is sole manager he cannot at any time be absent from the office, without risking a loss to the Company. And yet, as it is evident that our most advantageous sales are at home, if Mr Goldie were joined to him as a Manager he would be at liberty now and then to spend a little time at Glasgow, Dundee and other places in the North country, Salton etc very much to the Company's advantage and we think Mr Goldie's appointment needs little or no addition to the Company's expence. Messrs Tod & Anderson have only two per cent commission from us on their sales. They however we find charge Neilson etc 2½ per cent on their sales in partnership with us. The half percent they may be prevailed with to give up, and our partners will submit to give it to the Company, as they must give 2½ per cent commission to any other factor they employed. These sales in partnership, it may reasonably be thought, will so much increase as nearly to afford fund enough to satisfy all the allowance we now make to Mr Goldie.

If a sale of all the white linens was instituted at the Company's office here, by way of a Hall such as they have in Ireland to be open for ten days, once every two months from June to December. It would give a double chance of a market to the proprietors of the goods lodged here, and if they don't sell here, it will be no hindrance to their sending them to England. For they may be lodged in the Company's warehouse at Leith, while the hall is open, and only samples of them sent up to the office. If this scheme succeeds, it will probably bring buyers to Edinburgh, and increase the number of our own customers. As the making this attempt can be attended with no charges it should be tried, and what is got by the Company for warehouse rent, commission and their other trouble about it, will in so far be a fund for defraying our charges of management.

All of which is humbly submitted to the Court (signed) by George Drummond, Pat Lindsay.

To Tod & Anderson, London

15 July 1762

Having now consulted with the sundry gentlemen that are joint adventurers with us in linens that are consigned to your house and that yet remain undisposed of, they seem generally to be of opinion that the chance of selling with some more advantage when the West India fleets are arrived with their orders for goods is much greater than the hazard can be of keeping on hand till then and especially when it is considered that this year there has not been much above one half of the usual quantity made for sale, and in fact white linens are selling at the markets of Perth, Coupar etc fully as high if not higher than last year. I therefore desire you may wait the event of a demand from America which may naturally be expected to be considerable, and consequently raise the price somewhat in proportion to the cost.

The trade has been and is generally at present so discouraging that we cannot promise you quantities of any sort of goods. I must observe as to Silesias and white linens, both of which fabrics are much improved but from the lowest price goods gave last year few have been made, the weavers not having bread by their labour.

Ashes and in particular pearl ashes are of such an enormous price that I would not chose to have any of them for I now learn they are again gone up in price. And I flatter myself from the more attentive use of our home materials and a few cashube ashes to do without them and give as good colour.

Court of Directors

28 July 1762

In consequence of sundry conversations as to Salton Bleachfield, it was this day resolved that Mr Patrick Bannerman be desired to enter agreement with Mr James Armstrong the master bleacher at their field for performing all carriage to and from the field at the following rates viz six pence for each computed mile out and three pence per mile home for a leading which is reckoned 12 cwt for a cart or waggon and that he do exchange a missive with him for that purpose and that Mr. Armstrong's letter be transmitted hither and that proper checks be pointed out for ascertaining the number of carriages. As also it was resolved that the Company's three cart horses be sold in about 14 days hence by public roup, and that in the meantime these horses be put to grass to be fitted for sale and that all the Company's carts, tackle and horse furniture be then sold except those for the mill horse.

As also it was resolved that Mr Armstrong be allowed 24 cartloads of coals by the Company but he must drive them at his own charge, the value of which is computed at one and sixpence per cart load is one pound sixteen shillings. That Daniel Mackie and Alex Gray be allowed twelve cartloads each, they also to drive them at their own charge, value to both one pound sixteen shillings and that no perquisites of candles be allowed to any of them. And it is to be recommended to Mr Bannerman and Mr Armstrong to consider of, and as they shall see proper give orders for providing oil and burning lights in the lapping room and beetling room, it being the opinion of the Court that no candles should be used excepting a stone or a stone and a half of small bald wick candles to be employed for occasional purposes and further that the coals be put into some proper place of which Rutherford shall keep the key and give out coals as occasion requires, he always keeping an account of what is put into the coal house and the several purposes for which they are given out. The water for the servants meals shall be provided by such a woman as Mr Armstrong shall direct who shall come from her work at 8 and 12 o'clock and have the boiler ready by nine and one o'clock for the whole servants, after which the fire is to be extinguished or taken off.[1]

To Col[onel] Patrick McDual, of the 3rd Regiment of Guards, with the Allied Army in Germany

2 August 1762

You will have the trouble of this to have yet some further plague with your friend's affairs. There is belonging to your army one J[ohn] Mudie, who I believe acts as a commissary and who was lately a merchant in Riga. This same Mr Mudie owes the Company I act for £1545 by four bills.[2] He never declared any losses but declared himself unable to pay his debts and indeed it would be difficult for any factor as he was at Riga to show losses. There being no trust granted in their way of trade but *the whole was* knavery, dissipation and extravagance. He came over to London lately of which I got notice and caused him to be arrested. He then found Mr Steward, the West India merchant and his son in law, Mr Marjoribanks to be his bail. He then made an offer of four shillings in the pound in cash and his promise for six shillings in the pound more in two years, and that in full. The latter is not worth a sixpence and the other is hardly the interest incurred on the principal and therefore the Company rejected it. He the next day makes off for Germany, having obtained, I am told, an office worth in salary no less than three guineas per diem besides valuable perquisites against winter. He must appear in the court of King's bench or his bail must pay the debt. I am quite satisfied that Mr Steward would never have given bail for him without some good cause of interest or absolute security moving him thereto what ever his pretence may be to here or his other creditors and therefore it is my dear sir what I would after stating my case beg your help in this affair. His public office, which I believe is one of commissary of your army will easily bring him to your knowledge. It will then be practicable for you to find out what his profits are and with whom he is connected and in short what prospect there is of us recovering the money. He is a gay, easy, well bred, facetious fellow, speaks most languages and I fancy from these qualifications has been taken in a share with Sir James Cockburn and others in their forage or bread contracts with the government but at this I only guess at from Mr Stewart's being of his bail who is a near relation of Sir James's; his history you will please keep to yourself as I imagine the not

1 For a full account of the operation of this bleachfield see A.J. Durie, 'Saltoun Bleachfield, 1746-1773', *Transactions of the East Lothian Antiquarian and Field Naturalists' Society*, xv (1976), 49-74.

2 The Company were also pursuing Mudie's clerk, William Weir, in the Scottish Courts: Signet Library, Edinburgh, Court of Session Cases, 85:9 (1762).

divulging any part of it will the more readily bring about what is wanted to be known. I mean the knowledge of his circumstance as upon your information I will lay the whole stress of my future conduct with him.

Already I can see friends appearing for him to procure him an acquittance on his impudent offers of 4/- in the £ which considering how he cheated the Company and truly had no loss in trade, he by no means deserves unless you shall tell me no better than can be made of him. Were it not possible by means of the Marquis of Granby[1] or some of your folks in power to give him a hint that upon him doing justice to such a one only his office should be continued or made easy to him? I think power used to command justice is power well used and honorably or else I should not else have mentioned it to you. But all this is pointing at things I imagine proper or practical; you being on the spot and knowing particulars will be much better able able to judge what is proper to be done, and therefore I leave my cause wholely with you.

To Robert Paul, Walton Gardens, London

26 August 1762

My being from home ever since your letter of the 31st Ult. came to this office till within these two or three days past has prevented a reply being made thereto in course. I have now to say that at present there is no such thing as money in this country for laying out on any subject whatever. Such large sums of money have been remitted from hence for purchasing stocks at London within these two years that the exchange upon bills on London is risen to 25/- per cent for those of sixty days from the former price of 5/- to par premium. By this you will see how we are straightened in this part of the country. How soon money becomes more plenty I shall endeavour to find a purchaser for your stock in this Company and advise you in the meantime to apply for your dividends to Mr Tod in London which are paid half-yearly.[2]

To Tod & Anderson, London

11 October 1762

I have wrote to both Walker and Pearson to centre themselves in providing brown Fife linens to go by this ship as you desired and I daresay they will do

1 John Manners, marquis of Granby, was commander-in-chief of the British forces in Germany during the latter part of the Seven Years' War.

2 Robert Paul of Chatton Gardens, London, had subscribed for £500 of stock on 1 May 1747. His stock was finally sold only after his decease, and was transferred to James Guthrie, merchant in Edinburgh: BSA, British Linen Company Stock Transfer Book, 6/35/1.

all in their power. I am sorry to find you still complain of the thinness of Neilson and Sandeman's goods and of the diapers. There is no doubt but that the boiling of the yarns properly would improve these and every other fabric but then the expence that would occasion in such coarse goods would amount to from 6 to 8 per cent in the present method of boiling yarns which I have all along looked upon as a kind of prohibition to the practice. It is true that some few persons have tried it as far as to cost ¼d per yd, more for the shirtings, but then it is not boiled to purpose. I have lately got over from Germany directions for preparing the yarns in their way for Osnabriggs, Ticklenburgs, etc, and of which I have been making proof very much to my satisfaction. If this succeeds as hoped for, one can prepare any coarse linen yarns for them in such a way as not to shrink in bleaching for one third of the price for the present method even when done at the highest perfection with Pearl and Cashube ashes.

To Henry Davidson, London

11 October 1762

Your having shown a concern for and taken an interest in Thos Junor at Kirkcaldy occasions my giving you this trouble at present. He has been very unfortunate for these 12 months past: there has been a great stagnation in trade so that he has been little employed either as a weaver in making goods or as an agent in buying up goods for this Company in both of which ways he has for several years bygone been employed. But that is not all; about 6 months ago he was seized with a lingering sickness and tho' he has got well, his wife is taken ill and of six children has had many of them indisposed. The consequence of all this is that he has for his and his family's support made use of part of the cash entrusted to him for weaving and purchasing of goods to the amount of £30 or perhaps £40 and has nothing to give for security but his looms and household furniture. Business is now again revived but as agent for and acting in trust for a Company I cannot continue to give him further orders without first paying up the former balance.

What occurs to me is that if you would venture to give him a letter of credit with the Company for the amount of one or two hundred pounds as occasion may require on your putting that sum into his hands for the purchase of goods and saying that you would oblige yourself that he will make faithful account thereof of any time in two months after puting the same into his hands. But at same time expressly saying that you will be liable only for such balance as may be intimated to you and certified by both parties at the end of every two months from the date of your letter of credit. By this means I think he could be put into bread for himself and numerous family and not only so but into a means of repaying the sum he now falls short of and by keeping him steadily to business and short accounts, he will do you no hurt by your friendly support of him and thereby he will be double bound both by gratitude and interest to exert himself. I shall be glad to have your answer to this letter of which or its purpose he knows nothing.

To Tod & Anderson, London

1 November 1762

I duly received yours by private letter of the 26th ult complaining of the not sending to you white Osnaburgs either by Mr Neilson or by me for the Company as you had desired. And that the disappointment may be a loss to the Company for the future as at present. As to Mr Neilson, I cannot pretend until I hear from him particularly on this subject to give you any reason why these goods you desired were not sent. I only know in general that he has complained greatly of the poor and unprofitable proceeds of the goods sent by him to London and has for these many months by past been very much discouraged or to express it more properly quite intimidated. And therefore as I guess, it is that he has not provided the quantities you proposed to him. And I do not believe he or any man will launch out liberally in any one branch where from experience the hazard of loss is greater than the chance is for gain; unless that the factor were to stand a concern in the adventure. With regard to this Company's doings in and about their place, you will please know that I have not one-third of the weavers there was even two years ago. And those remaining from the Army are mostly old people very unfit for making the best white Osnabriggs. What of the weavers are good are employed in making Navy Linens, Sheetings and Osnabriggs of bleached yarns, the last two are mostly all sold in the warehouse here, and the other mostly goes to your house for sale.

As to the proposal of my being at London for four months, I do assure you nothing would give me greater pleasure than the contributing to the planning or the carrying on a business that should prove to the Company's benefit and our mutual satisfaction although I spent three times four months at my own particular charge. But I do not much flatter myself with any great success from it. At least I shall be very shy of proposing any plan to the Directors that is not upon joint account with others, as in that case it may secure the Company the interest of their money for the one half of the adventure. And though my particular interest suffers thereby, I shall save all sorts of reflections being cast on me either in private or in public without going to London. I know that great improvements are as yet wanting to the Linen manufacture both in the fabricating and in the upmaking and in the charge or cost for all these. But it is some danger I find to make some alterations as that will give offence somewhere or other. Not long ago I showed the public how to make up linens at half the expence, nay not one third of the prices paid public lappers, and thereby saved this Company in particular a charge of about £250 per annum but this has been attended with so much bad humour to myself and hurt otherwise to the Company. At the same time I had set about the improvement, I had laid my plan for procurring from Germany their account of preparing their yarns for loom either for sale or in the piece brown or when bleached. This I have procurred at some expence and the hazard of paying more. I am therefore resolved to stop short until I am repaid my charges at least and be satisfied that no evil will come at me from some unforeseen quarter as a return for either my application of time or moneys spent in trying to improve the manufactures. At almost every meeting for this long time past something or other has been said amongst the Directors of the apparently unprofitable trade that has hitherto been carried on with London and sundry propositions have been talked over as to amending it for the future, the enclosed memorandum will show you what is the most approved sentiments hitherto on that subject. And it greatly concerns the well being of the Company to have their trade with London put on a more established and sure footing.

To Tod & Anderson, London

30 December 1762

I have no more Osnabriggs at present of either brown or white than what you have by this fleet, and designed for Mr Beckford, as to Navy linens there are but few of them and mostly all bespoke for customers here.

Mr George Young at Coupar Angus has been here these some days by past settling his accounts with the Company on their concerns in joint purchases and as the loss on sales for 1761 has been so considerable he desired and has obtained leave to be quit of his joint concerns for the goods of anno account 1762.

Chapter Three
DEBT AND DEVOLUTION, 1763-1764

Meeting of the Court of Proprietors

7 March 1763

The Directors also laid before the Court a state of the trade of the Company from balance 1761 to balance 1762, and acquainted the Court 'That upon looking into a state of the debts due to the Company, they had found bad and doubtful debts to a great extent, which had made them come to a resolution to propose to this Court that the Company should give up their present method of trade, and betake themselves to copartneries and adventures in trade with other merchants, who should have the management of the purchases and sales, insure against bad debts and be paid a commission therefore, the Company advancing all the money necessary for carrying on the said joint trade at interest.

'By this method the Company would be as serviceable to the Country as at present, and would no longer run the risk of bad debts. And the interest of the money they should receive, together with the reasonable profits which might be expected by said joint ventures in trade, would in all probability turn out an handsome profit to the Company. This method has the further advantage that the Directors could inspect the whole of the Company's transactions, and give proper orders upon full knowledge of the fact, which was impossible to be done in the long detail of spinning, weaving, bleaching etc that the Company's business has hitherto been in the custom of undergoing; and considerable savings will be made in salaries to clerks and other servants necessary to be employed as the trade has hitherto been carried on.'

They further acquainted the Court 'That Mr McCulloch had by his letter of the 5th current addressed to the Directors demitted his office as Manager from and after the 30th of May next (when the yearly balance of the Company's affairs is to be made). And therefore it becomes necessary that a properly qualified person be chosen in his place. And represented that if it should be the opinion of the Court to alter the plan of trade as above proposed, the proper way of paying their Manager in time coming would be by fixed salary.'

To Tod & Anderson, London

31 March 1763

Yarns prepared in the new or German method makes much better cloth than those done in the old way of milling the yarns. The brightness of the colours I apprehend will be of no difficulty. If Mr Neilson can find a proper spot at Dundee, he is to get a man taught this art to promote it at Dundee. Mr Neilson sent to you lately some 9/8ths wide Osnabriggs which it's possible may be such as your friends want. As to the drapers not liking and their finding fault with our diapers, I am not conscious of any falling back in the fabric. But I know that when an article is not just in demand the quality of the goods is generally depreciated.

Meeting of the Court of Proprietors

4 April 1763

The Directors then acquainted the Court of Proprietors, that in consequence of the plan laid before the last General Court, they had been conferring with Messrs William Alexander & Sons, and Mr Ebenezer McCulloch, who have proposed to undertake the linen trade now carried on at the Company's warehouse in Edinburgh, and to enter into a contract with the Company for that purpose. But as the Directors were not empowered to conclude a treaty upon this head, they could only talk to these gentlemen upon some general articles vizt:

It has been proposed that the contractors shall as at the 30th of May next take the whole linens in the Company's warehouse at Edinburgh, and at the different bleachfields, either at an appraised value, or at the prime cost, as be agreed on. And also relieve the Company of all contracts they have come under for the manufacturing or purchasing of linens, and of their bleachfields and factories. And for a space to be agreed on, carry on that branch on the joint-account of the Company and themselves. That the contractors shall ensure the debts that shall come due to the copartnery, for which they are to have a reasonable allowance. That the contractors find security to the Company for a sum to be agreed on. The contractors to have the transacting of all purchases, sales etc and they a reasonable commission for their trouble. That the copartnery's books be balanced annually, the net profits or loss be mutually divided and paid. That these books be at all time patent to the Directors and Managers for the British Linen Company.

The Directors are encouraged to enter into this copartnery with Messrs Alexander and Mr McCulloch for these views. That they will thereby not only continue their present trade but also enlarge it by means of Messrs Alexanders' house who already carry on the linen trade to a considerable extent. And also that the Company giving up this branch of the trade on the terms aforementioned, will be free of all loss by bad debts which has hitherto sat so heavy upon the Company. And when the Company shall be freed of the great load of business which the trade now proposed to be put into the hands of these contractors necessarily laid them under, the Directors will have under their eye at all times the state of the Company's affairs and thereby be enabled to be more useful and attend better both to the interest of the Company and of the Country than they have hitherto been able to do.

It has been proposed, as a measure equally beneficial to Country and Company that the Company do advance money to manufacturers upon pledges of their goods, which the Directors do heartily approve of, and will as far as prudent carry into execution.

Court of Directors

9 August 1763

Since the 28 of July last when the copartnership of Tod and Anderson, the Company's correspondents at London dissolved, Mr William Tod, one of the partners of that house and formerly one of the Managers for the Company, had been employed to transact the business of the Company there; but that as yet the terms on which he was to serve them had not been agreed.

The Court ordered that he be paid for his trouble in acting for the Company at London as serving them as a factor for the disposal of their goods on the same terms as the aforesaid house of Messrs Tod & Anderson vizt that he Mr Tod shall be allowed at the rate of 2½ per cent commission and 1½ per cent warehouse rent on all goods sold for the Company deliverable at London while the amount of the sales does not exceed £15,000. And while they are under that sum to have allowance for paying or receiving moneys for the Company or making insurances or getting losses made good for them. But if the sales shall exceed £15,000 he is to abate one half per cent of the commission, but in that event to have one-fourth per cent on all bills negotiated for the Company other than for goods sold by him and one-eighth per cent on all insurances transacted, other than for goods consigned him, together with one and one-fourth per cent for making up all average or general losses with the insurers.

It having been represented that the contracts for the different undertakers for the north expire in [blank], and that the copartnery of Ebenezer McCulloch had now agreed to commence new contracts with the said undertakers for three years for carrying on the trade of dressing flax and spinning yarn, as more fully set forth in the scroll of the contract produced. But that in case the copartnery with the said Ebenezer McCulloch should not subsist for the aforesaid space, that then the British Linen Company are to relieve the said copartnery of that agreement and fulfil their engagements with the said undertakers for spinning.

To William Sandeman, Perth

11 October 1763

It will be obliging if you, if possible, can get all the linens on joint account for this season finished at the bleachfields and what part thereof cannot be sold at home they may be immediately consigned to London to any house you think will make the most advantageous sales; only if a new house advise me so I may get the directors to approve of the factor. You some time ago was in hope of considerable quantities of these goods could be sold at Glasgow; I should be glad to know if you can get any part therof disposed but in the meantime it will be very proper that you now begin to purchase for 1764 in which this Company is only to have the concern in the profit or loss but will advance you the value as formerly and as it is probable the goods now on hand of last year's trade may be sold before any of these you're going to purchase be got ready for the market, the which I think can be easily kept distance from the goods on hand; I am humbly of opinion it would be better to delay carrrying them to the debit of the ensuing year's purchases as goods are now upon rise but to endeavour to have them sold before January or February next in order to compensate for what we have lost by last year's acccount. If they cannot be disposed of before that time, it will be brought to transfer them in the way you propose to keep affairs cleared. It makes the settlement easy.

Court of Directors

21 November 1763

The Manager represented that none of his cash transactions since his entering on office had yet been examined by the Court and that upwards of £14,000 of notes wore out in the circulation lay by him ready to be cancelled; he therefore prayed the Court would appoint a committee of their number to meet regularly at the office to examine the cash, cancel notes and give him their directions in the management of the Company's affairs, of which he at present stands much in need, being harassed by the reports current against the Company's credit and the attempts to hurt their circulation.

He acquainted the Court of the letters wrote by Provost Drummond to the several Collectors of Excise in favour of the Company and that they have had a good effect in removing in part the prejudices entertained in the Country against the Company. For which the Court returned their sincere acknowledgements to Mr Drummond.

The Manager further intreated the Court to think on some still stronger method of preventing the effects of the county advertisements bearing 'That the gentlemen etc will accept of no notes but those of the Banks of Edinburgh'. These advertisements having greatly already hurt the circulation of the Company's notes and made the holders of them bring them in great quantities to the office for change; besides the payments made to the two Banks of Edinburgh in their notes to no less amount than £3000 weekly. That this run had already drained him of almost all the money he had received in payments and of the credit with the Royal Bank. And as the Company were disappointed of very considerable payments which should have been made at this season, it became necessary to provide immediately a fund for security against a further run. That what occurred to him as the most proper method of procurring a fund for this purpose was to apply to the Royal Bank (who have always been the Company's friends) to discount bills in the Company's hands payable in London and Edinburgh to the amount of £[blank].

The Court ordered that the Manager do apply to the Royal Bank for a loan of £5000 stg for account of the Company, and that the bills or bond to the Bank be signed by him and sealed with the Company's seal in presence of one of the Directors.

The Manager laid before the Court a letter from Ebenezer McCulloch and Company to him dated the 14th current and desired their directions thereanent. And he represented that the Copartnery had already got from the Company more than the £30,000 stipulated in the contract, it should now be thought of to what further extent they would want and how they were to be supplied.

Court of Directors

4 January 1764

The Court resumed the consideration of a letter from Messrs Ebenezer McCulloch and Company to the Manager received 3rd December last, in which they desire the Court to be acquainted that their sales for the first six months had amounted to £24,551 15/10, and that till such time as the opinion and the orders of the Court were had they would not draw for any more cash from the Company but provide what further cash was necessary from the other partners concerned, allowing them interest for their advances.

The Court resolved that Provost Drummond do acquaint these gentlemen that tho' in the present cirumstances of matters of this Country, they do not think it prudent or proper to advance further than the sum stipulated by contract of copartnery. Yet as Messrs McCulloch & Co seemed to think they could go further with profit, and that they proposed to borrow this money from others on the credit of the copartnery, they desired these gentlemen to meet with them on Friday's afternoon, the 6th current, and to bring with them a note of what money they had borrowed, and to what extent they intended to borrow in this manner.

A sketch of the Company's circulation of notes with the sums due by bonds and promissory notes together with a state of their cash account with the Royal Bank etc having been laid before the Court, the Court ordered that all pains be taken to call in the Company's debts, and that no new credits be issued, but that those to whom credits are already granted to be pressed for bills on London or returns on Edinburgh at short dates.

To John Auldjo, Aberdeen

8 February 1764

As to your Commission I wrote you fully 10th August last, what the Directors proposed to settle with you, & as it was the highest allowed to any, I hoped it would have been acceptable. The next day after writing to you I went out of town for some weeks, on account of my health. And now observe by your letter of the 13 August, you declined the the terms offered to you, on account of the resolutions of the Commissioners of Supply & Trustees of your Country against all those notes but those of the two Banks of Edinburgh. As these are now at an end, or in great measure so, I flattered myself that that you would not have insisted on terms so disadvantageously low, & which indeed the circulation will not bear. In a few days there will be a meeting of the Directors, to whom I shall show our letters of 13 August & 13 July. I know it will be most agreeable to them & it will be highly so to me that you continue your friendships to this Company but I imagine it were better that by encouraging your endeavours for bills you in that way double your commission for the year than that you ask more than double the Commission we pay to other of our friends, in the one way our mutual interests would be served, & as 21 days are allowed to you to make remittances in return for the notes, that article might often be in your favours.

To Tod & Anderson, London

21 February 1764

It is a great loss that we were not allowed to value on T[od] & A[nderson] as the sales fell due when the exchange was greatly in our favour. Mr Bateman writes in a strain in which I do not choose to reply but beg to refer you to his copy book of letters, if he keeps any.[1] He can have no excuse for so long

1 Bateman was the accountant appointed to sort out the financial affairs of Tod & Anderson, that copartnery being in the process of dissolution.

delaying to send the accounts and inventories wanted but more particularly for not examining the accounts of cash due sent him from hence and say I when that may be drawn for since it was not paid for when due. I hope you'll see that the Company are not losers by this delay, at least that they receive interest from those people to whom indulgences are given. As an excuse for not allowing me to draw, Mr Bateman thinks it proper to mark a note of the sums due by Samuel Jeffrey and Sam Touchet of which he says he has not received any payment, but you'll please observe that Messrs T & A stand insurers on the sales for Messrs Cowan & Sandeman which constitute a great part of these debts.

I have long desired a list of the sums outstanding on the sundry sales made by Messrs T & A and in that list there should be noted the date of the sale, the purchaser's name and the amount of his debt that we might if possible get accounts cleared with the sundry gentlemen who consign goods on joint account with us, but no accounts can be got from Mr Bateman, and he even thinks proper to tell me that 'till such time as he sends a clear and distinct account of what money it is possible to collect to answer bills which shall be due soon, any more I draw until I am advised it will be impossible for him to accept without a remittance at sight comes to hand the day they are presented and that they must absolutely be returned if not accepted by some of my friends under protest for my honour.'

This genteel epistle is dated the 2nd current and as I did not chose to draw to put it in this gentleman's power to throw dishonour on this Company's bills, I have waited tho' most impatiently for the fulfilling of this promise of sending these accounts but in vain. And I find now that I must take some other method to prevent the Company as far as in my power from suffering more loss by a discontinuance of this delay. I beg the favour of your advice and assistance in getting this affair put to rights.

To Mr [Richard] Neilson, Dundee

19 March 1764

If the notes in currently payable on demand, can be kept out of improper hands, I would rather choose that they were continued in the Country than brought up & returned to me, but otherways I must submit to that inconvenience, of this I shall be glad to have your sentiments freely—I was sorry to observe that your warehouse was broke into, but they seem to have been very civil thieves, & since you only miss one of the linens in the first hurry of a search, it is to be hoped it will also be found. If not there is no help for it—I dare say you will spare no pains to recover or find out how it has been disposed of. Since the goods on hand agree so exactly with your books you can be at no loss to adjust the inventory at 30 May which pray send up as soon as possible.

We propose to value the goods then on hand at Dundee, Edinburgh and London at an advanced price for rise of markets, interest and petty charges etc. You & I once agreed on the rate for Osnaburgs & the rate for shirtings but as it was not extended, I beg you will assist my memory if you can recollect what was proposed. If not, give me your own opinion.

To Mr [Richard] Neilson, Dundee

22 March 1764

Since writing you 20 current, I have been with My lord Provost who tells me that Mr Tod has wrote to the Board of Trustees that he is attending to the motion made in the House of Commons for taking off the drawback on foreign linens exported, & that they hope for success.[1] My Lord thinks it extremely proper that you continue with the other merchants of your place, in the application you mention 19th current to be intended by them. I observe in the votes in the house that this matter is at present under their consideration & that they have ordered an account of all Linens exported for some years past, properly distinguished, and the drawbacks and Bountys paid thereon to be laid before them.

As Mr Yeaman is just now here I propose by him to send you the £100 you desire in Company notes—I have not seen him since his return from thence but if he stays a day or two I will endeavour to remit the notes also to Mr Strachan—I am not fond of remitting the notes as you propose, nor would I choose that you should value on me for much more money. What notes on demand come naturally into your hands let them be retained & returned me, but do not strain the matter too far. No person who has a regard to the character will be accessory to the passing these notes into improper hands, & the measures used by the banks & us have already had the effect to discourage the trade, & made many of them who plied it, give it up—though still caution is necessary & I wish you & Mr Strachan to prevent as much as possible these notes on demand falling into improper hands.

To Mr [Richard] Neilson, Dundee

9 April 1764

As I wrote you formerly it is extremely proper that you prefer Messrs McCulloch & Co on equal terms to the bleaching & assorting of your linens,

1 The Board had instructed William Tod as their parliamentary agent at London to 'procure all relevant papers': SRO, NG1/3/9, BOTL 16 Feb. 1764. A bill was eventually passed imposing higher duties, and reducing the degree to which these were repaid (or drawn back) upon re-exportation to the West Indian or North American colonies: 7 Geo. III, c. 28.

both on account of their connection with this Company & I really believe it is your interest as Mr Tod always preferred the bleaching & dressing of these linens at Saltonfield to any other.

It is really inconvenient for me at present to be drawn on for more money, & you advised me a considerable time ago that for the drafts now made, you had picked up about £250 or £300 of the Company's old notes payable on demand to be returned to me. You may send these over per first opportunity & Messrs S & N will accomodate you with £50 of optional notes to buy a bill to remit Messrs M & Co. I beg that Mr Strachan & you may remit me largely for the notes sent by his desire. The balance in their hands is high and I want bills on Edinburgh or London if at the current exchange here on their arrival.

I imagine there must be some error as to the purchases for the west kirk poorhouse which shall be enquired into;—do you know the prices say now that transaction is entered in your books, both as to purchase and sale as the bales nos 25, 26, 27 & 28 they were marked B S C not BLC being linens consigned Mr Tod on the Company's own account. Messrs McCulloch & Co have followed their practice of numbering progressively all the bales they ship for this Company and where others are concerned distinguishing the mark by adding the initial letter of that person's name. This however must have surprised you & if you think it attended with any inconveniency I shall cause them alter it for the future.

As I wrote you Mr Young has not forwarded the letter about the yarns (whereof you send me a copy) at least it has not come to my hands, please enquire at him about it. I am sorry to see it wrote in so ambiguous a way, as to leave that triffling matter which has caused so much trouble and uneasiness etc, still undetermined and really to tell you the truth of it is left so I see no probability of its being settled amicably, the Directors and the other party being equally positive they are in the right. For my part I was out of town when the claim for damage was made and refused, and on my return found matters as they still stand. It is surely the interest of the parties that the yarns were sold immediately and that they mutually agree to cooperate in the sale, but this is declined by M[cCulloch] & Co as they allege that they have nothing to do with these yarns and the Directors on the other hand say they were delivered them according to yours and Mr Y[oung]'s agreement and that they were not consulted or advised about as to the picking of these from others which were sold before the demand for these were made. As a friend to both parties I wish heartily that the matter was settled.

Court of Directors

24 April 1764

The Court having taken into consideration the state of their trade with Messrs Robert and William Alexander and Ebenezer McCulloch in virtue of a contract of copartnery executed between the Company and them on the thirtieth of May last, and from many circumstances it appearing to them expedient that this copartnery should be dissolved in terms of the twenty-fifth article of the said contracts at the end of eighteen months from the said thirtieth of May. They therefore ordered Mr Goldie, the Manager for the Company to give notice to the said Messrs Robert and William Alexander and Ebenezer McCulloch personally or at their dwelling houses under form of instrument that the British Linen Company are in terms of the said article to dissolve the aforesaid copartnery upon the thirtieth day of November next, and the aforesaid intimation to be made six months previous to that day.

Ebenezer McCulloch & Co. to George Goldie [British Linen Company Office, Edinburgh]

5 June 1764

We desire that you will acquaint the Directors that it is full time for taking steps for supplying the North country spinners and Mr Richard Neilson with flax, we are yet in advance for last year's flax as the Directors declined supplying us with money to pay the bills drawn for it; the sum wanted for this year will be about £6,500 and will fall due between September and November next. The Directors will please now determine whether they are to do this themselves or enable us to do it, so as we take our measures, but as we are subject to warehouse rents and the wages of clerks in the copartnery's service, whoever makes the purchase, the Directors we hope will think it reasonable that we be allowed the usual commission on the sales.

We applied some months ago for liberty to consign sundry goods for London with which we were loaded at entering into the copartnery. This has been hitherto refused. We must therefore request that the Directors will now either relieve us from these goods, by taking them at first cost with interest or allow us to send them to London together with such others as may be necessary to send to that market, since they will be sensible that we cannot continue to pay interest for goods which are totally unsaleable here. We are stopping all purchases of goods but we are under a necessity of taking such goods as are now manufacturing by our orders previous to the intimation but which soon will be delivered.

You will also please acquaint the Directors that the linens damaged by bleaching to the amount of £400 7/- exclusive of interest lie at their disposal. We shall have an abundance of trouble disposing of the sound goods as the copartnery will soon be dissolved and therefore desirous of getting free of all such as we can legally dispense ourselves from.

Ebenezer McCulloch & Co. to George Goldie, Edinburgh

7 June 1764

Subjoined you have a note of the particular quantities of flax wanted for the North country spinners amounting in all to 90 tons, as to Mr Neilson he last year desired an importation to be made of about 60 tons of flax but this year he has not as yet required any to be imported on account of the high prices abroad but it's probable he may soon now demand that quantity at least for the support of trade and customers. There appears to be due betwixt and December or rather January next for goods sold to the amount of £13,300 or thereby, from which must be deducted advances made by Messrs Alexanders, Geo Young and our Mr E.M. to the amount of about £6,900, which necessarily must be repaid out of the first moneys coming in. There is besides the above £13,300 that may be expected in payments a supply of cash from yarns that may be sold in that period and what goods may be sold for money, but it is more than probable that the above sales and cash will not make up the deficiences by nonpayments on the above £13,300 due betwixt and January next.

About 4 or 5 months ago we intimated to all our manufacturers not to have a dependence on us for more than half the quantities they were in use to furnish the B.L.Co annually by reason we were uncertain what might be the event of the importations of foreign linens expected this year from Germany. It was however necessary to have a proper assortment so as to keep our customers and supply our bleachfield which we have endeavoured to the best of our power and judgement. The sundry manufacturers in the country and in this place with whom we deal may demand us to take goods to the amount of about £1800, and which we must accept of, if well done, and tendered at the present market prices, at any time in two months yet to come, but from that value will fall to be deduced about £1400 value due us for yarns. The goods we formerly wanted to consign Mr Hamilton were clouting Diapers and Sheeting. These goods are still on hand and you have herewith a note thereof. Mr Tod had an assortment of these diapers sent him not yet sold. Mr Anderson has another which has been sold to loss. Mr Hamilton promised on seeing the goods to make us sales without loss as he apprehended, and from some former experience we were inclined to believe he might do so, and this is all the interest we have in him to recommend him to a preference.

There are however sundry goods likely to be sent for sale to the London market occasioned by some interruption to our African trade which usually carried off quantities of these low-priced linens made up into what is called platilloes. We have wrote to almost all our usual customers, but as yet have received no orders or replies, and we shall now soon know the truth of the report that the trade has met with some interruption abroad, and if so must try for sale at London, as these goods are bought for printing as well as for exportation to Africa. In this event we will be obliged to employ factors in the usual way, and it is then to be considered what is the speediest way of bringing the goods into cash and with the most advantage in point of sales. We last year employed four houses vizt Mr Tod, Messrs Anderson & Davidson, Mr Hamilton, and Messrs Eadie & Laird, the last of whom proved both dilatory and unprofitable in their sales. The others acted with attention to our interest and of this we gave you an account stating the trade with London particularly.

Ebenezer McCulloch to George Goldie, Edinburgh

20 June 1764

In reply to yours of this date, we shall take all due care of the Sheetings you have asked to be bleached at Salton Field. And I shall also bleach those diapers of Mr Campbell's you mention. But we should be glad to know if the quantity you mention to be come and about to come from Neilson of Dundee is over and above a quantity of about 20,000 yards of shirting he himself bespoke room for about two months or six weeks ago as that will make a great difference to the profits of Salton field. We this year pay the same rent as agreed on by contract and have hired in servants for the season accordingly, but by the stop put to the trade we shall not have above ⅔rds of the quantity we could bleach there. We have provided about 7000 pieces. The master of the field says he can finish from 10 to 12,000 pieces so that you can safely engage for 60 to 80,000 yards of linen worth from 8d to 20d per yard brown to bleach this season and we should be much obliged to you helping us in this dilemma.

To George Blaikie, Perth

25 June 1764

I am favoured with yours of the 23rd current & observe you do not relish the proposals I made you of holding a cash account with this Company, on any other terms than formerly and though these are almost generally discontinued, I shall talk to the Directors in your favours and if they allow me shall continue to correspond with you on the same footing. In the meantime I shall by first opportunity forward you the £200 you desire. I entirely disapprove of the methods you mention to be used by some of our friends in your place in circulating this Company's notes, but as no such remittances are made me, I am at a loss to account for their conduct.

I would wish to have a conversation with you on this subject, or that you would write me a private letter mentioning the Persons who follow this practice—as you are particularly favoured in the continuance of your allowance in this circulation, I hope it will render you more zealous in this Company's interests and I beg the favour that the terms etc of our correspondence be kept to ourselves & not communicated to others. I wish to offend nobody, but I find this practice of allowing premiums has led to many abuses & it is extremely proper for this company to check them. As to their new banks I do not see anything to be apprehended there from, but that the gentlemen concerned will hurt themselves in place of doing a service. I mean if they do as they ought, bring Specie from England to answer their notes and not live on their neighbours, and the increasing of these Societys will evidently hasten the Parliament putting an end to all private banking which they are to have under their consideration this ensuing session.[1]

To George Blaikie, Perth

27 June 1764

I have yours of yesterday & note the contents. I am sorry that Mr Brown or any agents of our Neighbour Societys should use us so ill & I wish to prevent it as much as possible & will take well the Services of our friends in that Respect, but I do not choose to retaliate such injuries, for there is no end to that sort of trade and it is in my Opinion both dishonorable & ridiculous. I see you have got a third Bank with you which is very well, the more there are of them the sooner there will be some check put to the frenzy. It is not long since a Cobler erected a Bank as he called it at Tranent & issued notes which being in like and form to the Edinburgh notes passed for some little time among the Country people, till both they & he disappeared. There still remains a sufficient number of such Societys & they daily increase both with you & elsewhere. Leith & Bo'ness, I am told, have now each a Bank, & perhaps will soon have three. The mischief is, besides the risk the country runs by this abuse of credit, that none of these little banks bring one shilling of Specie from England, to answer their notes but in place thereof drain the societys who are at that Expense to supply the country.

1 A Bank Act was passed in 1765, the preamble to which referred to the need 'to prevent the inconveniences arising from the present method of issuing bills by banks, banking companies, and bankers in that part of Great Britain called Scotland': Checkland, *Scottish Banking*, 113-21.

To Alex[ander] Anderson & Davidson, London

19 July 1764

Your favours of the 7th July came to my hands only on the 16th, having been mis-sent and appears to have been at York. Enclosed is Geo[rge] Butt of the Tay's receipt for three packs and one bundle linen shipped by James Marshall, Newburgh, and consigned you for sale on his account. Mr Wm. Sandeman of Perth advises me of having shipped by the forementioned ship the Tay 3 Bales Linens WS N 91 92 & 93 consigned you for Sale on account of this Company & said Mr Sandeman, which you will please to advise me you are to account for this Company as usual & place the neat proceeds to this credit.

There have been so many delays & scandalous usage to this Company about messrs T & A's affairs that the Directors have resolved to put up no longer with the partners, blaming one another & different clerks is what we have nothing to do with nor will interfere in but that house must do us justice & exhibit a fair & just state of our effects & debts committed to their charge or we will take other measures to oblige all concerned to do so. It is become a serious affair to this Company & they are determined on immediate satisfaction being given. Let you and Mr Tod consider what they have suffered by keeping all their accounts open in which that house was concerned & you cannot blame this Company were they forever to withdraw their Consignments from both. Your delays have already deprived you of money as the proprietors of the goods would not consign to houses who had used them so ill. I still hope that you will eventually exert your duty & do all concerned immediate justice & prevent the certain consequences of a longer delay. You are sensible this Company are well disposed to serve you & your friends if you show them that you have their interests & your own honour at heart.

Ebenezer McCulloch & Co. to W[illiam] Boats, Liverpool

30 July 1764

We had the pleasure to receive your most obliging favours of the 23rd current ordering 2,000 p[iece]s of Silesias to be sent you at 10d per yard in 4 weeks. We are just now looking out the goods and hope to furnish them such as to merit your future favours to us. But it will take four weeks to cut, tie and paper these 2,000 p[iece]s and one week more to assort, packup and dispatch these goods so that you may be sure of having them laid down at Dumfries to any person's care you shall name on the 6th week from this date. In chosing these Silesias we will be necessitated to take some from ¼ to ½d per yd lower, and others from ¼ to ½d higher but on the average so as to come out at 10d per yd. It will not be practicable to send these goods safe and free from chaffing unless they are either packed up in puncheons or in cases of wood, and subjoined you have a note of the expence in both for your election, which you will be pleased to mention to us in course of post. If you will be as good as to give us your order now for these 5,000 p[iece]s Silesias you say will be wanted some time this fall, we could by having time to finish them up neatly and by due care in the chosing them, provide you much better and more for your liking than when called for in haste, and tho' your orders come early, yet the date of the credit will only run from the date of dispatching them.

Ebenezer McCulloch to James Armstrong, Salton

1 August 1764

I sent out yesterday my own cart with 120 p[iece]s Silesias to make a beginning in the upmaking of 3000 platillos I have just now got an order for. And of these 2000 p[iece]s must be ready in three weeks hence and the other thousand in eight days thereafter. I cannot imagine it possible for Alexander Gray and his present assistants to be capable to dispatch the goods in the time I am limited to without you give some special assistance. And for that purpose I desire you would cause Peter Stewart and Arch Howden to help us in this strait and I shall be willing and ready to give all of the lads to be employed in this job such additional gratuity as you think may be equitable and Gray says they deserve in proportion to their diligence. I have still complaints about their not being done up so neat and firm as the foreign and likewise that the paper is not so fine as it should be. Pray show this to Alex Gray and let him exert himself both in the firm tying up and glazing of the paper as I doubt not you will in the proper starching of the linens. I apprehend young Hill might be employed in this affair too. He certainly would serve well enough in holding to a lapper and save the labour of a better man. I pray that you see everything may be done to hasten this job.

To John Mackay, Cyderhall

16 August 1764

You will see by the docket of the account that all the former contracts of Spinning are thereby discharged, excepting only your agreement with Messers McCulloch & Co. for flax delivered last year part whereof is yet to be delivered by you in yarns to them. All which you will please to conform & approve of by a letter to me as Manager for the British Linen Company. I likeways will send you by Mr Sommervaile, two contracts for Spinning Flax into yarns, signed by me on the part of this Company, & which you will please sign & return to me one copy noting the date & place of signing, witnesses' names & designations. I refer you to the contract itself, which you will find conceived in the most favourable terms possible for your interest. As you insist on having the flax insured from Cromarty to Brora & Cyderhall at this Company's risk if not delivered at Cromarty on or before the month of August the Directors, though they would not stand insurers themselves, have agreed to allow you eight pounds Stg. this year in consideration of the risk in transporting your twelve tons of flax from Cromarty. This is because the ship this year cannot be expected sooner at Cromarty than the end of Sept. or sometime in the month of October next, you binding your self to insure this flax against sea risk at Edinburgh or London & to pay the expense thereof, & bear any loss which the underwriters may not be subject to. They intend that next year the flax ship shall come earlier in the season, & therefore they are to pay no money on this head to you, as you agree that if the flax is delivered at Cromarty any time in or preceding the month of August that the risk was to be your own without any allowance from them. If the flax does not arrive next year till September or October & you insist on it, the regulation in the contract, for this present year will also take place. All this you will also please confirm to me by a letter. I refer you to Mr Sommervaille for what the Edinburgh underwriters said about the opening a policy on that flax, I have wrote to London to enquire on what terms it can be done there, what they here seem to dread is the average[1] on the flax as transported in open boats, but this Mr Sommervaile does not seem to think of any consequence as it comes immediately to your own warehouses & under your own care in case of any small damage. But as the Company allows you £8 to account of this insurance, it will possibly cost you very little more to insure even against average loss at London if you think it necessary; but as to this I can say nothing till I receive a return of my letter.

I have now only to beg that you will give me distinct orders as to making this insurance for you, that no mistake may happen which in those matters is very dangerous. I hope this contract as it is still more favourable for you than any of the former will be expected as performed by both parties with the greatest ease of satisfaction as all the former were. It was really chiefly with this view & to satisfy all claims that this Company consented to sacrifice £8 on account of this insurance, which was not asked in any former contracts. As I hope often to correspond with you, & have daily occasion to write to London with bulky papers I would beg the favour you will procure from your friend Col. McKay who I hear is just now with you, two or three dozen of Franked Covers, one dozen whereof may be directed to you & the rest to Mr Willm. Tod, Merch. London. Mr Sommervaille tells me that small notes are much wanted in your country particularly in the months of September & October

1 'Average' denotes the special allowance made by insurers to ships' masters for extraordinary losses in trans-shipment. See John Mair, *Book-keeping Modernized* (Edinburgh, 1800), 607.

for bank bills & other good bills on Edinburgh & that it would be for this Company's advantage to send you some notes for procuring such bills. If you will take this trouble & answer for the goodness of the bills you send me, I shall be much obliged to you & provide you with what notes you advise me to be proper for this purpose.

Court of Directors

27 August 1764

The Directors ordered the sums demanded by Lord Milton and the Royal Bank should be paid, and that provision for paying these and the flax be made by pushing Messrs Ebenezer McCulloch & Co and the other debtors of the Company to make regular payments and in the meantime to discount as usual what good bills offer on London or Edinburgh and to issue cash credits to such persons concerned in the linen trade as shall be approved of and thereby to keep up the circulation of the Company's cash notes to eighty thousand pounds sterling in all.

The Manager informed the Court that in consequence of the approbation of Messrs Drummond and Kinloch, Wallace Gardyne & Co of Arbroath were allowed a credit in the Company's books per bond for five hundred pounds and that David Sandeman, Perth, was allowed a like credit for the like sum on William, George and Thomas Sandemans' security, of both which the Directors approved.

Ebenezer McCulloch to George Goldie, Edinburgh

10 September 1764

In the month of May you were pleased to intimate to us your resolution of dissolving the present copartnery against the 30th of November. Sometime after, you informed us of your inclination to enter into a new contract with us for the purchase and sale of linen only and to employ a capital of £20,000 in that branch. We were referred to Mr James Guthrie for the particulars of your plan, and after sundry conversations with him, we delivered to him in writing heads of articles for a contract, such as we thought equitable. Since then we have heard nothing from you or Mr Guthrie on that subject. As the time of the dissolution of our last contract fast approaches, and as it is of the greatest consequence to both parties that it be immediately determined whether we are to continue together or not, we must beg for an answer on that head. You will be sensible that if the trade is at all to be continued there must be no stop in providing goods for the current demands since we would otherwise be unable to answer them and our customers will go to others. We have with a great deal of trouble established an advantageous trade and obtained a set of the best customers in this country to take off our goods, as will appear by our sales and we would justly incur your blame if the benefit of our labour were lost to the Company without our giving you timely notice, to put it in your power to prevent it. We have hitherto gone on providing the necessary goods to continue the trade on the faith of it being your intention to do so. We have however been gradually lessening our stock of goods to accommodate matters to the proposed diminution of capital. But we do not think it prudent to go further without a certainty of your intentions. We must beg to know whether we are henceforth to confine ourselves to the liquidation of the copartnery's affairs or whether it is your intention to continue the trade, and execute a new contract for that purpose, as our conduct must be regulated by your answer.

To Robert and William Alexander & E. McCulloch, Edinburgh

13 September 1764

I am ordered by the Court of Directors of the BLC to acquaint you that they have this day received your letter of the 10th current & in answer thereto they have desired me to inform you that considering the present situation of the Company's affairs and of the country in general, they think it improper to enter into any new contract of Copartnery with you, and that you should therefore regulate yourselves accordingly in bringing in the Effects & debts of the present Copartnery as speedily as possible. They likeways expect you will punctually comply with the contract in paying in to the Company daily whatever sums you receive in the Specie that is paid to you. And I have got in strict charge to answer no further drafts of yours as you have already so far exceeded both the original contract and the after concessions made you for assorting the warehouse. The Directors desire that your books may be brought to a speedy balance to 30 April last & delivered into this office that they may be examined.

To J[onathan] Gray, Town Clerk of Haddington

22 September 1764

I am this moment favoured with yours of this date. You need be in no apprehension nor any of your friends on account of the notes of this Company that were forged. They were in all only four which two little rogues pilfered from their Book binder while the blank copperplates were binding by him. The books were found to want these four notes and they afterwards appeared at this office with forged subscriptions, were traced and the young men are in close confinement. One of them has confessed the other remains obdurate but both were formerly worthless dogs and this is only a more Capital Fault. The notes of this Company are filled up by the different clerks and you will observe a variety of hands, but these dated preceeding 1763 are signed by

Mr McCulloch and these dated 1st June 1763 by me as Manager for the BLC and both by James Gordon as accountant. I am obliged to you for your concern in observing these notes, but as there are no forged ones in the circle you may acquaint your friends thereof and remove their scruples as such things may be misconstrued & hurt our circulation. It was entirely without my knowledge that the paragraph was inserted by the Mercury on Wednesday.

To Messrs Jno. Anderson & Co., Perth

3 October 1764

If you have occasion for any of this Company's notes please advise me. Dr Mudie tells me he is to return to Perth on Friday. I, and with great truth, assure you that I am very far from believing you or any of this Company's correspondents in Perth make improper use of this Company's notes on demand. But we observe them come to our hands from Riders & they say they got them from the Bank of Perth. I will willingly pay value to these banks or their correspondents here for our notes but it is hard that they should give either these or our optional notes in exchange for their own to people who must have Specie or Bills on London of short dates. I am always for each Society paying their own notes, not laying that burden on other people which is really the case as I observe since these Banks were erected that a very large proportion of our notes which can be paid in here on cash accounts with the Edinburgh Banks come now by riders upon ourselves. If this is not remedied easily we must some other way put a stop to it. I wish to live in peace with every man and every society if possible, and think it is the interest of these gentlemen to be well with us and not declare war in this manner. These things I hint to you as our good friends and if you can advise me how we may remedy these causes of complaints, it will be obliging. I am sure I never gave any of them the smallest reason to complain of this Company who have been, you well know, of great use to your Country. I thank you for your promise of London Bills when you draw. They are at present very plenty and cheap here.

To David Sandeman, Dundee

3 October 1764

I was favoured with yours of the 1st Current and think you are extremely right in not launching deep in trade when Markets are so much glutted. I thank you for your promise of supplying me with bills against the term and circulating our notes for same. Wherein I can at any time serve you, you know you may command me. There will certainly be some salutory regulations next winter as to paper currency which will remove the present complaints. You may remit me the £100 you mention when you find a proper opportunity. What money Mr Neilson or our friends at Perth want, I will send them from hence. Bills on London are very plenty here at present and no buyers.

To David Campbell, Dunfermline

27 November 1764

I am very favoured with yours of yesterday enclosing one for Mr Tod which I have forwarded with John Grieg of the Mary & Janet [with] his receipt for the 4 packs diaper consigned to Mr Tod. I really wish for the cost invoice of these goods, as your not sending them with the London invoice may occasion their being overlooked as I suspect this may in some degree already have happened. I wish you to note to me how they stand with you. It will not I dare say be for your interest to overstock your factors in goods. You should certainly regulate your shipping by their sales and advices. The Directors of this Company will I dare say have no objections to your sending the goods you mention to Hanna and Son and will I know do all in their power consistent with the Company's interest to accommodate you. Mr Goldie is for this day in the country.

Meeting of the Court of Proprietors

3 December 1764

The Directors further report that of the debts deemed desperate at 30th May 1763, amounting per report of the Directors and Committee of Proprietors 4th June 1764 to Twenty-two thousand and thirteen pounds, there was recovered at 30th May 1764 Four hundred and twenty nine pounds, as since that time Four hundred and thirty one pounds stg.

[The Following Memorandum was incorporated in the Minute of the Meeting:]

A Short View of the Trade presently carried on by the British Linen Company.

The Company at considerable charge introduced the spinning of linen yarns into the Highlands of Scotland, which is now in such perfection as will afford them considerable advantage. This trade employs from about 6 to 8000£ of the Company's money annually, and is of the utmost consequence to the Country as no private society is equal to such an undertaking. The Company are at present in advance for this branch £5380.

The Company when they find it can be done with safety, and when they think it for the advantage of the Country, take ¼ or ½ share in the purchases of linen; and in that case they advance the whole money to the manufacturers or linen dealers, and wait their reimbursement from the sale of the goods. This at present supports a number of these manufacturers and dealers who from the smallness of their capital would otherwise be obliged to give up business. On this branch the Company at present are under advance for sundries £21,125 independent of their advance on account of the Copartnery with Ebenezer McCulloch & Company, £32,991. The Company likewise advance money on linens consigned to London, in which they have no share of the profit nor bear any part of the loss. In this way the linen dealer has the entire direction of the sales of his goods, and is not tied down to the Company's correspondents, but is at liberty to consign his goods to such houses as are of good credit, and who as he thinks, will render him the quickest and most profitable sales; the factors giving obligation to account to the Company for the proceeds when sold. On this branch are under advance £4166.

The Company advance to the manufacturers and linen dealers, ¾ value of the linens at the bleaching, by which they are enabled to sustain a long outlay of money, and at the same time to keep the manufacturing of linen agoing. On this branch, as it is the end of the bleaching season, the Company are only in advance £759. The Company advance money to the manufacturers and linen dealers for carrying on their trade, upon such personal security as the Company think consistent with their own safety, and on this branch they are now in advance £14,829. The Company have a bleachfield at Salton which is now valued at £3700 in their books. It is at present set at £200 rent, but if in their own hands, as in the year 1763, would throw off more than double that profit. In 1763 it cleared the interest of £5479 and left £549 profit.

The Company likewise discount bills, payable in Scotland and in England to the manufacturers and linen dealers. On this branch they are now in advance £11,918. The Company were in use formerly to pay considerably by way of premiums for the circulation of their notes; which practice they have now in a great measure done away with, as they have confined their circulation to what is absolutely necessary for the support of the manufacturers and dealers who have for some time past been dependent on the Company's friendship.

The Company from 30th May 1763 to 30th May 1764 carried trade conform to the above plan; and they are apt to believe from the offers of business made them in that way from all parts of this Kingdom, that they have been of real service to the manufacturers of the country. And it is evident, tho' encumbered with a load of debts due to them, which they could not command, they have on the above plan, in the course of one year, cleared £3781. And it is to be observed that before striking the above profit, all possible care was taken to fit the Company's accounts exactly and justly, that their affairs might neither appear in a more favourable or more unfavourable point of view than they ought; and further that the above sum of profit did not arise from accidental advantages, but from fixed and determined principles of trade, which if properly attended to, will always continue the same.

The court thereafter named Lord Kames, Messrs Whitefoord, Boyes, Guthrie, Tyler, and John Tod as a Committee of Proprietors, to meet with the Directors and consider the said state, and the above plan of trade followed by the Directors since 30 May 1763 (independent of their late copartnery). And also to consider of any proposals that may be made by their late copartners Messrs Alexanders and McCulloch. And appointed the Directors and said committee of Proprietors, after considering of said matters, to report their opinion upon the whole to the next General Court which is adjourned to Monday the seventh day of January next.

To William Forsyth, Cromarty

17 December 1764

I wrote you on the 15th current and agreeable thereto have this day made application to the Board of Customs here to allow you to return by the Expedition Capt Inglis for Leith the six tons of flax unloaded by mistake & what yarns you may have ready for Leith; as to all which the Board here have by this post given orders to their officers & Messrs A & G Guthrie the owners of the vessel have wrote to Capt Inglis. If that ship is sailed please to get an opportunity to ship the flax for Mr Richard Neilson at Dundee, where it is much wanted, but if that is not to be had you must just send it to Leith per Paterson's vessel as you proposed, advising me in all of these cases that I may make insurance.

I come now more particularly to reply to yours of the 26th Nov., 5th and 10th Dec. acknowledged in my last. Since things have happened thus with regard to Mr Anderson, it is a pity you had not allowed that flax to remain in the vessel as I wrote you formerly, & saved the trouble and expense of reshipping it but Mr Anderson deceived us all. As the Company have again taken all these contracts into their own hands we will in all things act so as shall [be] most for the interest of all concerned. And I beg to know from you against what time you would choose the next year's quota of flax should it be delivered at Cromarty. I am thoroughly convinced of the impropriety of its being late in the season but that we were obliged to submit to this year on sundry accounts. Pray yourself, & cause the other undertakers, keep the flax now delivered by this Company separate in every respect from any that may be delivered by Messrs. McC[ulloch] & Co. Send them the produce of their own, and this Company the produce of this. I must beg the favour that you will take the trouble to make out the accounts thereof with as great exactness as possible both for yourself & the other undertakers & send them to me. It surely can be done so as on the whole to make a very triffling if any error & your care & exactness therein will be a particular favour done me.

I observe you are to draw on Messrs McC[ulloch] & Co to this Company's order and to send me a full state of Harry Munro's effects, which is well. Pray, what is become of him? I see your brother has bought the damaged flax; I am glad to see that there is no great quantity of it and that you commend the shipmaster who shall be rewarded for his care. It gives me pleasure that the quality of the flax pleases you. I shall acquaint Mr Zuckerbecker thereof. When I have examined and entered the delivery of the flax I shall send the sundry undertakers their accounts. In the meantime you will please acquaint them of what I write you about this flax and the yarns from the former cargoes. From the quality of the flax you will be able to judge of each grist of yarn I may expect, and which I would like to know as nearly as you could guess for my regulation.

Chapter Four
DISENGAGEMENT, 1765-1775

Meeting of the Court of Proprietors

7 January 1765

The minutes of the last Court being read were confirmed. Thereafter the following report was made to this Court by the Court of Directors and Committee of Proprietors, vizt.

Edinburgh 31st December 1764. The Committee of Proprietors named by the last General Court report that having frequently met with the Directors, and with great attention considered the plan of trade presently carried on, and which was laid before the last General Court; They highly approve thereof, as equally beneficial to the Country and to the Company; two interests, which as as far as possible ought to be united in all the transactions of the Company.

The Committee particularly approve,

1. Of the Company's continuing to carry on the spinning of linen yarn in the North of Scotland, and of their importing flax for sale.

2. Of the Company's taking any share, not exceeding one half, in the purchases of linen when it can be done with safety; advancing the whole value to the manufacturers or linen dealers, and waiting the sale of goods for reimbursement. But are of opinion that the Directors should not deal very extensively in this article, as it requires a long advance, and can be attended with no considerable profit to the Company, and subjects them to risks, which in the concerns of a general company ought to be avoided.

3. The Committee approve of the Directors having put an end to the Copartnery with Messrs Alexander and McCulloch, not only for the said reasons, but also that they have had about £35,000 locked up since May 1763, which is extremely inconvenient in a Management which requires a quick circulation of money. On application to Messrs Alexander and McCulloch they find they have no proposals to make to the Company for a new contract.

4. The Committee approve of the advancing money to the manufacturers, upon getting the goods in pledge, and taking the persons in whose hands these goods are deposited bound to account for the proceeds when sold. And if the Directors keep their advance within three-fourths of the value, the Company

will be secure against loss. And when the sales are made at London, the Company will be supplied with money there for making their payments.

5. The same approbation is given to the advancing money on the pledges of goods at the bleachfields, and the Company's warehouse especially as this measure is greatly for the advantage of the linen trade, and highly acceptable to the Country in general.

6. The advancing of money to manufacturers and linen dealers upon good personal security is approved of. And lastly the Committee above all, approve of the plan for discounting good bills due to manufacturers, as a branch of trade both convenient and beneficial to the Company and to the manufacture in general.

As to the extent of each of these articles, the committee are of opinion that this must be left to the Directors, who can best judge of the interest of the Company, and how far from time to time these articles ought to extended.

Considering the handsome profits cleared last year by the care and vigilance of the Directors, independent of their copartnery with Messrs Alexander and McCulloch, the committee think the Court of Directors entitled to the thanks of the General Court; and they submit whether the General Court ought not to acknowledge their good offices accordingly. Signed Henry Home.

The Court approved of the above report and recommended to the Directors to continue the trade on that plan. They likewise recommended to the Directors to give in to the next General Court a list of such proprietors who have not yet paid up their calls, and to report what in their opinion will be the most effectual method for to procure their being paid up.

The Court further authorised the Directors and Committee of Proprietors who are continued for that purpose to concur with Messrs Alexander and McCulloch in winding up the affairs of the copartnery in the easiest and most amicable manner, and even to allow them some time longer than stipulated by the contract (if the Directors and Committee shall judge it proper) for disposing of their stock of goods.

Ebenezer McCulloch & Co. to George Goldie, [Edinburgh]

9 February 1765

We are sorry you should find so much difficulty in your banking department and would willingly give you every assistance. But as to the state you gave us of the funds that you suppose we may force in, we apprehend you may find yourself under some mistakes. The condition of our obligation will be fulfilled as exactly as possible, after the advances made, which were agreed to be replaced from the first payments, are satisfied. We are sorry for your opinion of Alex Flemming and since our proposal does not seem to suit your views, you will no doubt follow out the measures you see best. We have had dealings with Mr Flemming both in purchase and sale, but cannot discover any obligation we are under in honour or otherwise undertake for his debt to the Company; at the same time were it in our power, we would do everything consistent that could make the Company easy. We said in our former that the balance between the debit and credit of Mr Flemming's account was much about £12. But we may have made a mistake, tho' not quite so far as your clerks when they accumulated both debit and credit into one article of charge; upon your view of matters the Company's claim in place of £75 would only be £52 5/6, but we apprehend the matter on due consideration will appear different.

With regard to your letter of the 7th, it will greatly depend on the Directors of the Company themselves, whether we keep the warehouses as presently possessed for another year. For, if they allow of the stock of goods upon hand their being sold off to best advantage as called for, in that case we readily agree to possess the warehouses. But if the Directors mean to force a sale of the stock on hand by public roup, there will be but too much loss to sustain from that concern, without enduring more by engaging to pay such heavy rents, as the whole of the warehouses here amount to. If the Directors shall still however be for selling off the stock on hand by public roup, in that case E McCulloch will take the low warehouses, the counting room and warehouse in the intersale ['intersalle' or 'between-hall'], together with the packing house and pay such rent for the same as two skilled persons to be mutually chosen shall value them at. We are sorry that you should put yourselves to any inconvenience by printing your notes anywhere but here, for at any time you may command the use of the little writing room adjoining the upper warehouse and that without any stipulation for that purpose. Whatsoever solution the Directors may take, we mean to quit the warehouses at Leith at the ensuing term. We have been busied for sometime bypast in taking an exact inventory of the effects of the Copartnery, and hope now in a few days to be able to lay the same before the Directors and we are also as sollicitous to get in cash as possible, but still so as not to take indiscreet measures with people to whom we are much obliged for their custom.

Court of Directors

9 August 1765

The Manager laid before them a letter, 12th July last, from William Tod of London of which follows a copy; 'Sir, the British Linen Company have of late greatly reduced their consignments of goods to London, and I find several of the Proprietors there are informed that the Company intends to abandon the intention of their charter and give up all future concerns in the linen trade. I am satisfied this information is wrong, and that it is for very prudent reasons that your consignments are lessened. If you will look into the account of consignments made me for these two years past, you will find your payments not only pointed and regular, but you have drawn for the value in less than twelve months after the sales have been made. In my humble opinion a certain value of goods consigned to London in the manner you have done for these two years past, is equal to so much money invested in the funds at an interest of 5 to 6 per cent, which you may upon any emergency avail yourself of. And I submit to your Directors whether or not the continuance of that trade to a certain extent is prudent and necessary.

'As I am now in this country and will have an opportunity of conversing with sundry people with whom you have been connected in trade, I should be glad to know to what extent the Company would go in that branch for the ensuing year, and to remove every difficulty as far as in my power. I will agree for this year that in case the Company have any extraordinary demands, you may draw on me for the value of the goods consigned and if remittances for these drafts shall be found necessary, I shall charge no commission; by this means you shall always have the command of the Company's funds and have an opportunity of circulating your notes in the natural way as well as promoting the linen manufactures agreeable to your charter.'

Court of Directors

28 January 1766

The Manager read to the Court Ebenezer McCulloch's letter of the 10th current informing the Company that he is at Whitsunday next to give up the house now possessed by him, and also the warehouses occupied by him and by the company and the Manager informed the Court that in consequence of this letter he had, by desire of Messrs Young Muir & Kinloch, made offer of the warehouses to the Board of Trustees for a Linen Hall at the rent of seventy pounds per annum.[1]

The Court approved of the offer made the Trustees as to the warehouses, and ordered the dwelling house to be possessed by Mr Goldie, the present Manager, from Whitsunday next and his allowance of twenty pounds per annum for house set to cease from that time.

1 This was a scheme modelled on the successful Irish Linen Hall in Dublin (to which English merchants were said to flock), to try to draw English buyers to Scotland and reduce the usage of factors at London. George Goldie was put in overall charge.

Court of Directors

11 March 1766

The Manager acquainted the Court that he had now engaged a ship to go to Riga, in consequence of which the Directors ordered him to commission eighty tons of flax for Cromarty and Leith & to employ Zuckerbecker & Company as usual.

The Court having considered that Mr Bannerman, Minister at Salton had, when the bleachfield was last in the Company's own hands, a great deal of trouble about it, ordered the Manager to present him with a piece of Linen about four shillings a yard.

The Court ordered an advertisement to be put into the newspapers, that the Company were now taking in linens to bleach at Salton and desired the Manager to write the sundry Manufacturers from whom Linens may be expected to bleach that the Company will advance them for three or six months a half or two thirds of the value of what they send to the Company's field.

There was read to the Court a scroll of two circular letters, the one regarding the dissolution of the Copartnery and the procuration they have granted to Mr Goldie for calling in their debts, the other acquainting the Linen dealers that the Company now carried on the Linen Trade as formerly and could supply their friends with what Linens they were pleased to order, of both which letters the Court approved and ordered the Manager to get them printed & sent off immediately, and further to acquaint Messrs Alexander & McCulloch that the Directors thought it proper that Mr Goldie as their Procurator should take the Copartnery books into his possession and send off the accounts as soon as possible.

Court of Directors

24 June 1766

Present: George Drummond, John Young & Pa[trick] Lindesay Esqrs.

The Directors ordered the Manager to continue to advance money, on what Linens are sent to the Company's bleachfield and to take bills at six months date on the money so advanced and an assignation of the goods in security of the bill and to grant an obligation to the owner of the goods, that the Company shall deliver them on their receiving payment of the bill with interest.

The Manager informed the Court that on the eighth of April last he had laid before Messrs Drummond & Guthrie two of the Companys Directors a letter from Mark Stark of Dunfermline dated 31 March desiring a credit in the Company's books to Mark Stark & Company for One Thousand pounds Sterling (in place of their present credit for the same firm held on other security) on his, George Oswald, James Oswald, George Brown and William Craig of

Glasgow their joint bond, also desiring a credit of six hundred pounds for William Craig & Mark Stark (for a separate branch of trade) on his, William Craig & John Brown their joint bond—And that he had also laid before them letters from John Mackay of Tordarroch, William Forsyth of Cromarty and Joseph Forsyth of Dingwall proposing to enter into new contracts with this Company for three years for spinning of yarns, and a letter from David Melvil at Ceres and one from John Watson at Ceres dated 27 March as to their becoming purchasers of the Company's houses at Ceres; formerly the property of John Watson. And that he had informed these Gentlemen that James Robertson of Leith, formerly Manager under David Doig for Leith factory, was due the Company a balance of cash in his hands on account of that factory £237 3/0 for which he had granted bill, but had no other funds for payment of it save a small subject at Falkirk belonging to his wife who was willing to assign the same to a third person on behalf of this Company and Watt at North Berwick on their agreeing to discharge her husband of all claims they may have upon him and further that he had informed them that being obliged to go to the West Country the length of Falkirk on the Wednesday next, he thought it might be of use to go as far as Glasgow to attempt settling sundry of this Company's affairs there and that as he might be absent for some days it would be necessary to leave a procuration to some Person to act as manager until his return. He likewise informed them that he had received a letter from James Ingram of Glasgow acquainting him of James Ingram & Co their being obliged to stop payment and desiring this Company might sign a concert along with their other creditors—And he the Manager further informed the Court that he had received from the said Messrs. Drummond & Guthrie the following orders with which he had conformed viz;—

'That he should grant to Mark Stark & Co. a credit of one thousand pounds and to William Craig and Mark Stark a credit of six hundred pounds, both on the securitys mentioned. That he should renew the contracts for spinning yarns, with John Mackay of Tordarrach, William Forsyth of Cromarty and Joseph Forsyth of Dingwall, and to encourage the spinning of two hank yarns to allow an additional price for that grist. That he should not enter into any private bargain about the houses in Ceres but put them up to Public roup at the price offered for them by Melvil and Watson. That he should accept of the assignation from James Robertson & his wife and discharge the husband accordingly. That they approved of his going to Glasgow and ordered him to leave a procuration to Walter Hog, clerk to this Company to act as Manager in his absence. And desired and empowered him to sign the concert along with James Ingram & Co's other creditors.' The Court having resumed the consideration of the above affairs approved of and confirmed what had been done therein.

Court of Directors

29 July 1766

George Goldie Manager for the Company presented a memorial to the Court setting forth that sundry linen dealers propose to consign what linens they send to the hall (which is to be opened on Tuesday next) to his care for sale and that he thinks these types would serve to assort what remains of the Company's linens and thereby quicken their sale and that though it would cost him a great additional trouble as he must at any rate attend the hall for the Company's sales, yet he does not choose to accept of these concessions without the approbation of the Directors. The Court agreed of his making trial of selling what linens are offered him on consignments.

Court of Directors

1 September 1766

The Directors report that agreeable to the above states the profits on the Company's trade last year is £2713 8/9 and after deducting £493 19/10 of loss on sundry accounts prior to 20 May 1763 and the sum of £1729 2/6 wrote off from Salton Bleachfield to reduce it to its real value their stock appears to be £27,901 2/2, but as there are a great number of debts that may be esteemed doubtful included in the above, the Directors after the most careful examination are of opinion that a deduction of no less than the sum of £2002 5/9 will be requisite to make them good and therefore that the real capital of the Company may be valued at nearly £20,000.[1]

The Directors also report that the affairs of E McCulloch & Co are not yet so far wound up as to determine what profit or loss may arise from that concern. At the 30 May 1765 the Company were in advance on that account £30521 5/7 which at the 30th of May last was reduced to £11475 19/10 and as the whole outstanding debts are now under the care of the Company's Manager they are hopeful that before the Company's next Annual balance the affairs of that Copartnery may be brought to a final conclusion.

Court of Directors

12 November 1766

James Armstrong having received notice from the Directors of the Company to remove at this Martinmass from that part of the Farm of Maigrie which he occupies and as this Farm is situate close upon the House of Salton Hall

1 'Real capital' in the sense of realisable assets.

especially the West and North sides of the policy thereof, Mr Fletcher would be greatly obliged to the Directors for a lease of the said Farm at the usual rent and would engage to find carriages for the service of the Company at the present rates paid by them to James Armstrong for the same. And in order to enlarge the drying field, the Company may retain four or six acres next to the drying field as they think will best accommodate them. How the above is to be transacted Mr Fletcher submits to the Directors.

The Directors present having taken the above into their consideration are of opinion that it would be very inconvenient for the bleachfield to want the farm of Maigrie and therefore that they cannot comply with the proposal on the terms thereof, but submit it to the consideration of the next full Court of Directors whether or not it may be proper to make an offer to Mr Fletcher of the lease of both bleachfield and farm.

E. McCulloch & Co. to Messrs Mossman & Polson, Edinburgh

15 December 1766

When Messrs Alexander and I entered into partnership with the British Linen Company, it was stipulated that the set and profit of the bleachfield at Salton should run with the copartnery for one year after the dissolution of their trading concern, and accordingly the bleaching for the year 1765 fell under my immediate care and direction. In stating accounts, I have charged 5 per cent on the amount of the bleaching, being the usual factorage or commission allowed in such cases, for trouble, warehouse rent and servants' wages in receiving and again delivering the goods to the respective owners; as also I have charged £15 stg for the attendance and services of a clerk employed to pay the wages and keep the accounts of a field. There were from 50 to 60 servants employed during the season that behoved to be paid monthly; this clerk really costs £40 per annum, but I have charged no more than I thought an equivalent for his many writings on that service besides spending two days every month for 8 months in the country counting and clearing with the field's servants. The Directors of the Company are satisfied that something is due to me for both these services, but referred the quantum or rates to your determination. I believe I have stated no more than customary or equitable, but jointly with the Directors I leave them to your determination.

To John McDougall, Belfast

24 January 1767

You will as soon as possible after the receipt of this come over to make a mill at this bleachfield for the B. Linen Company. The mill will consist of one water wheel, four pair of rubbing boards and one washing mill also drawing machines for the boards, traversing machines for the beetling engine. There are likewise a good many repairs necessary to be done about the field. You will also do me the favour to hire three bleachers for this field, viz a boiler, a beetler & a rubber. I would have them sober, sensible and sedate people who know their business thoroughly. You may offer them their full Irish wages, but if they will not come over for that you may agree with them for a little more per week as you can get them to accept of, but I would not choose that it should be above one shilling more a week. As the B. Linen Company have fixed upon you for doing this job partly from my recommendation & partly from some of the proprietors of the Company having seen your work, it is hoped you will lose no time in coming over & bringing these three hands with you. The Company will bear your travelling expenses & theirs & as the bleaching season will commence in a few weeks the Company's business must suffer if you do not come over soon. Signed Sam Sinclair.

PS I should have mentioned to you that it is by the B. Linen Co's orders I have wrote for you to come over. That I have been master bleacher at this bleachfield this last season & am engaged for the next & that I hope it will be both doing yourself & me service to come here as soon as possible.

To William Adie, Dunfermline

30 March 1767

I received your letter of the 28th current & notice the contents. Mr Horn tells me he only gives the Dunfermline diapers a little beetling to make them pack into less bulk when sent away & at most they are only single beetled whereas yours beetled at Salton were all double beetled which we make serve for callendring when dressed at Salton, only they are put through Lignum Vitae rollers. So that I dare say you will find the beetling reasonably charged. The 7/4 table cloths are charged at prices Mr Stark paid Mr Horn last season which I daresay you will not think too high as the cloth, I am certain, the cloth was as well done. The diapers in your place are seldom ever either the length or breadth they are said to be; you know thick diapers always come short in the length & I don't know of any bleacher that will engage to make up lengths if the pieces are kept whole at both ends. I wish you would settle the affair of the damage per Mailer with him yourself as you know best what it was & I don't choose to meddle with it. As to the other damages I rather wish you would say what the damage on your cloths may amount to & you shall have credit for it & keep the cloths to yourself as they will sell better with you to the hawkers than here but I shall leave this to yourself.

Your packsheet was sent to Dunfermline with a bundle of Mr Stark's but if they have it not you shall be credited for it. I shall cause our warehouse keeper at Leith send a note of the charges on your bales & advise you what Diapers you send to Salton field this season. I wish you could send them by water to

Leith as the carriage is so high from Queensferry but if you cannot find a speedy opportunity send them per Mailler & be so good as distinguish the single & double Diaper in your invoice.I am assured Mr Stirling gives no difficient[1] this season and I assure you your prices of bleaching will not allow any.

To William Forsyth, Cromarty

9 January 1768

By order of our Directors I have to inform you that two or three days ago they heard that the Aberdeen Bank from a belief that we assisted the Thistle Bank in the very large demands they have lately made upon them have ordered their correspondents & agents to pick up our notes on purpose to make a run upon this Company.[2]

Nothing can be more false or injurious than the above supposition as we never had the smallest connection with the Thistle Bank & always showed the strongest inclination to be on good terms with the Aberdeen Bank. We therefore think the information given cannot be true and until we are certainly advised that it is, we will not take any steps against them but in the meantime the Directors beg of you to be on your guard to whom you pay our notes & endeavour by all means in your power learn without making the affair public whether anybody in your place is endeavouring to take our notes out of the circle. If you find there is, write me immediately all the particulars you can hear and what kind of value is given for our notes. I mean whether bills on London or Edinburgh or Aberdeen notes. The Directors depend on your diligence and prudence in this affair.

Court of Directors

26 January 1768

This day the Court entered into the following agreement with Archibald Horn bleacher at Salton Barley Mill, as to Copartnery concern with him in this Company's field at Salton viz—

That the Copartnery shall continue for two Years and this Company be allowed one hundred pounds sterling per annum for the rent of the Field.[3]

1 Sic—an allowance for shrinkage?

2 The Thistle Bank of Glasgow, founded in 1761. See Checkland, *Scottish Banking*, 106-7, 115: 'The Aberdeen Company right from birth [1767] found itself involved in a bitter note war with both the British Linen Company and the Thistle Bank.' This northern note war seems to have petered out in 1769.

3 The bleachfield was valued in the Company's books at £2,090 for the ground and fixed works. An inventory of utensils added a further £286. BSA, 5/1/2, Salton Bleachfield Journal, 20 Feb. 1768.

That Archibald Horn shall be allowed five per cent on the amount of bleaching & lapping Linens yearly for the trouble of his management, he being obliged to give his whole time and attention to the concerns of that field. That the utensils shall be valued by two neutral persons, the half of which shall be paid by Mr Horn to this Company.

That this Company advance the money necessary for carrying on the Trade on which they shall be allowed 5 per cent Interest.

That Mr Horn shall not bleach above two thousand pieces yearly of Linen at his own field.

That this Company shall have the appointment of a Clerk to the field.

That this Company shall hold one half concern in the field & Mr Horn the other half and the Profit on the Trade shall be equally divided or the loss equally sustained by the said Parties.

The Court ordered a warning of Removal to be given James Armstrong if he refuses to give a letter agreeing to give up the profession of the House he is now in at Whitsunday next.

To Arch[iba]d Horn, Salton Barley Mill

6 February 1768

I promised to put an advertisement in the papers about taking in cloth at Salton field but as you are best acquainted with the style of these things I shall leave it to yourself. Samuel Sinclair writes me today that he is offered Eight Guineas for his cow. Mr David Kinloch begs the favour you would take the cow from Sinclair and sell her to the person who has offered the 8 Guineas & receive the money & pay it in here on Mr Kinloch's Account any time when you are in Town. The Scroll of the Contract is now finished & will be sent you about the middle of next week. It will be obliging you say when it will be convenient for you to take off the Materials & Utensils &c at Salton field.

p W.H. [Walter Hog, the Company's Clerk]

Court of Directors

11 February 1768

A letter from William Bell as to the Warehouses presently possessed by the Company at Leith being read, in which he offers these warehouses for another year at Forty Guineas rent or what the Company want of them at proportionate rent. The Court ordered Walter Hog, their clerk, to wait on Mr Bell and take at reasonable rent what part of the warehouses may be wanted for the ensuing year.

A letter from George Mackay of Skibo and one from Alexander Somervail Manager for the Spinning carried on by the deceased John Mackay of Tordarroch [were read] proposing that in place of delivering over the Lint unspun at

Mr Mackay's Death in terms of the Contract, the same should be spun up by Mr Somervail and returned to the Company as formerly in Yarns.

The Court, having approved of this measure, ordered the money necessary for carrying on the business should as formerly be advanced from time to time to Mr Somervail's order.

A Letter from Samuel Sinclair, late bleacher for the Company at Salton, being read to the Court, setting furth his distressed situation and want of money to pay his debts in the Country and to carry him back to Ireland. The Court resolved as the Company did not bring him to this Country and as they have allowed him more than agreement, that they will not advance him any money for paying his debts, but that if he goes to Ireland they will give him Thirty or Fourty shillings to help him on his Journey.

To Eben[ezer] Hill (to the care of Alex[ande]r Forsyth, Forres)

20 April 1768

I have rec'd your letter dated from Kinghorn & am glad you got safe over the water. Mr Forsyth has already in his hands about £1200 of this Company's money. You'll please therefore only deliver him about £1500 more unless upon conversing with him you find that he has a view of immediately remitting near that Value in which case you may give him £2000 I mean independent of the £200 of Silver, all of which you are to deliver him. From Forres you will please proceed to Banff & leave with Dr. James Saunders the notes you may have left after settling with Mr Forsyth, which must not be under £2000. From Banff return by Aberdeen & wait on Mr Durward & Mr Leslie in that place. You will need to be particularly cautious: you have nothing to do there save receiving from Mr Durward or Mr Leslie what remittances they have to send here & therefore I think you have no occasion to make yourself known to any body or to hint where you have been or where you are going. Mr Ford at Montrose will have a remittance prepared for you as I fancy Mr Neilson will have also.

At Forres, Banff &c you should be as attentive as possible to every thing you hear that may be of use to this Company to know & of these things you should make notes in writing as they occur in particular to learn as much as possible the conduct of the Aberdeen & other Bank Agents. On the whole of your Journey you should on no account make a bustle & noise or discover your connections with this Company. You'll remember to send the man you carried with you back from Forres & if Mr Forsyth has a remittance of any value, remit it by him—[per] W.H. Mr D Grant is an Agent for the Old Bank.

To William Durward, Aberdeen

16 June 1768

We are advised from Banff, Inverness etc that your bank are very industrious in picking up our notes and from their not having sent any here for some weeks past, we judge they intend a run upon us. A little time will however discover if our conjecture is just. You may continue to buy for this Company what Dutch bills come in your way even at 22⅙ per cent tho' by all I can learn they cannot be negotiated to profit at that price. We yesterday sent by your carrier under cover to Geo Marr one thousand pounds stg which is put to your debit and of which please send our receipt. We are just now so scarce of notes that we were obliged to send in this small parcel two hundred pounds in five pound notes.

Court of Directors

21 June 1768

On Account of the Aberdeen bank having yesterday made a demand on this Company for £7300 of Specie, which obliged this Company to get from the Royal Bank £4000 in Guineas Ordered to send to Newcastle for Four Thousand pounds sterling of Guineas. And to write the Aberdeen Bank to know the reason of their making the demand.

The Court having considered the state of the different Agents their accounts Ordered the following allowances to be made them—

To Gilbert Gordon Dumfries on his account since 14 December last: £10. 10. 0

To Thos. & Jas. Arbuthnot on their account since 30 May 1767 to 30 May last: [£]7 7. 0

To Alexr. Forsyth, Forres on his account since do. to do.: [£]25

To William Durward, Aberdeen on his account since do. to do.: [£]20

To Alexander Leslie since do. to do.: [£]50

To Ormston & Lamb, Newcastle

22 June 1768

Your letters of the 17 and 20 current came here in course, the contents of which are duly noted. This will be delivered you by Mr Hill, this Company's cashier who has with him £4000 of bills on London for which please procure him guineas and dispatch him for this place with all the expedition you can. We will probably now need a weekly supply from you but this we will advise you some posts hence.

To Alex[ande]r Simpson, Aberdeen

22 June 1768

On Monday last a Gentleman gave in here £7300 of this Company's Notes & demanded Specie for them which he was accordingly paid. He said he came from your Bank. As this Company desire to live in peace with all their neighbours & are not sensible that they have given your Bank any just cause of offence I am ordered to write you to know whether or not the above mentioned demand was made in consequence of orders from your Directors. The Directors of this Company love peace & to carry on their business in a merchant like manner. They make runs upon no body but will not tamely be run upon when no cause of offence is given. If this is part of your Company's plan they must act accordingly but wish much rather to live in harmony with all their neighbours. I beg your answer in course. WH. [Walter Hog]

Court of Directors

18 November 1768

The Manager having informed the Court that Ebenezer Hill, the Company's Teller, had by an abstraction from the money lodged on the faith of his Initials on the Cash Chest made away with Six hundred and eighty pounds one shilling and nine pence sterling as per Account produced.

Ordered to get the Account attested by Ebenezer Hill and afterwards made out by Mr Gordon in terms of his Bond of Cautionary and to write his Cautioners acquainting them of the Affair & desiring payment of the contents of their Bond of Five hundred pounds.

The Court Ordered Ebenezer Hill to be dismissed from the Company's Service[1] and that Samuel Kinloch who has acted for these some weeks past as Teller should be continued in that Office until another one is appointed.

Ordered to inform the warehouse keeper at Leith that the Company will not have use for his service after Whitsunday next and to write the factor for the proprietor of the warehouse that the Company do not intend to possess it after said term of Whitsunday next.

1 According to C.A. Malcolm, *History of the British Linen Bank* (Edinburgh, 1950), 89, Hill was a man of extravagant habits and 'theatre-going'. His freedom did not last long: he was reported to be a prisoner in the Tolbooth in 1769, while the British Linen Company vigorously pursued his cautioners through the courts for compensation. George Goldie, Manager for the British Linen Company v. William Nisbet, Linen Manufacturer in Edinburgh, Thomas Dick, Shoemaker there, Alexander Flemming, Linen Manufacturer at Kirkliston and Robert Pearson, Linen Manufacturer at Largo. Signet Library, Edinburgh, Court of Session Cases, 74/2, (1769).

Salton Bleachfield Journal

12 December 1768

Profit and Loss d[ebto]r to cash £2 15/-. Paid James Merrilees for Ale and Spirits for the Servants' Dinner 28/-. John Fell for beef and Mutton 20/ 7½d and for Bread, Barley and Salt 6/6.

Profit and Loss d[ebto]r to cash £1 18/-. Paid for Andrew Rutherford's funeral.

Expences on Bleaching d[ebto]r to Cash. Paid Andrew Rutherford's widow his wages, being 33 days @ 1/-.

To James Urquhart,[1] Byth [Aberdeenshire]

10 April 1769

I wrote you 5 current and now send you John Paterson of the Janet of Leith his receipt for the flax and yarns you ordered in yours of the 13 and 30 Ult., amount per invoice as above, ready money prices £33 0/7d. Mr Arbuthnot has now sent me your letter to him dated 13 March and I have desired a manufacturer to purchase your utensils. When they are shipped, you will be advised, and Messrs Arbuthnot & Guthrie tell me they are to pay the money. The preparing the yarns for Osna[burg]s will cost you one penny per spindle but there are few people can do it of the proper German colour except one Brown, a bleacher at Baldovie near Dundee. I shall send you some patterns of Osnaburg with the utensils. The coarsest kinds are made of 6 & 8 cutt yarns for wafts and 12 & 14 for warp The best of 16 cutt warps and 10 & 12 cutts for wafts.

To William Forsyth, Cromarty

15 April 1769

Your yarns per Robertson came safe to hand and are now under examination. Jas Carroll paid the shore dues but I have not yet got account of the amount. I have advised with the Directors about the importation of this year's flax for you and they propose that if agreeable to you and your brother it should be commissioned immediately as from the last letters I had from Riga both the price and the exchange were remarkably favourable. They think you will by the same save more than you will lose in point of interest by commissioning the flax sooner than the time proposed. Let me hear from you as to this in

1 Urquhart, the proprietor of the estate of Byth, had started to feu out the planned village of New Byth in 1764. There is a reference in an account written in 1793 or 1794 of King-Edward parish to a house intended as a linen manufactory, 'and for some time used as such', recently converted into a chapel of ease: *The Statistical Account of Scotland*, ed. Sir John Sinclair (Edinburgh, 1791-8), xi, 402.

course. You cannot expect that Zuckerbecker & Co. will lie out of their money any time on our account nor indeed would I incline to ask them to do so. As to Mr Drummond's acceptance, part of it is already paid here and as it is inconvenient to take the ballance in your place, I wish it remitted here with interest. When you want money I can send you a draft on Inverness which I fancy will answer you and accomodate this Company as we find bills very scarce here.

To the Widow of Thomas Zuckerbecker & Son, Riga

19 May 1769

The purpose of this is to desire you to purchase for this Company Fourty tons of flax Vizt. Thirty-two tons of best Lithuanian Rakitz and Eight tons of best Drujaner Rakitz, provided that you find the market and the exchange favourable. I propose sending Captain Lansdale's vessel for it about the beginning of the month of July next so that you may buy the flax on receipt of this letter or any time before the Captain's arrival as you see it most for the Company's interest. I beg you may be particularly careful in sending the flax of a good quality and of a bright white colour. You will as usual draw on Messrs. Clifford & Sons of Amsterdam for the amount of this flax who will confirm to you the credit I have fixed for you with them.

Mr. William Forsyth of Cromarty writes me 'You may mention to Madam the widow of Thomas Zuckerbecker & Son that I will order for my account by Captain Lansdale's ship with the flax about 2 thousand cubic feet of best fir logs and 2 hundred best red wood fir deals 3 inches thick and from 18 to 20 feet long which they may reserve and set aside for my account until Captain Lansdale arrives at Riga.' I have wrote Mr Forsyth to correspond with you himself on this subject and fix a credit for the amount of the timber wanted, which I doubt not he will do.

I do depend on your care in the purchase of this flax as yarns here are such a drug that it requires the very best materials to make them of to cause them to sell.

To Alex[ander] Simpson, Aberdeen

22 May 1769

I have today a letter from you of the 19 current in which you inform me that your Company have considered several informations they have from their friends and correspondents they have in different parts of the country whereby it clearly appears to them that the faith of the treaty which this Company made with yours has not by this Company or their agents been duly observed in matters of real consequence, particularly that you have informations of entire credit that our agents have been in practice of industriously picking up your notes and substituting this Company's notes in their place and that they have even acted in confederacy with the agents of the Thistle Company of Glasgow and supplied them with the identical notes they have so collected. In justice to this Company I do assure you that we have neither directly nor indirectly countenanced the picking up of your notes either for our own or for other notes. And that we have not in any manner of way been acting or assisting to either side on the dispute bewteen your Company and the Thistle Bank. Nor have we employed any agents in your three counties since our agreement with you. I therefore do not hesitate to assert in the strongest manner that the informations given you as to this Company are altogether groundless.

Our Directors love peace and good neighbourhood and therefore would not willingly give cause of complaint to any Society but to yours they had a stronger motive to act a friendly part, as they had engaged their honour to do so, and they are extremely surprised that you could suspect them of infringing a treaty so solemnly made. You will observe that it was a positive article of the agreement that it was to subsist for 12 months and that no alteration of measures was to be taken by either party without two months' previous notice being given to the other. In that time if you are pleased to point out to me the particulars of the information given you, I shall be more able to satisfy you but if on the other hand your Company are determined at any rate to break off the treaty, this Company will assuredly take proper measures to defend themselves. I shall be glad to have your answer in course.

Court of Directors

29 June 1769

Isobel Rutherford's petition, the wife of Andrew Rutherford who met with an accident last season at the Company's field at Salton by which he lost his life, having been read. The Court ordered her a peck of meal, each week for some time to come.

To Archibald Horn, Saltonfield

22 August 1769

I am favoured with yours of the 18, and shall acquaint you when Mr Rankine's soap is sent here. He has some excellent kelp coming from Skye, but perhaps it wont arrive in time for you to use this season. In the meantime you may be provided at Largo with kelp delivered there free on board at £3 10/- per ton. Mr Pearson wants his linens returned to the [Linen] hall as do the Proprietors of the GW & IW diapers and sundry others complain of their being so long delayed by which they are daily losing sales. Mr Pearson is to send you 20 P[iece]s more this week to bleach and there are some goods here to be bleached and some to be cleaned. Advise me first if you can do them. Send us a cart and let it be loaded with the goods wanted at the Hall.

To Lord Elgin, Broomhall, Dunfermline

30 April 1770

Messrs Stark & Millar of Dunfermline sent here John McPhie's bill dated 31 May 1769 & payable the 5th July thereafter on John Menzies in Aberdeen for £14.17.6 and Mr William Keir's bill 20 March last at 10 d[ays]/d[ebit] on Gavin Hogg for £62.13.9 [total of] £77.11.3. These they paid your Lordship Value for. We have wrote Mr Menzies & Mr Hogg to order payment, but to no purpose as the bills lie here still unpaid. You will please give your Directions about them as I imagine it will not answer any good purpose to keep them here. The Directors expected more operations on your Lordship's Account than which have hitherto been made upon it. It will be obliging that you give directions for paying your men in our notes.[1]

Court of Directors

3 May 1770

Mr Goldie the Manager when at Glasgow on the 23rd ultimo on this Company's business, had his pocket picked in the Inn where he lodged of £26-6/ of which £9-12/ was paid him by Wm. Craig for a bill on Oswald & Comp. sent him by this Company to negotiate and £8-14/ of a sum paid him by Wm. Craig to account of an acceptance due by him to this Company. The Court considered that the £9-12/ was the property of this Company and therefore the loss fell upon them, [but] with regard to the £8-14/ they considered Mr Craig as liable for it but if he refused to pay it, ordered that it should also be borne by the Company.

To W[illia]m Christie[2] & W[illia]m Christie jun[io]r, Stirling

4 May 1770

I received your letter of the 30 ulto which the Directors had yesterday under consideration but before they came to any resolution as to giving you a Cash Credit, they desired me to write you that if it is equally convenient for you they would rather deal with you by discounting bills payable at 3 m[onths], if that method will not answer they beg to know to what extent annually your

1 The 5th earl of Elgin had both collieries and limeworks in the area of Dunfermline, and had founded the port of Charlestown in 1761 to allow the shipment of his estate's products.

2 William Christie, merchant and dyster, had been provost of Stirling several times since first holding office in 1743.

operations would be on an Account of £500. Our Rules require that at least four times the sums of the credit given should be properly circulated in the Company's Notes every year. The Directors have agreed to delay the payment of your bill due at Whitsunday to Martinmas next. When it falls due you shall be advised that it may be renewed.

To Provost Alex[ande]r Chrystie, Montrose

21 March 1771

Mr Hog has reported to the Directors the conversation he had with you as to your becoming Agent for this Company at Montrose and they having approved of the terms mentioned by you. You will please call at Mr John Straton who will deliver ten parcels which contain each two hundred pounds sterling making in all Two thousand pounds sterling which we have entered to the debt of Thomas Chrysties' sons. To prevent any mistakes we shall note to you the terms upon which we understand this Account is to be opened and shall subjoin what directions we think necessary for conducting the business properly. In the first place this Company will pay you one quarter per cent commission on what notes you may circulate for them and will replace to you what postages or carriage of parcels you may pay on their account. This Company will take the risque of the money they may have occasion to send you and will also run the risque of the money you may have occasion to transmit us, and as we are perfectly satisfied that you will not make a purchase of any bills but what you believe entirely good and such as you would take on your own account we agree to free you likewise of risque upon this Article. Inclosed you have a copy of the credit side of Mr James Ford's account since 30 May last; it will sufficiently explain and point out to you the nature of his transactions and the channel in which his remittances came. As to the other parts of the business we have to observe to you. First it is necessary to keep our cash altogether separate from your own and that you send here weekly a State of the Cash on hand, particularising what of our notes you have to circulate & what other notes or Gold &c you may have on hand to remit us. We allow you to give what Exchange may be current in your place for bills on London and shall for your government note to you weekly the course of Exchange here. For bills on Edinburgh we have found the par at your place to be about 10 days, from that to fifteen days you may take them without discount. Bills payable on Glasgow are less valuable as we pay a commission for negotiating them there but these you may also take at currency with you, which we suppose may be about par for bills at sight or bills at one or two days date. We never allow our Agents to discount long dated bills but if you find any good ones offering at or under three months date you may advise us and they be laid before the Directors.

We have as much as possible discouraged the practice that some people have of going about & picking up of other notes. We think it mean & not calculated to serve any good purpose, at the same time as we expect our friends only to use our notes in their payments. What other notes come in the common course of business through your hands you will please remit as follows. Edinburgh, Glasgow, Ayr & Dumfries in parcels addressed to me. If you cannot find an opportunity coming immediately to Edinburgh, send the parcels to Mr Richd Neilson, Dundee who will forward them here. Dundee notes to Mr. Richd Neilson. He gets bills for them from the Dundee bank & remits these bills here. Perth notes to Mr Geo Blackie which parcels may go to the care of Mr Neilson if you cannot find an opportunity going directly for Perth. As to Aberdeen notes, we are under engagements with that bank to take none of these out of the circle and therefore what of these come through your hands, you will please use them again in your payments. We have now only to beg that you would pay some attention to the operations of Mr Ford & Mr Paton as to picking up our notes & advise us that if any improper practice is used against us, we may get the matter explained by their employers. Please address your letter to Mr Geo Goldie, Manager for the British Linen Co.

Court of Directors

21 March 1771

Mr Goldie informed the Court that he was ordered by his physicians to take a journey for his health to the South Country, to which the Directors agreed.

Court of Directors

26 March 1771

There was read a letter from John Fergus & Son as to continuing their account until May next and longer if between and May next they make proper operations, and as to abating them something on what yarn they may want this summer from what the other Kirkcaldie people pay who take less quantities.

Ordered to allow them to operate on their account until the 30th May next and if between and that time they make proper operations to continue their account on trial for another year and to give them the yarns one half penny & spindle below our ordinary prices as also three and six months credit on what they buy.

To James Gilchrist, Edinburgh

29 March 1771

As you are going to London in expectation of getting employment there as a Clerk in a counting house, the Directors of this Company have ordered me to give you this letter, that you may have an opportunity of showing it to any person that may wish to know your character. During the time you have been in this Company's service, which has been from the year 1763, you have behaved yourself honestly, soberly and have given great attention to your business. This Company are so much satisfied of your integrity, capacity & ability that I am also desired to assure you, if you do not find employment in London, you are heartily welcome to return to your place here.

Court of Directors

18 April 1771

Mr Guthrie reported that he had waited on the Directors of Douglas, Heron & Co[1] and spoke to them about Mr Ford's operations for their Company at Montrose and that they had promised to write Mr Ford to discontinue picking up our notes and to desire him to meet with our Agent Provost Christie weekly in order that they may settle the Exchange on bills properly and otherwise concert measures for carrying on their business amicably and without either prejudicing the interest of the Society for which the other is employed, and that he had promised that this Company would give the same directions to their Agent. Of which the Court Approved and Ordered a letter to be wrote Messrs Christies & Sons accordingly.

Court of Directors

16 May 1771

The Court read a letter from Thomas Stewart, Secretary to the Old Bank, intimating the resolution of the Directors as to now receiving our notes in payment to which they ordered the following reply to be made:[2]

'Gentlemen, Today I laid before the Directors of the British Linen Company Mr Stewart's letter of the 15th Current, intimating your intention of receiving the notes of this Company in payment at your bank and and after Monday next and that it would be agreeable to you an Exchange was made at your office each day between two and three o'clock afternoon.

'I am ordered to acquaint you that this Company will regularly exchange with you as you direct and that in this and every other particular they will be happy to cultivate a friendship and good understanding with your Society—Signed p WH.'

1 Otherwise known as the Ayr Bank, it had been formed in Nov. 1769. Its Chairman, the duke of Queensberry, was the current Governor of the British Linen Company, having succeeded the 3rd duke of Argyll in 1762.

2 Checkland, *Scottish Banking*, 126, sees this establishment of a twice-weekly note exchange as an important measure in allowing the two senior Scottish banks 'a measure of jurisdiction over the others'.

Part of a note of the Company for One pound being presented for full payment. Ordered the note to be paid for as entire on receiving an Affidavit as to the other parts being destroyed and a discharge and obligation that the parts wanting shall be repaid if they appear.

Walter Hog reported that the late Lord Elgin[1] owes this Company £1500 on an account settled 30th May last. Ordered to inquire the situation of Lord Elgin's affairs, and who is his Doer, and lay the information before next Court.

Court of Directors

26 December 1771

The Court took under consideration the claims made by Richard Neilson against this Company for allowance for his transactions on our Account and for loss on Shirting Linen bleached at Salton field in the year 1766. Ordered to write Mr Neilson that the Directors do not think his Claims well founded but if he inclines to abide by them this Company will submit them on their part to the determination of Sir William Forbes and will claim from Mr Neilson a commission on the whole of his transactions made on his proper account and on the Linen concern with him.

Ordered to write George Chalmers & Comp[any] that the Directors do not incline to continue their credit for bills at Dunfermline but will give a credit for £500 on a Cash account with proper Security.

The Directors took under consideration the present State of Salton Field and ordered Walter Hog to go there and converse Mr Horn and that he should report to next Court a State of the Affairs of that Bleachfield and if he had any opportunity of seeing Mr Fletcher they authorised him to make Mr Fletcher an offer of the Field and the Utensils at £2000.

Court of Directors

14 January 1772

Walter Hog reported that he had in consequence of the orders of the Directors of the 7th current waited on Mr Horn at Salton and intimated to him that this Company did not incline to continue the Copartnery business of bleaching for another Season, but that Mr Horn had observed it could not well be given up on account of the principal Servants at the Field being considered by him as engaged for another year. The Directors having taken this circumstance into consideration, they agreed to continue the Copartnery business for another

1 The 5th earl of Elgin, to whom the Manager refers, had died two days previously on 14 May. What was to complicate matters was that his son and heir, William, died only two months later on 15 July.

year and that the Servants should before the end of it have proper intimation to provide themselves otherwise.

To David Flint, Board of Trustees

28 January 1772

The Hon[ora]ble Board of Trustees for Manufactures &c in Account Current with the British Linen Coy Credit.

1760

May 20 To Premium on Yarns Spun in the Interior parts of the Highlands in consequence of the Minute 3d August 1759

Total 14136½ spindles.

Jan 13, 1762. To paid Freight of sample Linen from London £0 2/5d . £352 10/8.

By Premium paid on 4859½ spindles at 6d £121 9/9. Balance due the B. Linen Coy £232.0.11.

To David Flint, Edinburgh

3 February 1772

Inclosed I send you a State of the Honorable The Board of Trustees their Account Current with the B.L. Co balanced by £232.0.11 due this Company being for premiums on Yarns spun in the interior parts of the Highlands agreeable to the Contract with the Board in 1759. The Vouchers as to the Yarn spun in the highlands are ready for the Inspection of any of the Trustees who will take the trouble to look them over. The Charges & Losses which this Company sustained on that Contract greatly exceed the Sum Stipulated with the Board of which also whenever the Trustees desire it vouched Accounts shall be produced. You will please lay the Account Current now sent you before the Board at their first meeting that they may give orders about the payment. Be so good as now also order payment of the rent of the Linen hall due at Whitsunday last & the delivery to me of the Receipts in favour of James Alexander & on the faith of which I have by your desire advanced money to them.

Court of Directors

16 April 1772

The Court read a letter from William Forsyth of Cromarty desiring this Company to fix a credit for him on Amsterdam to reimburse the Widow & son of Thomas Zuckerbecker for thirty tons of flax to be purchased by them for him and proposing to allow this Company One per cent commission on the transaction. The Court Agreed to his proposal and Ordered the Manager to fix a credit for Zuckerbecker's Widow & son with Clifford & Son of

Amsterdam to the amount of £1200. And to inform Mr Forsyth that the Court has agreed to this transaction only to oblige him as they consider it as rather out of this Company's line of business.

There was read a letter from Thomas Christie & Sons of Montrose wanting liberty to continue to receive Merchant Company[1] notes which they think will be of advantage to the Companys circulation. Ordered to allow them to receive these notes as formerly on payment.

To Messrs Clifford & Sons, Amsterdam

18 April 1772

I send you inclosed a letter to Madam the Widow of Thos Zuckerbecker & Son of Riga ordering Thirty Tons of Flax for Mr Wm Forsyth of Cromarty & giving them orders to draw for the Amount upon you as usual. You will please therefore honour their draughts for that cargo to the extent of Twelve hundred pounds Sterling & when their Bills appear advise me & I shall either remit you for them from hence or Order your reimburse by a credit on London.

To William Forsyth, Cromarty

18 April 1772

I wrote you the 13th Current. On Thursday the Directors took under consideration your letter of the 4th Current & ordered a Credit to be fixed at Amsterdam for the Amount of the Cargo of Flax ordered by you from the Widow & Son of Tho Zuckerbecker which I have accordingly done to the amount of Twelve hundred pounds Sterling & have this day forwarded your letter to Riga, at the same time the Directors ordered me to inform you that such transactions are rather out of the line of this Company's business. On the 16 Current I paid your Acceptance for Thirty Six pounds Sterling to Alexr. Forsyth dated 13 October at [Cromarty] & have placed it to your debit. I have received your letter of the 9th current with the invoice of your yarns per Captain Robertson, & advising the freight £6.17.6 which shall be paid him. I shall also pay him what money he calls for to the amount of Forty pounds Sterling. Your bill to Hugh Graham & Co for £10.3/ is paid & placed to your debit & I further debit you One hundred pounds Stg sent you by this night's post under two franked covers. Be pleased to let me have your receipt for that sum in course.

1 The Merchants' Banking Company of Glasgow, founded in 1769: Checkland, *Scottish Banking*, 107.

Court of Directors

6 August 1772

There was considered a Memorial from James Gordon[1] the Company's accountant desiring an increase of Salary and some allowance for the first years his son was in the Office. Ordered to inform him the Company will not increase his Salary and that they do not consider he has any claim for his Son. To give him Thirty Guineas as a present from the Directors.

The Manager reported that Richard Livingston, Clerk at Saltonfield, had a prospect of being engaged by Messrs Cadells & Sons for a longer time than his Company can have any use for him.[2] And that John Gifford, Clerk to Johnston & Smith, was out of employ and was well recommended. Ordered to let Livingston go and engage Gifford in his place for some months.

James Guthrie proposed to open an account with this Company as Secretary to the Board of Trustees for lodging money at 4 per cent to be drawn for as wanted. Ordered to agree to Mr Guthrie's proposal. And to allow James Grieve at Harden to discount £400 more of bills than the sum mentioned 30 ultimo.

Ordered to write the Carron Company that as they have since the beginning of the present troublesome times drawn weekly £300 in place of £200 as formerly agreed on that they must either again restrict themselves to £200 weekly or grant bills at the end of the month at 4 months date.[3]

Court of Directors

21 January 1773

The Manager informed the Court that the Royal Burghs had named him and Neil McVicar as Commissioners to go to London to sollicit Parliament for aid to the Linen Manufacture and wanted to know if the Directors approved of his going.[4]

1 James Gordon had been in the Company's employment for many years. In 1755 'A Plan of Books for Manufacturers' by him had been shown to the Board of Trustees for approval by David Doig and Ebenezer McCulloch: SRO, NG1/1/13, BOTM 7 Feb. 1755.

2 The bleachfield at Salton was in its final season before its sale and conversion into a pleasure ground. In Dec. of that year the stampmaster at the field notified the Board of Trustees that as the 'business was given up at Salton, his employment was at an end': SRO, NG1/1/20, BOTM 2 Dec. 1772.

3 This was a time of immense financial strain on the economy generally, the Ayr Bank having failed on 25 June. Carron Company was under particular pressure. Several of its partners were in grave financial difficulty and David Hume reported to Adam Smith that Carron itself was in danger of bankruptcy: 'Carron Company is reeling, which is one of the greatest calamities of the whole, as they give employment to near 10,000 people'. R.H. Campbell, *Carron Company* (Edinburgh, 1961), 133.

4 George Goldie gave evidence to a parliamentary committee appointed to enquire into the state of the linen trade. He was again in London in Mar. of the following year to give evidence as to the extent of the depression in 1773 in the linen industry in Scotland. 'Four whole counties, Glasgow and Paisley

The Court Ordered him to go to London and appointed Walter Hog to act as Manager in his absence as authorised by minute of 20 June 1770 and the general procuration granted him in consequence thereof.

To William Forsyth, Cromarty

19 July 1773

Your letters of the 13 and 15 current are before me. Messrs Fergus & Son have been here today and I have finished the bargain with them except as to the length of credit which they insist shall be nine months. As I think them safe and see no prospect of selling any part of your yarns to others, I have ordered the yarns to be sent them even tho' I should be obliged to settle at the nine months.

To Carron Company

20 July 1773

I have received your letter of the 17 current but the patience of the Directors is so much worn out in waiting your St Petersburgh remittances that they have today ordered me to insist peremptorily for the payment of your two Acceptances lying here past due. I have therefore sent out one of the Company's Clerks in order that you may remit one by him & prevent further trouble. The Directors meet again on this business on Thursday & I hope to be able to report to them that these [illegible word] old bills are paid.

Court of Directors

23 July 1773

The Directors had today a meeting with Mr Gascoigne relative to the affairs of the Carron Company when the following matters were agreed upon.[1]

That the bill due by the Carron Company on 5 March last be instantly paid by a bill on Walpole, Clark & Bourne.

That the bill due the 2d August next, be then paid either in Money or a bill on Walpole & Comp., or by good bills on London under six months to run.

That the bill due the 3d April last shall be retired in the same manner on the 10th August next.

included, out of 6000 looms, had 2500 unemployed, that the proportion of those that were in general idle was at least a third; that out of a certain district in the county of Sutherland 600 out of 1800 spinners had emigrated, and so in proportion in several other places': *Scots Magazine*, xxxvi (Sept. 1774), 479.

1 Charles Gascoigne, a leading partner in Carron Company, had a remarkable ability to disguise the full extent of his debts (Campbell, *Carron Company*, 136), but eventually the British Linen Company ran out of patience and in Nov. 1775 put his affairs into sequestration.

And that the Partners in the Carron Company as expressed in their Charter shall execute a Bond to this Company binding themselves for Mr Gascoigne's Transactions with this Company. Upon these conditions this Company are to continue the weekly supplies of £300. After the Charter is in force but if the Carron Company fail, this Company are to stop the weekly supplies but not otherwise without giving them three months intimation.

To Carron Company

23 July 1773

I have received your letter of the 22d Current which I laid today before the Directors when Mr Gascoigne attended & they have agreed to the following terms vizt that the bill due the 5th of March last be paid today by a bill on Messrs Walpole Clark & Bourne London. That the bill due the 2nd of August next be then paid either in money or a bill on Walpole & Co or good bills on London under six months to run. That the bill due 3rd April last shall be retired in the same manner with the one due the 2d of next month on the 10th of August next. And it is understood that as soon as you are in possession of the St Petersburg remittances the Directors shall have it in their option to receive an equal Amount of these bills upon their delivering back to you the bills deposited at Six Months & that the Partners of the Carron Company as expressed in the Charter shall execute a Bond to this Company, binding themselves for Mr. Gascoigne's Transactions with this Company so far as respects the weekly supplies of £300 after the Charter is in force.

Upon these terms the Directors agree to continue the weekly supplies, provided the Current Bills be regularly retired either with Cash or bills on Messrs Walpole & Co at par. And it is likeways understood if you fail in the above engagements that this Company are at Liberty to stop the weekly supplies but not otherways without giving you three months notice of their Intention. I shall soon send you the above mentioned Bond so as it may be executed before the operations under your Charter commence.

To Alexander Christie, Montrose

26 July 1773

The Directors of the B. Linen Company received your letter of the 17th current in answer to which they desired me to acquaint you that they will at all times think themselves happy to have it in their power to oblige you. As acting for a public company, they did not think themselves at liberty to give any of the Company's money for the purpose you mention but themselves contributed and paid me ten guineas to account of the Northesk Bridge.[1] I have placed it to the credit of Messrs Thos Christie's Sons and desired them to pay it to you.

Court of Directors

30 December 1773

It was Represented by the Interim Manager that W[illia]m Fleming who was proposed to be employed to make clean copies of the Directors' Minutes which have fallen behind had a prospect of being otherwise engaged and for a longer time than this Company intended to keep him, and that he seemed to be a sober diligent young man. The Court ordered to engage him for a year certain at the rate of Thirty pounds per annum and so soon as James Rowe could again attend his business to employ Fleming first in bringing up the Minutes and sorting the old vouchers &c that when these old matters were brought up the Court would consider & direct as to his future employ.

Court of Directors

27 January 1774

The Interim Manager reported that Alex Gray, writer to the Signet, had called on him yesterday and desired a meeting with him on Saturday next to go through the Articles disputed between this Company and Ebenezer McCulloch their late Manager in order to bring about a settlement.[2] Ordered not to meet with Mr Gray until Mr Campbell Agent for this Company shall be satisfied of Mr Gray having a preferable right to any balance that may be found due to Mr McCulloch.

The Interim Manager further reported that he had yesterday received a card from Mr Stewart Secretary to the Bank of Scotland intimating that the Bank had come to the Resolution of offering One hundred pounds sterling of reward for discovery of the forger of their notes.

The Court having resumed the consideration of the forgery which has lately appeared of this Company's One pound notes dated 6 Sep 1770. Ordered in the first place to stop issuing our one pound notes dated 6 Sep 1770 that as they

1 The Northesk Bridge cost £6,500 and was completed in 1780.

2 Alexander Gray was engaged by McCulloch's creditors to recover for their benefit what monies he could. It was Gray, for example, who handled the sale on 4 Apr. 1775 of McCulloch's stock in the British Linen Company to Hugh Corrie, WS. It is unlikely that the £2,300 of paid-up stock realised more than perhaps £1,100 or so, given the Company's financial position. BSA, British Linen Company, Stock Transfer Book, 1746-98.

come in they are to be put up in £400 bundles which are to be reckoned and sealed up by the Directors.

Next. That a sufficient quantity of Guinea notes shall be prepared with all possible expedition for issuing as occasion requires. And that the following Advertisement be immediately inserted in the Courant Mercury & Advertiser viz.

'British Linen Office, 27 January 1774.

'The British Linen Company give notice that a forgery has appeared of their one pound notes dated 6 Sep 1770. The forged notes are done on common paper: the figure of the woman & ship are ill executed and appears faint and the strokes of the letters in the copper plate print are less full or broad than in the real ones.

'The Waving, Water mark round the edges of the real notes is imperfectly imitated by draughts with an instrument which are so deep in the forged notes that have already appeared as to cut the paper in some places quite through. The words of the Water mark in the Real notes are BRITISH LINEN COMPANY.

'And these can be easily distinguished from the forged notes by holding them to the light when the word LINEN which runs across the note appears distinctly. The Seal is also attempted to be imitated but very imperfectly.'

Court of Directors

4 July 1774

The Court had under consideration the State of Messrs Wm Tod & Company's Account with this Company from 30 June 1773 to 30 June last. And also the terms on which our account with that house is in future to be carried on and authorised the Manager to write Mr Collon, partner in the house of William Tod & Coy, the following letter viz—

'Sir, I mentioned today to the Directors of this Company the conversation I had with you as to settling this Company's account with Messrs William Tod & Comp of London prior to the 30th June last. As also the Terms on which their account with Messrs Wm Tod & Coy is in future to be carried on. As to the first the Directors understand that interest at the rate of 5 per cent is to be allowed on this Account on both sides from 30th June to the 21st October 1773 and on account of the unexpected alteration of circumstances agree to take interest at the rate of 2½ per cent from the 21st October to the 30th June last. The commission as formerly. As to the Second this Company are to have interest at the rate of four per cent on what money may be over remitted and lie on Messrs Tod & Co's hands on the account after the 30th June last and they are to pay at the rate of five per cent for what they may be due Messrs Tod & Coy after that date. And this Company are to allow a commission of five shillings per cent on all bills drawn at a shorter date than thirty days and the usual commission of three shillings & four pence per cent on all bills drawn at Thirty days and upwards. But in order to accommodate your house and in consideration of the interest allowed by them, this Company propose not to draw at shorter date than forty days unless where the conveniency of this Company requires it. I am &c. Signed for the British Linen Coy, Geo Goldie Manager.'

The Court thereafter recommended to the Manager to get a Bond from the Partners of the House of Messrs William Tod & Coy for the £8000 lying in their hands of the money borrowed of Mr Pringle.

Court of Directors

25 August 1774

Agreeable to the recommendation of last General Court the Directors have caused make up a state and valuation of the old doubtfull debts and a list of such of the later debts as are in a stagnate state and on some of which a loss may probably be sustained.

There is reason to believe the old doubtfull debts will produce a considerable sum above that with which they are charged in the Company's Books but it is supposed this overplus will fall something short of indemnifying the Company of the loss that may arise upon the list of stagnate debts. The Directors report that from the 30th of May 1773 to the 30th of May 1774, the Company's Gain agreeable to the state affixed, was £1510.16.10 and that the Affairs of the Company are now in such a situation as gives great reason to hope that their Capital will in future produce a reasonable return to the proprietors. The Directors therefore report it as their opinion that the Company's Capital is at present worth £23721.12/ being Fourty eight per cent on the Seven Calls made on the proprietors and that a dividend of 4 per cent may be declared on that Capital (which will amount to £948.17.3) payable out of the profits from the 30th May 1773 to the 30th May last. After which there will remain the sum of £1382.2.1 as per Account annexed to go to an insurance account for making good the debts on which loss is apprehended. And the Directors recommend it to the Court to have in view to have annually (if the profits of the Company can afford it) a sum carried to the insurance account that a fund may be provided to make good any losses that may hereafter happen.

Court of Directors

23 September 1774

There was read a letter from Richard Neilson Dundee wanting this Company to discount his bills on Mr Goldie at the Linen hall at 6 m[onths] date in the same manner as is done by his bills on Wm. Tod & Comp. London.

Ordered to write him that this Company cannot engage to discount his bills in common at 6 m[onths] date but when he wants it done as a particular favour the matter shall be considered.

There was read a letter from Doctor John Roebuck of Bo'ness offering a composition of five shillings in the pound for his debt but without Cautionary.[1] Ordered to agree to the proposal, not departing from our present security until he pays 5/- per pound and guarding against the other creditors taking legal measures to the prejudice of this Company.

Ordered to get a double iron door put upon this Company's vault.

There was read a letter from Mr William Tod of London dated the first Current with a Petition to the King for a renewal of this Company's Charter, also a Power of Attorney to Mr Tod to present the said Petition also an Affidavit by the Manager as to the Utility of the Company, of all which the Directors approved, and ordered the Petition and the Power of Attorney to be sealed with the Company's Seal and Signed by Mr Goldie as Manager and Secretary.

To John Roebuck, Bo'ness

26 September 1774

I laid your letter of the 21 Current before the Directors wherein you propose that they will accept of five shillings in the pound composition on your debt to this Company with interest on said composition from that date, the composition to be paid in six equal portions the first payment to commence six months after the Company's agreeing to your proposal & the other five payments at six months distance & so that in three years the whole composition & interest will be paid.

The Directors are disposed to agree to the proposal on receiving the above composition & interest & to discharge you of, or to assign to any of your Friends, the debt you owe this Company but you will please observe that they cannot agree to it but on the following express conditions. Viz that the proposed payments be regularly made & that until the said composition is fully paid they will not discharge you of or assign to your Friends any part of the debt you are due them. And if you fail to make good any part of the composition within three years from this date or if any of your creditors shall within that time attach your effects or pursue any measure different from this Company, the Directors hold themselves at liberty to take any measures they

1 John Roebuck was another major partner in Carron Company, and in common with the others had suffered heavy losses. He was made bankrupt in 1773: Campbell, *Carron Company*, 17.

may judge prudent for securing this Company's whole claim against you after deducting what partial payments may be made by you before that time.

To Alex[ande]r Fleming, Kirkliston

26 September 1774

On Friday last the Directors had fully under consideration your memorial & Mr Hog reported to them what had passed at the meeting of your Creditors[1] and they gave me orders to inform you that they do not consider themselves at liberty to depart from their original agreements. They therefore expect that you will immediately grant your personal obligation for the remainder of your composition & that you will assign the outstanding debts in corroboration of the payment of that obligation. I return you the memorial inclosed.

Court of Directors

24 November 1774

The Court having considered the proposals given in by Messrs Wm Tod & Coy as to a Contract between them and this Company respecting our account with them came to the following resolutions. Viz Agreed that the Company shall continue to remit all their bills and notes negotiable in London to Messrs Tod & Coy.

Agreed to allow ¼ per cent commission but would wish to have it settled on the whole transactions in order to have the account conducted in as simple a manner as possible and because it appears to be unreasonable to pay a higher commission on short dated bills should the Company have money not bearing interest in the hands of Messrs Wm Tod & Coy. But they will recommend it in the strongest manner to the Officers of this Company to conduct the account in such a way as to occasion the least possible inconvenience to Mr Tod's house.

The Directors Agree to pay one half per cent commission upon Bills returned to the Company under protest for non payment. The Directors are willing to lend any sum not exceeding Eight Thousand pounds sterling to Messrs Wm Tod & Coy on the conjunct Bond of the Partners for a term of years not exceeding Six and bearing interest at 5 per cent.

1 Fleming, or Fleeming, had sustained severe losses in trade and also as a result of a serious fire in 1769 at his factory in Kirkliston, even before his unfortunate involvement in the affairs of Ebenezer Hill, as already noticed. He came to an agreement in 1770 as to a schedule for paying off his debts to the British Linen Company and other creditors: SRO, CS233/M4/14. As part of this programme his stock in the Company (£200) was sold in May 1775.

The British Linen Company are to have liberty to draw when their occasions require for Ten Thousand pounds sterling over and above the amount of bills &c remitted Messrs Tod & Coy accepted and due in two months.

The British Linen Company are to be allowed interest at 4 per cent for such of their money as may be in Messrs Tod & Cos hands not exceeding Seven Thousand pounds sterling.

The Directors do not think it mercantile to enter into a Contract for a term of years, but being sensible of Mr Tod's friendship to the Company propose to make a minute in their Books expressive of his good services and to recommend it to their successors to continue their correspondence with his house.

As it will take some time to bring this Company's Affairs into the train of this agreement the Directors propose it should not take place until Candlemass next.

The Court in consideration of William Flemming having been employed in transacting the Company's cash matters with the banks etc which is attended with some risk, ordered to allow him five pounds additional salary for the year commencing 1st of December last, and to allow him in future at the same rate of thirty-five pounds per annum.

Court of Directors

1 September 1775

Present—Mr Fyffe, Mr Campbell and Mr Corrie.

The Directors having taken into their consideration the present State of the Exchange between this and London. Ordered to buy London bills from the Correspondents of the Company at ¼ per cent discount & the difference of the interest until due. And to induce Richard Waddilove to give the Company the whole of his bills. The Court judged it proper to take them without any other discount than that of the interest. And they gave a discretionary power to the Manager to take the other Drovers' bills from ¼ per cent discount to par at sight as he shall see it for the Company's Interest.

Court of Directors

5 September 1775

There was read a letter from William Christie junior of Stirling mentioning that he, John Stevenson weaver in Stirling & Charles Rattray weaver in

Boberdin[1] had contracted for furnishing plaids & hose to a Highland Regiment now raising in America[2] and that they would at different times want advances to the amount of Six hundred pounds for carrying on this business. Ordered to advance these Gentlemen on their bill or bills payable at a date not exceeding three months to the amount of Six hundred pounds.

To Mr Christie Jun[io]r, Stirling

5 September 1775

I am favoured with yours of yesterday the Directors have agreed to the advance of £600 for the purposes & on the joint Acceptances of the Weavers mentioned in your letter of the 25th ulto. You may therefore send the bills from time to time as you have occasion for the money. They have also agreed to discount your bill on John Napier this date at 3 m[onths] £101.5/- for which I have put up £100 as you desired to be sent by the carrier or any private hand you desire to call.

1 Boberdin is almost certainly a tired clerk's rendition of Bannockburn. 'For a long time, all the tartan used by the army has been manufactured at this village': *Statistical Account of Scotland*, xviii, 394.

2 Hostilities had already broken out in the American colonies, with the skirmishes in Apr. at Concord and Lexington, and the battle of Bunker Hill in June.

Appendix
NOTE ON THE MANUFACTURE OF LINEN

It may be helpful to sketch the key steps in the manufacture of linen, an industry now virtually extinct in Scotland. There were five main steps from raw material to finished product.

Flax was harvested by pulling. Though it could be and was grown in Scotland on some scale, most flax used in the industry was imported, either from Holland or Russia. Scottish farmers disliked flax as a scourging crop, and one with uncertain yields: despite frequent attempts to encourage the growth of more flax in Scotland, these had little long-term significance.[1]

The next stage was to prepare the flax for spinning. The seed had to be 'rippled' out of the heads, and then the flax was loosely retied, and taken for steeping under water in river backwaters or in lint pots, specially-made pits. The purpose of retting, the name of this process, was to allow the outer bark to begin to separate. The flax was then taken out, dried, and and beaten with mallets ('scutching') so as to remove the bark entirely. The final exercise was that of 'heckling', the combing of the stem so as to release the fibres, a dusty, demanding task.

When the fibre was ready, it was spun up on a spinning-wheel, the yarn being measured by winding on a reel, and then sold for manufacture into thread or cloth. This was exclusively a female task, some spinners working full-time, others not, but an activity in which many households were involved. Sometimes the finished yarn was sold in an open market to weavers and manufacturers, but increasingly the latter gave out flax and then collected the yarn back, the spinner being paid for her spinning rather than the yarn. To prevent embezzlement, the yarn received back was weighed to make sure that it tallied with the weight of the flax given out.

The yarn was then woven into cloth on a handloom. Whereas spinning was a female occupation in the eighteenth century, handloom weaving was a male preserve. If the weaver were an aspirant to better-quality work, he took the

1 Flax from the Baltic was imported in bundles of 12, 9 or 6 heads. The best was generally reckoned to be the growth of the province of Marienburg (Marienburg Clean), followed by Drujaniar Rakitzer, with the lowest quality known as Badstup or paternoster.

precaution of boiling the yarn to remove the dirt which the spinners' fingers had imparted. He also made sure that the yarn he used, whatever the type of fabric he was to weave, was of a consistent quality and free from knots. The cloth from his loom could be sold brown (unbleached) or white (bleached). It had first to be inspected for a small fee by an official (the 'stampmaster') of the Board of Trustees for Fisheries and Manufactures, who checked for the consistency of weave, it being a well-known malpractice to put the best work on the outside of the folded web. The stampmaster also measured the length and breadth of the cloth, which were marked on the end of the cloth, and stamped it with a thistle stamp showing his name and the location of his office. Should a buyer find deficiencies, he was entitled to compensation not from the weaver but from the stampmaster himself, which was intended as an incentive to the official to do his duty carefully.

The final stage was the bleaching and finishing of the cloth. At its simplest, bleaching involved a programme of steeping of the cloth in an alkaline solution, washing it out in clean water, and then applying a dilute acid, this being repeated until the cloth was thoroughly clean and 'white'. This process could take, depending on the weather, as many as five to eight weeks. The cloth was then either beaten with mallets ('beetling') or put through the cylinder (a species of mangle), to get the surface as smooth as possible.

GLOSSARY

A. FABRICS

Britannia: The name given to a species of fine linen manufactured in the West of Scotland. Also known as 'Irvine Linen'.

Buckram: A coarse fabric, sometimes gummed for use as a lining.

Cambric: A very fine linen made in imitation of the French fabric woven around Cambrai, and therefore sometimes called 'French lawn' in Scotland.

Caroline: Cambric as renamed by the Board of Trustees.

Check: A cloth of varying quality, but usually in Scotland a fairly coarse fabric with a simple pattern obtained by crossing stripes of dark and light colours in the warp (q.v.) and the weft (q.v.) to produce a chequerboard effect. Used, for example, in upholstery.

Coleraine: A medium-quality linen in imitation of the Irish.

Diaper: A medium to fine cloth used for table-cloths, napkins or cloths, e.g.'Clouting Diaper'.

Dimity: A coarse to medium priced fabric.

Dowlas: A coarse, low-priced linen.

Garlix: A fine bleached linen made in imitation of the Continental fabric of the same name.

Edinburg: See 'Osnaburg'.

Glasgow: Striped muslin: a fine, thin and light fabric.

Holland: A very fine linen made in imitation of the popular Dutch fine fabric.

Huggabag: A stout coarse fabric suitable for towelling.

Lawn: A very fine linen fabric of the Cambric (q.v.) type.

Muslin(m): A delicately woven, fine linen fabric.

Navy Linen: A broad Osnaburg (q.v.).

Osnaburg: A coarse to medium priced fabric, made in imitation of the popular German fabric from Osnabruck. Also known as 'Osnabrigg'. Re-named 'Edinburg' by the Board of Trustees.

Paisley: Muslin neck cravats.

Platillo: A low priced linen: a kind of coarse Silesia (q.v.).

Pomerania: A medium-weight cloth modelled on the German fabric of the same name.

Sailcloth and *Sacking:* Strong fabrics for use as their names suggest.

Silesia: A medium-quality linen made in imitation of the German medium-priced fabric from Silesia.

Ticklenburg: A strong coarse fabric similar to Osnaburg (q.v.).

Valencienne: A fine cloth made in imitation of the French fabric manufactured in and around that town.

B. TECHNICAL TERMS AND MEASURES

Ashes: Burnt wood, weed or kelp ashes commonly used in bleaching to make an alkaline solution.

Beetle: To flatten the surface of a bleached fabric by beating it with wooden mallets, either manually or mechanically.

Birquet (Barquet): The Russian equivalent of the Dutch shippound, a unit of measure of weight used in the Baltic trades, 300 lb in the case of flax.

Brown: Unbleached.

Buck: To soak cloth in a warm alkaline solution.

Caim: See 'loom'.

Callander: A set of rollers which flattened out the cloth.

Cutts: See 'measures of yarn'.

Ell: A measure of length for cloth (37 inches); the Scots ell was approximately four-fifths of the English.

Grist: The thickness of the yarn, often expressed in weight (lbs) per spindle.

Hank: See 'measures of yarn'.

Harl: The outer bark of the flax.

Heckle: A process of combing out the flax fibres after the flax had had its bark removed by retting (soaking in water) and scutching.

Hundreds: See 'reed'.

Kiltage: Ballast or mastfasting.

Lapping: The process of pressing and folding the cloth after it had been bleached and in the case of fine linen starched.

Latching: To enable cloth to be pegged out for washing and drying during bleaching, loops were sown at two-yard intervals on to the edges of the webs.

Loom: The warp yarn was first stretched betwen the leys or front and back beams, and the shuttle with the weft threads thrust forward by the weaver, his foot pedal or 'treddle' opening the shed to allow its passage. The caims or cambs were the heddles which opened out the shed of warp yarn so as to allow the passage of the shuttle.

Matts: The packages in which flax was shipped.

Measures of yarn: One *spindle* of yarn was defined by official regulation as 14,000 yards in length, and contained four *hanks* of 3,600 yards each, or 48 *cutts* of 300 yards each.

Measures of cloth: The length of cloth was measured by the Board of Trustees' stampmasters in yards rather than ells. The breadth might be one yard wide, or expressed in some fraction thereof such as quarters. Four quarters, typically expressed by clerks as '4 qrs', was a cloth a yard in breadth: '6 qr' would be one and a half yards wide, and so on. Table linen and napkins were made in a particularly varied range of sizes.

Mill: The mechanical rolling of yarn after cleaning so as to make it even.

Porter: See 'reed'.

Quil: A bobbin or pirn on which the yarn was wound.

Reed: The part of the loom, like a closed comb, by which the warp theads were separated out. The finenesss of a fabric was determined by how closely the intervals (or 'dents') in the reed were spaced. When the 'sett' of the weave was designated, it referred to the number or 'hundreds' of intervals in the reed every 38 inches.

Reel: This was the instrument on which the yarn from the spinning wheel was wound. In Scotland, by law the wheel was 90 inches in circumference.

Selvedge: The edge of the cloth.

Sett: See 'reed'.

Selvedge: The edge of the cloth.

Smalts: A deep blue dye, used to finish cloth.

Sour or *Sower:* An acid solution used in bleaching, which was made from bran or cow's milk. Sulphuric acid was increaingly used from the 1750s onwards to replace these natural acids.

Tow: The coarsest part of the flax first heckled out.

Warp: The threads stretched lengthwise in the loom. Some weavers employed specialist warpers to prepare their looms for them.

Waterfold: After bleaching, the cloth was folded rather than rolled for despatch to market.

Web: The woven piece of cloth, which varied from 50 to 100 yards in length, depending on the fabric.

Weft or *Woof:* The crosswise threads in the loom which were pushed up the warp threads by the weaver's shuttle.

Whiten: To bleach, a process applicable both to yarn and to cloth.

INDEX

SCOTTISH HISTORY SOCIETY

OFFICE-BEARERS AND COUNCIL
1995-96

MEMBERSHIP

Membership of the Scottish History Society
is open to all who are interested in the history of Scotland.
For an annual subscription of £15.00
members normally receive one volume each year.
Enquiries should be addressed to
the Honorary Secretary, whose address
is given overleaf.

SCOTTISH HISTORY SOCIETY

109th ANNUAL REPORT

Presented to the Annual General Meeting by the Council, 9 December 1995

Some progress has been made during 1995 in bringing the publication schedule up to date. The 1993 volume, Sir John Clerk's *History of the Union of Scotland and England*, edited by Douglas Duncan, was issued to members during the year. There were further delays with the 1992 volume, which had originally been intended to precede it–*The Scottish Office: Depression and Reconstruction, 1919-1959*, edited by Ian Levitt. This volume has been with the printers for some time, held up by technical problems, but its issue is currently imminent.

Two further volumes are also in page proof, and will shortly be printed. The 1994 volume, *Miscellany XII*, will include 'A question about the succession, 1364', edited by A.A.M. Duncan; 'The autobiography of John Hay, 1st marquis of Tweeddale, 1626-1672', edited by Maurice Lee, Jr.; 'Letters of Lord Balmerino and Harry Maule, 1710-1713, 1721-1722', edited by Clyve Jones; and 'Strike bulletins from the General Strike in Scotland, 1926', edited by Ian MacDougall. The 1996 volume will be *The British Linen Company, 1745-1775*, edited by Alastair J. Durie. Publication of this volume is being assisted by sponsorship from the British Linen Bank, which in 1996 is celebrating the 250th anniversary of its charter.

Publication of these volumes will still leave a gap for 1995, but it is hoped that this will be filled in the course of the year by one of the numerous volumes on which work is proceeding. In particular, good progress is reported with *French Military and Financial Documents Concerning Scotland During the Reign of Henri II*, edited by Elizabeth Bonner, while progress is also still being made with *The Black Book of Coldingham, 1298-1430*, edited by Joseph Donnelly, and with *Scottish Migration, 1740-1920*, edited by Allan Macinnes, Margaret Storey and Marjory Harper.

There are several other volumes which have been accepted for publication but which are in less advanced stages of preparation: *Clan Campbell, 1550-1583*, edited by Jane Dawson; *Miscellany XIII*, for which a number of items have been accepted; *Minutes of the Mid and East Lothian Miners' Association, 1894-1914*, edited by Ian MacDougall; *The Duke of Montrose's Buchanan Estate, Stirlingshire, c.1680-1787*, edited by Alexander Gibson; and *The Diaries of General Patrick Gordon of Auchleuchries, 1635-1699*, edited by Paul Dukes and Graeme Herd. It seems that the prospects of returning to, and maintaining, a regular annual publication programme are good.

The Society's financial position continues to be healthy, the subscription continuing to be held at £15.00.

Mr Bill Scott retires after holding the post of Honorary Treasurer for the last four years; and Dr Pat Torrie retires after four years as Honorary Secretary and for six months as Assistant Treasurer to the late Professor Ian Cowan. The post of Treasurer will be filled by Dr Iain Hutchison, and that of Secretary by Dr Steve Boardman. Dr David Ditchburn has resigned as Publication Secretary, due to pressure of work. Council thanks him for his services to the Society. He has been replaced by Dr Fiona Watson. Council also expresses its gratitude to Mr W. Mackay who deals with misdirected genealogical queries; and Mrs V. Wills who cares for the stock of books.

The three members of Council to retire by rotation are Mr Iain Flett, Dr Iain Hutchison and Mr David Sellar. To replace them, Council recommends the election by the Annual General Meeting of Dr Norman Reid (St Andrews University Archives), Dr Dauvit Broun (Glasgow University) and Dr Eleanor Gordon (Glasgow University). Any other nominations, made by at least two members of the Society, should reach the Honorary Secretary not less than seven days before the Annual General Meeting.

The Council recommends that a minor amendment is made to the Society's constitution. In Clause 7, 'Office Bearers', after the words 'Publication Secretary', the words 'or secretaries' should be inserted.

The membership of the Society stands at 492 individual and 206 institutional members.

SCOTTISH HISTORY SOCIETY

INCOME AND EXPENDITURE FOR THE YEAR TO 30 SEPTEMBER 1995

1994			1995
£			£
7561.81	Subscriptions		10663.56
500.00	Income Tax on Covenants Recoverable (estimate)		413.00
481.75	Sales of Past Publications		600.85
-82.19	Less: Insurance		-98.00
0.00	Royalties		0.00
2985.06	Interest on Bank Premier Account		3834.78
76.61	Interest on Bank Current Account		253.28
11523.04	NET INCOME		15667.47
	Costs of year's publications:		
0.00	Printing	-10860.00	
-197.77	Typing & Photocopying	-375.10	
0.00	Literary Editor's Honorarium	-450.00	
0.00	Postage & Packing	-780.08	
-543.43	Purchase of Software	0.00	
-410.00	Printing Leaflets	0.00	
-156.00	AGM Expenses	-190.50	
-124.94	AGM Postage	-119.65	
-140.85	Other expenses	-155.28	
-50.00	Subscriptions & Donations	0.00	
			-12930.61
9900.05	CURRENT ACCOUNT SURPLUS		2376.86
3000.00	Bequests & Donations		0.00
12900.05	TOTAL SURPLUS FOR YEAR		2376.86

BALANCE SHEET AS AT 30 SEPTEMBER 1995

1994		1995
£		£
1.00	Stocks of Unsold Publications	1.00
1500.00	Debtors (Income Tax Recoverable)	1450.00
65198.22	Bank—Premier Account	65533.00
2874.16	Bank—Current Account	5326.24
0.00	Creditors	0.00
69573.38	NET CURRENT ASSETS	72310.24

CAPITAL ACCOUNT

1994		1995
56673.33	Balance at 1 October 1994	69573.38
12900.05	Surplus for Year	2736.86
69573.38	Balance at 30 September 1995	72310.24

SCOTTISH HISTORY SOCIETY

ABSTRACT ACCOUNT OF THE CHARGE AND DISCHARGE OF THE INTROMISSIONS OF THE HONORARY TREASURER

1 October 1994 to 30 September 1995

CHARGE

				£
1		Cash in Bank at 1 October 1994		
	a	Sum at credit of Premier Account with Bank of Scotland	65198.22	
	b	Sum at credit of current (Treasurer's) account with Bank of Scotland	2874.16	
				68072.38
2		Subscriptions received		10837.11
3		Past publications sold		600.85
4		Interest on Premier Account		3834.78
5		Interest on Current (Treasurer's) Account		253.28
6		Tax Recovered on Covenants (1991-92)		463.00
7		Sums drawn from Bank Premier Account	5000.00	
8		Sums drawn from Bank Current Account	14702.16	
				84061.40

DISCHARGE

				£
1		Subscriptions refunded		173.55
2		Cost of publications during year		11640.08
3		Literary editor's honorarium		450.00
4		Typing and photocopying		375.10
5		Costs of insuring stock of unsold books		98.00
6		Costs of AGM		190.50
7		Costs of postage re AGM		119.65
8		Office bearers' expenses		155.28
9		Sums lodged in Bank Premier Account	4761.48	
		Sums lodged in Bank Current Account	10158.92	
				13202.16
10		Funds at close of this account		70859.24
	a	Sum at credit of Premier Account with Bank of Scotland	65533.00	
	b	Sum at credit of Current (Treasurer's) Account with Bank of Scotland	5326.24	
				84061.40

STIRLING, *31 October 1995.*

I have audited the Account of the Honorary Treasurer of the Scottish History Society and certify that I am satisfied that proper records appear to have been kept and that the above Account is a correct statement of the transactions recorded during the year.

H.B. PEEBLES
C.A.